The Summertime of Our Dreams

The Summertime of Our Dreams

On Mateship, Mortality and the Road Home

Michael Pascoe

Published in 2022 by Ultimo Press,
an imprint of Hardie Grant Publishing

Ultimo Press
Gadigal Country
7, 45 Jones Street
Ultimo, NSW 2007
ultimopress.com.au

Ultimo Press (London)
5th & 6th Floors
52–54 Southwark Street
London SE1 1UN

A catalogue record for this
work is available from the
National Library of Australia

NATIONAL
LIBRARY
OF AUSTRALIA

The Summertime of Our Dreams
ISBN 978 1 76115 101 9 (paperback)

10 9 8 7 6 5 4 3 2 1

Cover design George Saad
Cover images Beach © Svitozar Bilorusov / Trevillion Images; father and son by
EpicStockMedia / Shutterstock; dog by choosangyeon / Shutterstock
Typesetting Kirby Jones | Typeset in 13/19 pt Adobe Garamond Pro
Copyeditor Simone Ford
Proofreader Pamela Dunne

Printed in Australia by Griffin Press, part of Ovato, an Accredited ISO AS/NZS 14001
Environmental Management System printer.

The paper this book is printed on is certified against the
Forest Stewardship Council® Standards. Griffin Press holds
FSC® chain of custody certification SGSHK-COC-005088.
FSC® promotes environmentally responsible, socially beneficial and
economically viable management of the world's forests.

Ultimo Press acknowledges the Traditional Owners of the country on which we work, the
Gadigal people of the Eora nation and the Wurundjeri people of the Kulin nation, and recognises
their continuing connection to the land, waters and culture. We pay our respects to their Elders
past, present and emerging.

For family,
for friends,
for love

Every time I draw a man I involuntarily think of my father.
For me, all men are Don Jose.

Pablo Picasso

*

As I sd to my
friend, because I am
always talking, — John, I

sd, which was not his
name, the darkness sur-
rounds us, what

can we do against
it, or else, shall we &
why not, buy a goddamn big car,

drive, he sd, for
christ's sake, look
out where yr going.

'I Know a Man', Robert Creeley

The times

These are times you might read about, not live through. This is something you imagine, not experience.

But it is real, it is happening.

You know it before you believe it. Your ears hear the doctor's diagnosis/the jury's verdict/the government edict/the banker's decision/the ambo's shout/the policeman's order/the thug's threat and your mind nods along while comprehension lags, trying to place the pieces of a world upturned.

'This can't be happening.'

As you will your gut into the reality you start to understand how the millions before you didn't understand either, didn't read the signs, didn't grasp calamity unfolding, were unprepared, were lost in history's turmoil, thought their mass grave impossible even as they dug it.

We're out of practice. Mass disasters don't happen here, not in our lifetime. The plagues and total wars and famines and deaths in the thousands and millions are confined to television screens. Even our hard times remain relatively soft in the broader, longer scheme of things.

Other people's individual tragedies have gone on regardless.

And their sun does never shine.
And their fields are bleak & bare.

And their ways are fill'd with thorns.
It is eternal winter there.[1]

In groups sometimes, in planeloads. Perhaps whole communities when fire or flood or landslide tear through. Bad, terrible, but this, this, indiscriminate ... everyone?

And the comprehension comes – it has always been every one. The single diagnosis and mass verdict, the individual execution and the genocide: One person, however many.

One person facing mortality. We're born to this.

Jim

My friend Sergio tells bad news with a quiet reticence. It comes with a note of warning in his voice, of apology. His Italian heritage coming through stronger with a certain diffident movement of his head. He's sorry to be telling you, but here's the thing …

Jim McCormack has inoperable prostate cancer.

Jim, our schoolmate, our old teammate. Sergio and Jim were boarders together from Year 8 at Nudgee College. I joined them in Year 9.

Big Jim.

As a boy, a solid block of fast muscle – the sprinter. Country boy, such a country boy. Wild bulls couldn't get past him on the field. Fearless with the ball. Go down yourself and he'd be there, driving over you, driving back the trampling boots of those days. Solid of body and character. Intelligent. Zero pretension, absolutely none. So straight up. First pick to have beside you. Strong Jim.

He stayed strong as a man – stronger than we knew. Quiet in a group but people listened when he spoke. If he asked a question – often in a self-deprecating manner – you felt compelled to find your best answer. A great laugh when it came.

3

Oh fuck. What is there to say? Any treatment? How much time?

Serge had few details then. The news wasn't being broadcast. It would turn out to be a few years, but only a few.

'He said something about the treatment: they could operate but it wouldn't stop it. He said he wouldn't do that to an animal so he wouldn't do it to himself.'

I could hear Jim say that, in a measured deep rumble of a voice. Just a fact, not making an issue of it. A cattleman. Livestock, dogs, wildlife – birth and death, all part of life.

Max

On our local walks, my dog and I sometimes come upon an ancient terrier, deaf, blind and tottery, as he's allowed a slow piddle and uncertain sniff upon the verge. I wonder at what point the balance of companionship and an animal's drive to live yield to quality of life and death, a tipping point in living dying. Empathy and sympathy swamp declarations on Twitter of final visits to the vet.

I am guilty of once being dismissive of the extent of grief that is possible over a pet's death. Decades ago, as a stand-in host on *The Today Show*, back-announcing an American package on a boom in people seeing psychiatrists, unable to cope with the death of their Fido, their Simba, their Radish, their budgie. I was enough of a country boy myself to differentiate between people and animals and was maybe influenced by Evelyn Waugh's *The Loved One* on American attitudes to death of all kinds. I can't remember exactly what I said but the careless meaning was along the lines of silly Americans and their trick cyclists, they needed to get a grip.

'The switchboard lit up', as the saying goes. I was not the stand-in *Today Show* host much longer.

Our very dear Max died sometime early the Wednesday morning before a Christmas. He was lying in a flowerbed in the backyard, near his favourite spot for sunbaking in cooler months.

He must have grown tired of the embarrassment and inconvenience of his back legs no longer working as well as they should. Maybe he had just grown tired, being 14 years and four months, old for a dalmatian, a century in our money. So he went to sleep among the agapanthus, pushed his way in and expired, sparing us the vet decision.

Max was a happy, loved dog, a generous soul, an excellent companion for a walk or to have lie on your rug, a great help in the kitchen in case anything dropped and needed cleaning up.

He grew up with a bunch of boys growing up, so he had been provided with entertainment. Unlike many dogs, he was forgiven his indiscretions. He was never belted, never worked, never urged to be savage, never had to worry about going hungry – though his eyes might have said otherwise when he thought it was time for dinner.

Being a particularly handsome liver-spotted dalmatian, he received more attention from small children than most dogs. Patted, grabbed and chased by random small strangers for 100 years, yet it was always suffered with good grace.

Aside from us, he most liked fellow doggy dogs (chocolate labradors his favourite flavour – he turned gay for choc labs). He was wary and suspicious of those breeds he suspected were more closely related to wolves and considered himself above any small dogs that yapped at him. ('Don't even ignore them.')

Cats were for chasing, except for that one that didn't run away, that stood its ground and arched and hissed and stopped him in his tracks a metre away, confused and uncomfortable. Stupid cat not knowing The Order of Things. We decided it never happened. What cat?

The yard became neater when no longer a big dog's toilet, the house smelled sweeter without the lingering hint of his particularly foul farts. Possums, blue tongue lizards (sorry) and – from younger, quicker days – the occasional slow dove and mouse did not miss him, but anyone who had the chance to ruffle those big soft spotted ears surely did.

We were better for having had Max, for him increasing our ability to love another, for the pain of missing him, for making us more human, my sons' first lesson in death.

The boys, by then fine young men, buried him where he liked to snooze in the sun. He seemed happy to sometimes have sheets flapping over him from the washing line. Now they always will.

There is no theological debate about the presence of dogs in heaven, only about whether they run the place.

A friend replied to that statement that they probably are in charge – all those souls full of unconditional love, bounding about convinced that whatever they are doing at the instant is simply The Best Thing to do. Which is how it should be.

That is all good; life and death and love and pain and heaven being run by dogs. And in the general scale of things, we know Max was a dog. I won't write 'just' a dog, but he was a dog, an old dog, when so many people suffer massively greater loss and tragedy, unthinkable tragedies.

But, still, what to do with the scraps? He was a dog, a scavenger by distant heritage – there was nothing he drooled for more than a fine plate of scraps. Christmas dinner with the leftover turkey on the plates of those with eyes even bigger than their stomachs, you simply throw that out?

We felt a little guilty. There would have to be changes. Smaller servings. Forced finishing of unloved takeaway curries. No more wanton wontons. Or maybe not.

It's just when someone at a dinner party leaves a juicy piece of beef that was too rare for them, we forever think, jeez, Max would have loved that.

I know a bit more about death now. I wouldn't back-announce the American package that way – every death is theirs alone.

The girl with long hair

You are not too young to die; someone has to make the averages work, has to spread the business around.

The median age at death for an Australian male in 2019 was 78.8 years, 84.8 for females. Half of everyone who died was under those ages, half above. That's a lot of men not making 80 and then our deaths bunch up dramatically thereafter. Great clumps of us blokes fall off the perch in the peak dying range of 85 to 89. Time's up. 'Come in, Number 86, time's up!' Women half a decade later.

Yet children, young people dying …

We are social animals, hardwired with a sense of equity, of fair play. Instinctive pathos.

I was fine in the chemo room, riding it. Didn't worry me. The basement floor of the Royal North Shore Hospital's main building, maybe 30 chairs spread out with the odd partition. Didn't want Judy to accompany me – wouldn't let her. (She's not good with needles, even other people's needles, let alone cannulas.) Some patients had companions along, ending up equally bored, I'd think. Each to their own.

For me, it was one of the relatively less evil bastards – diffuse large B-cell lymphoma – with a pretty good prognosis. When pushed for the odds, the doc said better than an 80 per cent chance of matching my cohort's five-year life expectancy. And if you survived five years, that was a cure. So notwithstanding my cohort's ability to shuffle off for other reasons, better than a four out of five chance of beating it, of living for more than five years. Pretty much.

And people worry about a 1-in-100,000 chance of a blood clot from a vaccine, a 1-in-1,000,000 chance of a fatal blood clot. Pretty funny.

Different strokes – and cancers – for different folks. Some chemotherapy with the expectation of a cure, some the hope, some to extend life, a trade-off between time and side effects.

The orientation session: a video of chemo patients talking about how it was for them, some of it personal, mostly the usual side effects.

And it is usual, there's nothing unusual about cancer. If you haven't yourself or don't have a relative or friend who's danced with it, you must have beaten the trend into social isolation and stayed there.

There were two other men in my session, both a little younger than me. We nodded smiles of positivity. The nurses took questions and handed out goody bags – mouthwash, moisturiser, toothpaste allegedly helpful for handling dry mouth syndrome, jellybeans, an electronic thermometer, a card that would get you seen to immediately if you came in through the emergency department.

Take your temperature twice a day, they stressed, avoid opportunities for infection. Your immune system is drastically suppressed. (It will stay deficient for many months and longer.) If your temperature rises, if you have a fever, don't wait – come straight to emergency at any time.

'We had a patient, he developed a temperature during the night at home but thought he'd wait for morning before coming in. He was dead in the morning,' a nurse warned.

'Is that what you'd call a side effect?' one of the blokes asked.

You can quickly like someone. He'd do me as a chemo companion.

I didn't see him again. I like to think he did well.

Chemo. Nothing for it but sitting, reclining, while the drugs, the selective poisons, drip into veins. I had Jim's example, what I had learned from him three years before: be considerate, be patient, remember the nurses' names, thank them. The nurses, direct, cheerful, from a dozen different countries, instilling calm. A privilege to thank them.

For me, a few hours of reading, texting, tweeting; it was fine. Except: A bit of a reaction to one of the drugs in the first session – the big bad red one, the one you can have only one course of or it wrecks your heart – slowed proceedings down. I had to come back the next morning to finish off. Tidying up, taking a plastic cup and muesli bar wrapper to the bin, there was a young woman sitting down in a chair, about to start. She had long dark brown hair flowing about her as she moved, beautiful hair, shampoo-ad hair. She looked ... young and bright and the future of the world.

'What are you doing here?' I thought. 'This is no place for you, you're too young for this.'

And I had to leave quickly.

The daughter of friends died so young: a young mother with a two-year-old daughter, a young daughter herself, young wife, diagnosed with bowel cancer when she was pregnant.

Trying to tell Judy about the woman with the long hair caught me, stopped my words.

The statisticians summarise dying too young as premature deaths measured by years of potential life lost – YPLL. They count the burden of mortality in YPLL. If dying before the age of 75 is considered premature, a person gone at 65 would have 10 YPLL. A person dying at 18 would have 57 – so much more lost than had.

There were 1,020,762 YPLL in Australia in 2019, but statistical method doesn't capture the YPLL with others. There's the 32-year-old mother's 43 YPLL, but there's another 43 YPLL with her for her daughter, and another 43 with her husband, maybe 40 with another child never to be, 15 or so with her parents. Scores of YPLL accumulating, immeasurable and lost.

But we're not too young to die.

The drive

Come for a drive. It's a good one if you like a drive, probably isn't if you don't. Too bad. Door's open. Bit crowded but plenty of room. The car's good. Actually, the car's great. They've all been, they all are, whichever one we're in. Measure your life by the car you were in at the time. Just go.

But you don't really start a long drive when you start, even when it's a metaphor, a skeleton upon which to hang your ghosts, a couple of particular drives amid a floating compilation of a lifetime's driving and the last one.

Oh, you can be on your way, hopefully in the right direction, ordering your thoughts, but for the first bit your mind is back in the house. What did you have to do? What did you mean to do? Who were you supposed to call? Checked everything was turned off, the lights with the timers turned on? And did you bring everything you need? What have you left behind? You can be kilometres down the road before leaving the inertia of home.

And then you can get ahead of yourself – when will you arrive? Will the entry permit at the Queensland border be OK? Take the highway or Epping Road to Lane Cove Road quicker at this hour? The new toll road? That sort of thing.

It takes a little time to leave behind whatever you have left behind, to be on your way with this particular drive, to accept the solitude of your car and yourself and whatever scrapbook of your life you carry with you.

'I am the Toad! The motor-car snatcher, the prison-breaker, the Toad who always escapes! Sit still, and you'll know what driving really is ...'[2]

Poop-poop.

But you can be unlucky, you can have the radio on for traffic news and they play The Proclaimers' 'I'm on My Way'. Turn the radio off but it continues, threatens to keep echoing between your ears from here to Queensland. Mentally overrule it with Talking Heads' 'Road to Nowhere', settle in and finally start.

And take time.

Settle in to the time you have, the time to enjoy the experience of the car and the journey, the machine and movement, the kinetic wonder of landscape circling and wheeling, to feel the movement through the curve of your own space and time.

Some of us feel that more, some less, some not at all. From an age when the ability to drive was freedom and cars needed to be driven, when you felt and heard the partnership of car and driver, listened to the engine to be told to change gears, changed gears and told the engine, drove, *drove* into and through corners, up hills and as far as you cared, drove for the driving. You could fill a road trip's soundtrack (cassette tapes before CDs before MP3s before Spotify on your phone) with odes to the automobile as means of escape, paeans to speed and life's journeys.

Glad to be underway, to be away with the promise of the New England Highway and country and wide skies and an open twisting road rising and falling and your own thoughts.

Thoughts of the many times I've driven this thousand kilometres from Sydney to Brisbane over four decades. More than four decades.

The scrapbook's pages flutter about as if I still have the Alfa Spider with the roof down, flap past the young couple's annual pilgrimage in a Mitsubishi Sigma to visit family and their favourite beach. The young family, the madness of driving that far with babies and toddlers. The less young family requiring three rows of seats and teenagers' boredom – the Peugeot 505 wagon, the Nimbus, the MPV, the big Chrysler Voyager. The couple again. A series of Alfas. By myself often enough.

Never by myself. Always company – the company of ghosts. What else be memories of life? Increasingly with ghosts and their intimations of mortality. A dose of DLBC lymphoma can do that to you as the time passes from the end of treatment, survival time the only measure of cure. The chemo leaving a damaged immune response with a virus about can do that to you, too. The scarring of a few years of caution.

With Jim now, with him whenever I'm out of the city by myself in the years since his death, but particularly this drive north and through his last country.

A strong ghost after our conversations about life and dying, never mind that we had said little or nothing to each other for most of our lives, reviving an unspoken brotherhood that outlives us in memories while memory itself changes.

It was a brotherhood that began as 13-year-olds in 1969 on the Nudgee 'flats', half a dozen rugby fields that stretched away to the east down the hill from the first and second ovals, paddocks beyond them to a mangroved creek and swampy land, Nudgee Beach somewhere in the distance. The flats were a long way down from the Italian renaissance façade of St Joseph's Nudgee College fronting Sandgate Road, the public image of an archbishop's desire that 'a residential College be made available for Catholic boys, especially those from country districts'. The Nudgee of 1891 in fields north of Brisbane a long way from the landmark GPS school now in the suburbs, blue-and-white-striped Edwardian blazers a long way from the rag-tag soul of the flats.

Most boys started at Nudgee in Year 8 and had had a year to establish their hierarchies before the granting of conditional half-fees allowed me to join them in Year 9, a solitary new boy to be assessed, measured for worth in the fit of the boarding school.

The 110 or so members of Year 9 were divided into three streams by the mix of subjects chosen. Jim and I didn't overlap in any classes and played different summer sports – we might not have exchanged a word in the first term. Jim wasn't a big talker anyway.

And then the rugby trials. Coaches might or might not correctly grade talent, a player can have lucky or unlucky trials, but the boys know soon enough. I was in the under 14Bs for the first game. The 14As barely won a lineout that Saturday and Rollo broke his collarbone, a combination that elevated the new boy. I can see 13-year-old Jim, already a quality back-rower, assessing the tall, skinny second rower, quickly knowing my strengths and weaknesses, accepting them as we trained three afternoons a week, fought the enemy on Saturdays and played touch or tackle among ourselves the rest of the time for the next four years and in the athletics team together as well, building complete trust. Easygoing mates trained to the point of instinct to cover, to assist, to help as bodies collide and fall.

After my final Year 12 exam, I didn't see or talk to Jim for 30 years.

I'm remembering childhood and youth more, remembering mistakes and regrets more while decades of adulthood, of 'success', feature little. Adult failures, too – there are more of them. From mistakes made in selecting this or that boy for a junior representative team to words left unsaid, or said when they should not have been, they float back unbidden.

And whole decades can go largely missing. I am reminded by grandchildren now that so much time must have been spent with the boys when they were small, so many beach holidays, and they're not recalled in more than flashes, can't be dialled up to be re-run, to be savoured. So much time lost, decades disappeared. Tidying some of her mother's jumble, Judy found a photograph of me with the older three on a beach, a young man with a reddish-brown beard and three beautiful blond boys. I would relive that day on a beach over and over forever – but I can't.

It would be a worry if I worried about such things, so I don't. Jim, getting closer to death, told me he was spending more time with his early days, of the surprise he had in feeling an almost overwhelming happiness when visited by someone from his wild bush youth.

'Memory is a funny thing, Michael,' he said.

Drying up

For 36 hours I could not think of the name of the rectangular piece of cotton or linen used to dry plates and cups and glasses and cutlery after they are washed. It was frightening. I could tell no-one.

I had been struck by a black-and-red tree waratah print while walking through a nearby market. Strong, rich colour on linen. I don't often buy such things. Often? Maybe twice in my life, that I remember. No, thrice – I overlooked setting up my first flat, in Hong Kong.

They have simply existed in the kitchens of my life. I've not wondered where they came from. Other people bought them, gave them, left them, whatever. I bought the Pod & Pod tree waratah because it was beautiful, because the sight of it appealed, not because of the thing it was.

And then, some days later, I couldn't think of the name of this lifelong kitchen constant, this colourful utilitarian thing hanging from the oven handle. 'Dishcloth' kept coming to my mind but I knew it wasn't. I don't have a dishcloth. Never have.

I disliked washing and wiping up. Tedious, repetitive. It was the domestic job I hated as a child. I was happy enough to take out the rubbish, tossing the edibles to the chooks, burning the rest in a 44-gallon drum down the back behind the men's lavatory.

We had two outhouses in the backyard – theoretically, one for any prisoner in the lock-up, one for the family. In practice, one for the males of the household, one for the females.

Feed the chooks, bring in the eggs. Run errands. Literally run them – how fast could I get up to the Cooks Corner shop and back? But wiping up was boring. Long before dishwashing machines, please at least stack the dishes and let them drip dry. There was an advertisement for a dishwashing detergent: 'Drip Dry! No Streaks!' I remember as I write now, for the first time in many decades, that I once intentionally dropped a plate when I was ordered to help. Pretended it was too hot and slippery for me, to show I shouldn't do it. In the old police station house in Petrie, a broken white plate on the lino floor. The wood stove in the alcove off to the left. The sink with a single tap from the tank stand beyond the window.

Fooled no-one. A flash of anger from my father. His big hands in water too hot for me to ever bear, not much water, water boiled on the stove or in a yellow ceramic jug with a Bakelite lid.

I am sorry, Dad. I am sorry I broke the plate and was a petulant child. I am more sorry I didn't want to take, didn't take, the opportunity to be with you in that old kitchen and work beside you. To be a small boy being helpful with his father. I would relive that.

Washing up had its revenge for 36 hours. When I tried to think of the name, 'dishcloth' would come to me and I knew that was wrong. 'Leave it,' I told myself. 'Don't try and it will come.'

But it didn't. The fresh, stiff linen heavily impregnated with colour – useless for drying anything while new – hung from the rail of the oven, taunting me every time I entered the kitchen.

Is this how it starts?

I could have googled 'cloth used for drying dishes'. It would be a capitulation and would not erase the fear. I wanted to know if I could remember.

The second morning, I did. 'Tea towel,' I thought, could have shouted. For a day and a half I could not think of the name for a rectangle of linen used to dry plates and glasses and cutlery. And I couldn't tell anybody.

Words written and spoken have been my living, my life. They were there without thought, as automatically present as tea towels in a kitchen drawer. Sometimes now the right word doesn't come. I have to search for it, stop, hunt, google. They used to appear with no hesitation at all. On my feet, speaking, phrases on my tongue without thought. 'Never lost for a word.' Jim envied that about me. Strong, fearless Big Jim. Jim who lived his life in constant anxiety and never let it show, never told anyone except Sue and, eventually, me.

And now I take some small pleasure in most effectively stacking the dishwasher, solving the puzzle of making everything fit.

A man can always find a way to fit one more thing into a dishwasher his partner has packed.

Kitchen Tetris.

The conversation

A microscopic monster came hunting, a blindly purposed thing that is not actually alive but takes life often enough. A plague was back, reminding us a plague always would be back, pricking our hubris.

There was the gap between what we might know and what our gut believed, a gap that took a little time to fill, then was filled quickly by fear.

That provided lots of company for those of us already jogging a little closer to life's edge – the shadow of mortality cast more widely, our vulnerabilities sharpened. The old – the virus defined 'old' as 70, a shock to everyone who was 70 – and the immuno-compromised made themselves scarce. 'Comorbidities' found its way into general parlance.

Judy's 96-year-old mother, Maureen, locked down in St Paul's Northbridge, phoned a dozen times a day, asking the same questions, requiring the same explanations. Are you coming to see me? How are you? Where are you? Can I come up to your place? What is it? Is everything all right? Are you all right? What's going on? When will it be over? Sobbing sometimes, depressed often, calm and rational about it occasionally, forgetting the last conversation and the letters we sent. It would not have helped if she had heard the initial arguments for letting the virus rip – 'it only takes the old'.

Maureen is quite deaf. Hated the fiddliness of hearing aids, didn't want to wear them and lost two sets. The shouted conversations down the phone are wearing. But she has her moments.

'This virus, why don't they just shoot it?'

Once, after Judy yet again explained that COVID was particularly dangerous for elderly people: 'Oh, there aren't any elderly people here, not really. I'd say maybe in their thirties.'

Our delusions only vary by degree. You don't – or I didn't – immediately accept the consequences of 65 years and leaving most of my lymphocytes back in the chemo room. Being elevated to prime target status as COVID went hunting seemed … improbable. I passed people on the street a little carefully, aiming for more than the 1.5 metres. I held my breath as joggers approached – sweating, blowing hard – envisaging clouds of panted virus swirling from them. Yet I continued to buy takeaway coffee from the neighbouring restaurants, wondering where the barista had been, who he or she had socialised with, how their unmasked breath must fall as the milk was poured into my morning flat white, how long the virus could live on a coffee cup.

What are the odds? We're always taking our chances, but a feature of the initial fear was children of siblings and friends cracking down on their parents, reading the riot act of stricter social distancing, insisting on doing the shopping for them.

Wait for the conversation when they decide their parents are too old to drive.

Jim knew the odds and carried on, accepted the finality of advice that, when we started writing, he would be unlikely to make Christmas. He was never deluded about his outlook in our conversation, sought not optimism or pessimism. It was. His clarity helped me. Helps me. That's what he wanted to do – help.

We fell into writing to each other almost by accident and became able to talk in a way that we couldn't face to face, not initially, not for nearly all our lives.

Before our writing found its rhythm, its drive, the conversation was largely unspoken – the handshakes, the eye contact and nod that you hope carried the meaning you intend for a bloke sentenced to death. Brief words at the end of conversations about nothing.

After Sergio told me, I tried to ensure there was time to share a meal whenever I went to Brisbane, or at least a coffee at his regular local in Ascot on the way to the airport. If it was just a couple of us, maybe a quick question, clumsily putting a calling card on the table.

'Mate, how are you going?'

'Doing OK. Taking it as it comes.'

Sue

It was more for Sue that I first wrote, sent them a link to a podcast on August 3, 2015 about something we had discussed over coffee in Brisbane that morning rather than talk about cancer.

Great to see you both today – you continue to inspire me with your strength, Jim.

They shared the same email. I signed off 'love', an easier word to use writing to Sue and Jim than Jim alone.

Jim was 34 when they met, Sue two years older. He'd been sober for three years. Sue had been divorced for six. Jo was nine. Catherine was born 18 months later. Jim's three girls. Sue was left-wing, Jim predictably country conservative. It became a regularly told story, the way enrapt couples repeat stories about themselves, that Sue was a university student outside the showgrounds protesting the 1971 Springboks tour, risking the Queensland police batons, while we rugby-loving Nudgee boys were driven past in our buses to the game.

'Jim first asked me on a date to the movies, New Year's Day 1990,' Sue wrote. '*Sex, Lies and Videotape* – we both loved it. We were inseparable from that day on.'

Said simply and truly. There are couples like that: inseparable, totally bound to each other, living in each other's life, unable to imagine life without the other, always in love. Mutually dependent, some might sniff. Recipe for eventual heartbreak.

Their marriage might have seemed claustrophobic if you didn't know them. Jim didn't much like travel, so they didn't travel much. Jim had a big trip to the US before they met and that was all his international holidaying. He disliked the beach. The boy from the bush, in love with endless land, had a fear of the endless sea. So there wasn't much of that either. He drove the family to a beach when the girls were young and stayed in the car while Sue played with them in the sand.

There was work. There was the responsible use of money. When he had some good fortune, when work and investment paid off, he bought the small farm at Rosevale, a couple of hours from Brisbane, a surrogate for the family property he and his brother Tom, still boys, had brought back from ruin to debt-free and then sold. 'It was like cutting off your arm.'

Rosevale, every farm, needed attention to not lose money, required steady work, called with the peace, the deep soul of the land, the beauty of its hill rising up behind the house with a view to the Great Dividing Range, the hidden grove of ancient grass trees, the resident mob of aptly named pretty-faced wallabies, the horses and cattle that were in his blood, the master horseman teaching his girls to ride, the care of the animals and land. Sue, the city girl, the university student protester, the lawyer, gave herself willingly to it, to Jim's certainty and loyalty and sobriety.

Yet in some things, maybe Sue was the more conservative, Jim more liberal, more accepting of life. The context doesn't matter now but that podcast link was mainly for Sue. And sending it moved a friendship formed as schoolboys, brothers on the rugby field, beyond the solidarity of blokes, breaking the dam of masculine reticence.

August 3, 7.55 pm

Thanks, Michael. It was good to see you today too ... not sure about strength, but I'm just playing it day by day.

A lingering doubt in the back of my mind that it could unravel badly sometime, but I suppose I will still be doing the best that I can.

My goal would be to die with a smile on my face ... It is going to happen anyway, so might as well try to accept it and be part of the experience. Seems to be a very valuable time of one's life, and many people do not have the luxury of being given notice.

Those two men in Bali, Chan and Sukumaran, inspired me greatly. They literally stared death in the face and sang their way out. They could have possibly done more good in the last few years of their lives than many of us could do in a lifetime. They inspired me, anyway.

Dick was good and helpful today ... he is a good man.

Thanks for your love and support ... You, Serg, Dick and quite a few others. I am surrounded by very good people, with my Sue leading from the front.

Sue and I listened to the link you sent ... thank you ... change doesn't come easy to this old boy ... but change things will and do.

In a positive way, my irrelevance astounds me.

Don't normally sign off love to my old Nudgee mates ... but I will try here.

Thanks, Michael ... I hope my death whenever it may be can make your life and those of my family better.

Love Jim & Sue

p.s. Sergio's father to Fr Jim Spence:
How are you Frank?

I'm dying Father (said Frank with a smile on his face).

August 4, 12.01 am

Jim and Sue

Funny how Chan and Sukumaran inspire you and you in turn inspire me. Maybe 'funny' isn't the right word for it, but I think you know what I mean.

It would surprise me if you were playing this any other way than the best you can, which, you being you, is very fine indeed. I don't think people fundamentally change much as they grow older. We hopefully learn from our mistakes and experiences, mellow a bit and become more accepting if we're lucky, but the inner person – the strength of character, the sense of fairness, the steadiness of eye – doesn't seem to change much at all. And the people who were pricks mainly remain pricks too. So the love you're feeling and giving is no surprise.

My eldest brother, Brian, died just short of his 58th birthday. He had lived most of his life overseas and only came home near the end of his cancer. A couple of days before he died, he told me he was surprised at the love he was shown. Family, but also friends he hadn't seen pretty much since he left Nudgee who found out he was back in Brisbane and supported him. I think we form bonds and understandings in those years that are simply part of us, a sort of brotherhood we share among those we respect that we don't talk about but is real enough.

And to have a great love, to have Sue, is an enormous blessing. So many people miss out on that. That's what we end up achieving or not.

You puzzle me though by saying 'in a positive way, my irrelevance astounds me'. I'd like you to explain that to me, to help me to understand what you're thinking.

I'm looking forward to my next visit as an associate member of the Ascot/Clayfield Gentlemen's Coffee Club. See you soon.

Love
Michael

Timing

I christened it the Ascot/Clayfield Gentlemen's Coffee Club, primarily convened by Sergio whose office was across the road. It became a routine when Jim was in town, sharing a little time and conversation. I'd get there occasionally, or with some warning of a Brisbane visit and time, Serge would organise dinner at a local restaurant for whatever old mates were around.

'You couldn't find a better man, a nicer man, than Jim,' Sergio told me at some stage with a quiet intensity. What makes a good man, a man without betters, I wondered. And Sergio as good and kind as any.

Five years later, in another conversation with another dying schoolmate, Kev Carmody, we formed the considered opinion that you never know anyone as well as you know the boys you lived with, growing from childhood together through puberty and youth into fledgling young men – but still boys.

'We hadn't learned to bullshit yet, Pas, we hadn't learned to hide everything.'

And people didn't change. The boys who were good people stayed good people; those you didn't trust you wouldn't trust.

Kev, another athlete, rugby player, 16As teammate, a boy with a sense of mischief if he became bored, a sense of fun, a surfer in good shape at 65 – except for the multiple cancers killing him. Kev not quite believing he could be too weak to climb the stairs without assistance. Kev still talking about what changes he would make with the business, not planning to die, in and out of acknowledging Death's timing.

> *Because I could not stop for Death –*
> *He kindly stopped for me –* [3]

Timing is not a strong suit of Death's. Spare me the epitaph 'He died doing what he loved'. It's been said about friends and colleagues with kind intentions, applied to all manner of celebrities and unknowns. Adventurers unsuccessfully tempting fate atop mountains and below oceans, catching tigers by their tails. Gardeners among their rose bushes. Suburban lawn bowlers upon the green. It can be meant as a testimony to perseverance, dying with your boots on, going down fighting. More often it's posed as well-meaning comfort, delivered with that saddest of little qualifications, 'At least'.

Bugger that. I'd prefer to go doing something I hate. Better still, about to start doing something I hate.

'Well, that got him out of mowing the lawn.'

'He'd just assembled his shoeboxes on the dining table for his annual wrestle with the tax return.'

'And the flowerbeds remain unweeded.'

Or the detritus of a lifetime remains unsorted, tumbling out of wardrobes, stuffed in boxes and drawers, filling shelves, piled up upon itself in the attic, children's kindergarten drawings and sports trophies, newspaper cuttings, once favourite shirts and ties, coats as limp upon their hangers as they have become upon me.

Last thing I want, being snatched from doing what I loved. While skiing, gliding down an empty mountain on a clear windless day when dry snow squeaks beneath the skis, lazy curves choreographed to Mozart's Piano Concerto No. 21 playing in my head, as close to the sensation of flight as I'll get without feathers. Not now, Death, can't you see I'm enjoying myself? Bugger dying while doing what you love.

It could be worse: straight after finishing any of the mind-numbing routines or the physically painful – felled upon the freshly mown grass, collapsing after the root canal work, collapsing after paying the bill after the root canal work. Spare me that.

As if there is a choice.

On a drive, on this drive, his timing wouldn't be too bad to take me beginning the crawl north in Sydney morning traffic, not later when it's more likely – at speed on a loved road up and over across the tableland under skies as open as the farms. I wouldn't miss the tedium of commuters dutifully lining up for their daily jam, idling in the queue at the first traffic lights, the local tendrils of the city's vast root system, veins feeding them onto secondary roads for a slower drive to join primary roads to merge by centimetres into the clogged main arteries draining towards the towering heart.

But veins don't feed into arteries and arteries don't drain. I'm confusing my arteries and veins, mixing my metaphors early on this drive, confusing my sappy tree roots and mammalian blood pipes, unnaturally entwining them. I'd back the roots to win, to strangle the blood like a ball of heartworm in a dog.

Somewhat similar but very different are veins and tree roots. Diagrams throw up a facile similarity – all that branching out, if roots don't mind such language.

'We don't "branch out", you idiot beast of the sunlight. We root out. We stretch and invade and take possession. No airy waving in the breeze here, no effortless expansion against air. We fight for every millimetre, pushing, insinuating, invading your pipes and structures, cracking concrete if we care to, taking over everything you've built in time, outlasting you, passing you, seizing our ground and holding it, holding on for dear life at times while upstairs does the fancy swaying and waving. We stay. We last. We're here forever while you pass over and blow away like leaves. Have us snake out, if you will, or even creep, but we'll not branch. Tell upstairs to root out for a change.'

Roots would be like that, with a John Cleese voice. Gnarled and put upon, every blind discovery a slow one, endless time for reflection and muttering in the absolute dark. Mostly just being there, immobile in the weight of earth, silently absorbing molecules – water, this and that mineral, former particles of life for life. Existing, waiting. In some eventual end, triumphing.

Underrated, roots. We claim to 'put down roots' when we're growing from them, our roots making us. We may branch out, but we're always coming from our roots, the strength of them holding us.

And that's why roots are not veins: roots acquire the good sustenance; veins rhyme with drains, draining the depleted blood. It's the arteries that push the rich red oxygenated stuff to feed cells. It's the arteries that will dramatically spurt if you slice them, pump life out of you quickly enough. It's the arteries that flooded seats and floors of the fatal car wrecks stored in the police station paddock of my childhood, gone sticky black by the time I could explore them – a perk of being a country policeman's son. You don't want to strike an artery unless you want to strike an artery. Timing again – and the trajectory of chance.

August 4, 7.25 pm

G'day Michael

The line about my irrelevance … I thought I had better try to explain in print, as sometimes words fail me in person.

I know it could be thought of as negative or even depressive, which was why I paraphrased it in a positive way … I think Tom's death finally brought it home to me … Tom took a lot of life very seriously in many ways, which made him quite good at his job, but also obviously distressed him at times.

The feeling of irrelevance I find very freeing … no more than the blades of grass or the little ant … I'm a very small part of a very big picture.

Nothing profound or new … not for everyone, but it makes me happy.

It helps melt away any embarrassment or humiliation I might feel … helps me deal with regrets I might have … and as I said to Suz the other day, if I had any success, it would help keep me humble.

Look forward to catching up at the Ascot Gentlemen's Coffee Club … Some members freak out if conversations get too deep and meaningful … I like to talk about life, death and all those human emotions we have … Although sometimes it freaks me out a little too.

Strangely, I would like to share my death with someone … but is that just my ego at full throttle, in a direct contradiction of my irrelevance thinking? It is an area people seem to not want to go to … let's talk footy.

One of the nurses at the oncology ward was about to start her master's degree in palliative care … I wanted to say to her interview me, but it didn't seem right. Crossed too many boundaries in the professional patient/medical relationship.

All about me this email, Michael … Hope your stay in Brisbane was successful … I will start to feel uncomfortable about over-sharing soon.

Thanks for your care, old mate.

Love Jim

Pollard and dung

Splashes of memory and incident comprise the amalgam of drives north; different cars, different seasons, different company, different reasons. Memory stacks, cuts and shuffles them. At the Fullers Road intersection with the highway at Chatswood, I am dealt vivid recall of being stuck on this stretch of road on another April drive, the April Jim died.

Leaving Sydney under appropriately grey sky and desultory autumn rain, a not-young Nissan broken down just here, its hazard lights flashing more slowly as I look at them, a battery dying, blocking a lane, slowing northbound proceedings when it shouldn't be so bad going against the citybound flow – me and everyone else on an already rain-retarded morning.

'You're driving up?' they'd all ask. Even over the phone I can see faces reflexively contorting, that quizzing squeeze of muscles that lift the upper lip and squint the eyes. It's the look that says 'you're crazy', as opposed to the look of mild surprise when the eyebrows lift and widen the eyes, a look that merely asks 'really?'

'Why don't you fly?'

'Because I want to drive.'

'You're crazy.'

For a while in the congestion, I thought they might be right. I could be there in no time. But I didn't want to be there in no time. That time I wanted to drive and feel the time and distance pass around me as I moved through it, feel the country as it moved through me. To try to feel country as Jim felt it. To have a sense of travelling and hence arriving. Time to think and not think at all.

We merged, taking my turn to slide behind the big silver bum of a LandCruiser in the gap left for me by a truck. I raise my hand in acknowledgement, not that the driver can see it, high above the Alfa. I can see that LandCruiser now but the name of the local I chatted with in the park yesterday eludes me.

We merge well, mostly, in Sydney. It's rare to come across an arsehole unwilling to yield a single car space. I'm vaguely proud of that. We're in it together. A team sport. This is society functioning. Be nice. Get on with it.

There's time to take in the girl in the fogging-up Nissan. She's indistinct behind the misted glass but I know how she'd look: she stares straight ahead or down at her phone, shadowing in her long black hair, not wanting to meet anyone's eyes as she's embarrassed to be inconveniencing so many strangers; she's anxious that she's doomed to be hopelessly late; she's annoyed the NRMA hasn't arrived yet; she's saddened that she can't afford a better, more reliable car. She feels hopeless and hapless and I would like to tell her it's all right, it doesn't matter, we'll all still get where we're going, to offer her a sympathetic smile that she wouldn't understand and might well misunderstand. 'And some old goat just leered at me, thought it was funny that I was so fucked. Bastard.'

But she doesn't look and couldn't really see through that glass and I couldn't really see her. I know nothing of her other than surmising she's young because there's a P-plate half-jammed under the numberplate. We populate the gaps in knowledge to suit ourselves, make assumptions about people, mistake good for bad and vice versa, become defeated by complexity, find it easier to let matters slide, to let it go, to forget.

And too late find you've let too much slide, open a wide door for regrets. Myrtle Ryan, the encouraging, forgiving matriarch, said not to worry too much about the sins you commit, it's the sins of omission that will damn us, the law of unintended consequences hard at work. Myrtle delivering philosophy to a child over the noise of the milking shed, the pulse of sucking machines and cows bumping the stalls, hooves on concrete.

The memory of a traffic jam has me back in boyhood on the Ryans' farm. I can smell pollard and cow shit, iodine and bleach.

Time.

August 5, 11.52 pm

Jim

Thanks for being open with me – I feel privileged that you are – and for explaining what you meant by the irrelevance line. I've not considered death in that light.

I can see part of what you may mean – that we're all bit players in a vastly larger drama; or perhaps a feeling that could have settled on people in the trenches, that we do our best, our part, but we're not individually responsible for the outcome of the war. That if we do well, well, that's good, but if we don't completely succeed, if we die, well, that doesn't much matter. We've tried.

(And the trenches mention allows me to say – since we are being more open than just retreating into the blokes' code of footy or whatever – that I have always thought and told my family when I found out you had cancer that if I ever found myself in a trench, you were one of a bare handful I would want beside me. Just as well I'm beyond conscription age then.)

But I don't know why you should have any feelings of embarrassment or humiliation. That certainly doesn't make sense to me.

Re the desire to share your death with someone, I'm assuming you don't mean the sharing and support and love you're receiving from your family and friends now.

I won't offer to literally share death with you just yet (!) – but if you would like to write what you're thinking and feeling, I would feel very privileged indeed to receive it and respond as a conversation and perhaps try to use it in some way down the track. You write well – clear and direct. You have a story and stories I would like to hear and understand. You have obviously thought about mortality at length when most of us try to avoid the topic.

I hope I haven't misunderstood. Please ignore these paragraphs if I have.

I also think that if you would like the oncology nurse to interview you for her master's, bloody well volunteer that willingness to her. She could be very appreciative. In keeping with the ants on blades of grass idea, why not?

I'm just sorry that I can't often get to the Ascot Gentlemen's Coffee Club. Or does this conversation in print work well as part of the mix of conversations you're having?

And don't feel uncomfortable about oversharing with me.

Love
Michael

Cedric

I'm trying to remember what Nissan the girl was sitting in. She hasn't slid away to wherever all the inconsequential memories go. A Gloria? A Pulsar? Not young enough to be a Tilda. Nowhere near old enough to have been a Datsun though – the Datsun 1600, the Datsun Sunny, the Datsun Bluebird. One of those whitegoods models anyway. Such names the Japanese come up with, especially the anti-marketing department at Nissan. The Murano. They named an SUV after small, carless Italian islands famous for glassblowing. The Cedric. What local importer could ever let his Japanese master foist the name Cedric on a car? For that matter, what could Yokohama be thinking with the Cedric in any language? If it was the greatest thing on four wheels, you still couldn't buy a car called Cedric.

And my first car was a much-used Datsun 1600. After it was purchased, I found a receipt from a garage in Perth in the back of the owner's manual. It had done some travelling that wasn't reflected on the clock. Datsun 1600s were supposed to have a bit of oomph. Mine didn't, a white box with narrow wheels that had a tendency to get bogged if they strayed an inch off the bitumen. I had looked at an MGA rag top for the same money but thought I would be sensible instead. The MGA was older, it was English and wouldn't be as reliable, it only had two seats and the soft top would leak and be constant trouble. In the end I've had to live with the fact that I chose a Datsun 1600 over an MGA as my first car. Call me Cedric.

My father helped me buy it, a teenager by himself no match for a seasoned used-car salesman in a yard opposite the Brisbane Exhibition Ground. The salesman's name was Kelly and Dad called him Ned, suggesting we were being robbed as he tried to talk a few dollars off.

And I realise now that Dad would have been feeling as I did when I helped my boys buy their first cars – pride in being helpful, in being able to help, in having experience, in being a father, enjoying the chance to be useful for a teenage son, hoping it will be a good car, that the boy will be happy with it, father and son bonding in the First Car rite of passage. My father's love for me was in that white box with narrow wheels.

And my sons would have been feeling as I was back then – wondering if Dad knew what he was doing. I didn't show him that Perth receipt.

When I was young, in early primary school, I knew the name and origin of every car on the road. I suppose there weren't so many models or manufacturers to know back then. The Holden, the biggest seller by far, was just the Holden for its first couple of decades with mere initials to specify models before the names really started. First was the Premier to justify the cost of options loaded onto what was still the Holden. Then the Kingswood and the big flashy Brougham with an infamously thirsty V8 engine. But the Brougham was just a little bigger Kingswood, and the Kingswood was just the Holden.

'A little bigger' – that makes sense, the sort of sense that could name a car Cedric.

Introducing a smaller car, a little littler, the Torana, made the difference. Holden dealers had sold the Vauxhall Viva but this was the Holden Torana, and so the Holden couldn't just be the Holden anymore. It was the Torana or the Kingswood and then came the Commodore. They called a car the Commodore – a naval rank, the title of a sailing club Pooh-Bah. 'That chap is the club commodore, Cedric.'

Mick Donohue had a Torana. The two of us drove from Brisbane to Canberra in it – 12 hundred kilometres or so – over a long weekend for Serge's 21st when he was at ANU. And back again.

I wouldn't let my boys do anything that stupid, but we did then, taking our chances. People mostly don't need to now, flying for less cost and no time. Country boys still would. Drive half a day to play a game of football and then back again. Taking more chances.

August 7, 9.05 pm

G'day Michael

We are pretty much on the same wavelength … I never intended sharing my dying would involve dying with me … A little above and beyond the call of duty.

Just need a little covering fire as I singlehandedly storm the enemy trenches. Dying is a solo pursuit, I think.

The oncologist said she thought I would die this year (definitely, she said) … but I take it as it comes … Possible I could still be here this time next year, so I don't worry too much … Quality not quantity is my overwhelming desire.

The years from 17 to 30 were rather traumatic ones for me … Haven't had a drink since 1986, so after a few years of getting back on track, the last 30 years have been kind to me.

I think of sharing my dying experiences so as to help others … Observing Tom's death so closely has made my experiences to date much more acceptable and understandable to me.

That nurse in day oncology would have been an ideal outlet, but it wasn't to be … We will see what eventuates down the path.

I'm sure a bit of ego involved in such desires … The thing is, I think I have already helped Sue, Jo and Catherine.

Tom didn't want to talk or even acknowledge death … I said to him once: 'I don't know what is happening to you, mate, but all I can think is it must be ok … because it happens to all of us, everyone we have known, everyone we know … it must be ok.'

It's ok and as natural and maybe even as exciting as birth … Both birth and death can be a little painful and messy … Full of fear and apprehension.

I would like my communication with everyone to be mutually beneficial … it's not really communication otherwise.

Your perceptions of me are sometimes flattering … I am a simple and flawed soul, like most others, I suppose.

You have carved out a great career in an industry where most would fail … It is a credit to you.

All having a laugh about the Ascot Gentlemen's Coffee Club … print can be as good as words, so we shall see you whenever we do.

Thanks, old mate.

Jim

The dance

To be invited to walk beside a dying man, a good man, to be asked into his mind as its existence is counted down, to be offered his eyes into the abyss, to know another soul in the honesty of the deathbed. A privilege.

For Jim to watch Tom die – Tom, his trailblazer, his big brother – while knowing he was dying himself …

Tom was a larrikin, Sue told me. Impulsive, funny, charming, sometimes wild. Jim said Tom was loved by everyone, always forgiven. He wore purple flares in Mitchell when the only dress code was RMs. He bought a Mini Moke and an Alfa, both on a whim, both totally unsuitable for the property. He introduced Jim to all the music that he loved, played at full volume in a Datsun 180B that lasted much longer than the Moke or the Alfa.

Tom phoned Jim nearly every day. And then he didn't.

What wasn't there was the eeriest thing about the plague. There's a talent in seeing what is missing, in looking for the opportunity cost, the counterfactual, understanding what is not said. Cultivate an ear for the hound that doesn't bark and it's everywhere. Starting a drive north with a compassionate leave pass during the first lockdown, it was school uniforms.

Schoolkids' delivery time, all those North Shore parents, mainly mums, in their trucks. Dangers to shipping, I've sometimes harrumphed, as they crisscross the city, dropping off and collecting their Isabellas and Chloes, Williams and Lachlans. Missing.

It was a poor excuse for peak hour on this road. Real traffic starts with tradies' peak hour in the dark, then office workers' and schoolkids' peak hour and I don't know who it was that comes along next but there are plenty of them. The same in the afternoon, only the tradies and mums – and more grandmothers and grandfathers – hit the road together, a surge from 2.30 pm in utes and trucks and vans and mums' taxis and loosely driven SUVs merging into the daily long march of the masses into suburbia and night. Everyone starting earlier to try to beat the traffic with everyone else. The four-hour peak hour.

Or sharing your air in packed buses and trains, queuing for the privilege. The workers and secondary school kids – not all have chauffeurs – would be streaming into Roseville railway station now. On the other side the Roseville College girls would be drifting out in their burgundy blazers and blue-checked dresses, some of their Panama hats worse for wear, none in a hurry.

Despite the train line, the bus stops on my side of the road in these parts would still have a smattering of the tribal colours of the upper North Shore private schools and the less ostentatious state high schools. The more crowded southbound stops had different species among the preponderance of office workers – all shapes, sizes, colours and ages but uniformly glum.

Public transport. Society working. Don't scream. Don't go mad when the crowd surges forward on a railway platform, when bodies squeeze in on each other, when a crowded lift stops halfway between floors with a jolt. We're in it together. Hold on. We do that, mostly.

I caught the Redcliffe bus from Petrie to De La Salle Scarborough for Years 6, 7 and 8. In the last year I sometimes sat alongside Carmel Egan – almost a scandal. No-one our age did that. Her father had replaced mine as the Petrie sergeant and she lived in what had been my home, the police station house. Carmel was bright and pretty with the most beautiful tanned skin I had ever seen. Carmel was an exotic name for me at the time, almost Carmen, the only opera LP in my family's eclectic mix of records, a black album sleeve with a dramatic slash of red for the silhouette of a woman. She – Carmel, not Carmen – wore blue-and-white-rimmed glasses and the Brigidine Sisters' Soubirous uniform that I can't quite see now – I think a brown-and-green-checked beige summer dress. She was a bit younger, in Year 7, and I wasn't sure if she wanted me to sit beside her, if she hated me for it the first time, but the girls always got on first and thereafter sometimes she would sit by herself a little apart from them with space for me but looking out the window with no other hint of welcome. We barely spoke.

That must have been towards the end of Year 8. I went off to board at Nudgee the next year and we left Petrie the year after, moved into Brisbane. After that I saw her just once, at the Nudgee dance in Year 12. She was smaller and we cheated in the progressive barn dance, skipping a couple of partners to say hello, glad to see each other, but Eileen Williamson and I were a number then, so I let the barn progress.

The innocence of school in 1972. There was no inviting partners, no sanctioned pairing off. Bulk orders were put in by the college for girls from the Catholic schools. 'Hello, St Rita's? Nudgee College here. Annual dance at the Homestead Hotel this Saturday. Send us a busload of your girls.'

The barn dance was designed to shuffle the pack early on and you were supposed to take back to your table whoever's hand you were holding when the music stopped. Maybe life's a bit like that.

Those of us who thought we had a girlfriend or were working on it had to find and finesse a partner exchange in a room of 450 teenagers – Years 11 and 12 and a sprinkling of the more presentable, older-looking Year 10s, promoted for one night by the brothers to ensure there were excess boys to cover for those with no interest or too shy and would spend the night in huddles in the bathroom or foyer. The embarrassment of a Year 12 girl left by the music for the night with a Year 10 boy judged a lesser evil than being left partnerless. There were clusters of girls as well.

We mostly tried our best, the drive of our hormones overcoming our fear of failure in the face of the unknown. Some boys were worldly, seemed to know how. Or claimed to. Others were not. Some of the country boys, perhaps not particularly talkative anyway, could appear lost. I wonder how Jim fared at those dances, that strong, earnest, kind brick of a fearsome teenager, who looked and listened more than talked but could also crack the biggest smile and a deep laugh that had honest warmth right through it. If the barn dance had stopped with a country girl, with a girl who asked him about horses … I suspect the odds were against it. I have no idea and certainly didn't care. Eileen had to be found and swapped.

Ghosts on journeys – Roseville schoolgirls to a Nudgee dance nearly half a century ago to Jim. I don't know how he fared with girls back in the bush after school. I didn't see him for three decades after we left Nudgee. When we began to catch up with each other's lives again, I didn't ask and he didn't volunteer. He was married to Sue and had two daughters and that's all there was to it, that was all that mattered in his life.

August 11, 7.42 pm

Jim,

I'm writing on a plane on the way to Perth. The speaking work I do – where the money is these days, journalism being what it has become – tends to come in lumps, with August, thankfully, a busy month. I enjoy the Perth flights when someone pays for me to fly up the front. The phone can't ring, there's no email, the food and wine and service all very civilised. There's time to think and write and read. And re-read.

If you want to – and only if you are happy to – I would like you to tell me more of those 17 to 30 years when I have no knowledge of you. What made them traumatic, what realisation hit you that led to giving up booze. It doesn't surprise me that you had the strength to do so once you decided to. Heavens knows that's a rare thing, the world awash with people who can't, in one form or another. Without knowing anything about it in detail, it's that inner-strength thing that I think I recognised in you long ago without ever analysing it. Something instinctive about that. And I suspect might say something about your strength now.

Sharing your experience is mutually helpful. Well, I hope it is for you. To spread your thoughts more widely, I can try. Can't promise to succeed, but I can promise to try. Off and on (mainly off) I have been thinking of trying to write something that is a combination of a love of country (the country itself, not the nation) and a contemplation on getting older and death – the eventual preoccupation of we baby boomers. I have an idea and have started and stalled on something that would be 'faction' – largely factual but with packaging around it. I could use – and attribute – your musings. It's a thought. Think about it.

I know that there are people who have written cancer diaries, but it's not a genre I've felt like pursuing. This, rather obviously, is your death, so it's a matter of how you want to play it. Other people who have written about their experiences, well, that's theirs.

I also suspect that our views of death are broadly similar, albeit that mine are considerably more theoretical than yours. The old management analogy of involvement and commitment and a plate of bacon and eggs applies – the chook was involved, but the pig was committed. I like to think I have a 'rational' view, like you. A bit of the death-is-part-of-life idea, a bit of it's-inevitable-so-make-the-best-of-it. Your suggestion that it is like birth takes that a step further.

But, as said, my appreciation is theoretical – a mere chook at present.

It's a good while now since Serge told me you had inoperable cancer. How long? I don't know how much detail you gave him back then, but he confided something along the lines of you deciding not to take some sort of treatment at the time, something about 'you wouldn't do it to an animal'. Was that your thinking or has something been lost in translation?

I think I understand something of what you say about the effect of seeing Tom die. When your big brother dies too young, maybe the shock goes out of it. As mentioned, my oldest brother checked out at 58 – actually a few days short of that birthday. For me, that has contributed to a degree of 'it happens', if you know what I mean.

There are other deaths that are too cruel to contemplate, to lose a child, most obviously. One of my youngest son's friends topped himself just a year out of school. It was absolutely out of the blue, a total surprise to everyone. A smart, handsome, popular, happy boy. Tim's year had more than its fair share of early deaths. One of them was an Australian schoolboys' rugby representative, drowned during a Thai full moon party. He was a risk-taker. As someone said, if you drew up a list of the class, from least-likely-to-die-young to most-likely, those two boys would have been at either end, yet they died within months of each other.

That is another dimension. I don't know how it connects or doesn't connect with your thinking. Tell me if it does.

I don't know if those sorts of thoughts are covering fire in this particular trench or become inbound shells instead. The last bit of dying might be solo but your journey has lots of good company. If, mainly from a distance via email, I can travel with you, I would feel privileged.

And re your comment about ego being a factor in wanting to share the learning, that opens another whole area of what's healthy about ego and what's actually being helpful. I'd say forget any idea that it's anything less than a good idea.

Over to you,
Your not-too-bloody-old mate,
Michael

The school

Driving north again. A school zone warning lights flashing, 40 kilometres an hour. Some school zones get flashing lights, some don't, some have radar traps. Lindfield Primary has a speed radar, up at Wahroonga it's the full red-light speed camera.

The cunning red-light speed camera. Run the red and you're caught with a flash, and so you should be too. I don't understand people driving through a red light. One night in Crows Nest by myself, late, starting off as the light turned green on Hume Street crossing the highway, something, someone, my Dad, made me pause and look left – a big car powering up to the intersection and I realise he won't stop, just sailed right through at speed. He would have collected me if I had taken off as usual. Glass and plastic and metal across the bitumen, maybe a 70-kilometres-per-hour impact amidships, my head whiplashed to the left and then smack back into the B-pillar. Don't know if the first Alfa 156s had side curtain airbags. My skull smashing and blood and tissue among the glass as the car rolled. Or if he hit a little forward of centre, he'd spin me back into him broadside and he would ricochet off onto the footpath, the light pole, the shop window – they sold blinds and overhead fans. The explosion of car on car, the physics of the combined three tonnes of metal at 70 kph, every action having an equal and opposite reaction, this one an almighty bang, the echo of glass and then silence.

Prangs don't burn as much as the movies have you believe. Shot bodies don't dance or fly as Tarantino makes them. It would seem silent at the corner of the Pacific Highway and Hume Street on a late midweek night, the blast deafening for a moment before the noise rushes back in with the last tinkle of glass crystals. Check for injuries, there'd be that, for bleeding, for death. Probably not, but maybe. The B-pillar could do it. Good chance.

How to die – fast or slow? No warning or weeks, months, years to plan and ponder? Jim was grateful for the time. I wonder how many times you die while waiting, how you live dying.

No excuse for running a red light, but speed up a little to catch the green, the amber, to avoid the red-light camera and, snap, the speed camera gets you instead. Cunning. They've had to add the speed camera because the red-light camera made people speed. That's us. Take a dangerously narrow little road, widen it, and people will drive faster and with less care and it's just as dangerous. That's us. The Law of Unintended Consequences rules our lives and we never see it. Otherwise it would not be unintended. That's us.

I've done this drive for a funeral only once, Jim's, but feel to have driven to that one every time since, driven with him. Still driving to a funeral. I've flown north for eight of them when I stop to count: my father, my mother, my oldest brother, my brother-in-law, Sergio's brother, Jim's brother, my friend and former early-morning colleague Rossco, Sergio's mother.

I would have liked it to have been nine but I didn't know about Myrtle Ryan's until it was over. For several years my second mother, my favourite holidays spent on the farm. In another culture I would have called her Aunty.

No-one told me Myrtle had died until after the funeral. I regret I did not attend as my absence may have said something to the living that I deeply did not intend. Afterwards, when I found out, I meant to write, but somehow did not. The address was not immediately available. I wasn't quite sure what to say. And then it was too late, or just late and I am slack and a coward and let it slide.

An older friend from Hong Kong days, David Bell, was killed by pancreatic cancer while the virus was at large. I visited him twice in palliative care at Greenwich, not one of the hospitals they were trying to keep empty in anticipation. We shared a half bottle of St Hallett Blackwell shiraz. Siew, Caroline and Jack – his wife, daughter and grandson – left us alone for a while. He was doing well, he said, no pain, but he hoped he might be able to go home with palliative care there. The pancreatic had its way quickly with him. He was dead before I could visit again.

David's was a COVID funeral, broadcast online. A camera high in the back corner of the crematorium chapel left his immediate family of widow, daughter, two sons and partners indistinct, distant and alone. Another time would have celebrated his 79 years with a crowd, a large one, to salute his joy, his conviviality, his generosity.

The benefit of going to a funeral: sure, to celebrate a life, but as much for your presence to try to say something to the living that is too hard to express in words. Not because you can't find them, or not necessarily because you can't find them, but because clichés have grabbed them all. I could not think of anything to write to Siew.

A neighbour died the first day of the second Sydney lockdown when funerals were reduced to 10 people. She had battled Parkinson's for decades, long beyond the odds. Her forever bravely ebullient husband and six steadfast children supporting and caring for her throughout. A massive circle of relatives and friends and barely enough numbers allowed for her direct descendants, not for their partners. The balm of ceremony reduced to the distance of shadows on a computer screen.

Sometimes there is nothing that can be said, when the suffering is palpable and when any words of comfort would be known to be lies because there is no comfort. For the death of a child, never.

I have not felt such silence, such mute mutual sorrow, as standing among several hundred people outside the college chapel – there was no room within – as Will's parents were led out after prayers the Monday after the Saturday he died, still days before his funeral. The Riverview community didn't wait for the funeral to gather at such times, driven together to share pain. The funeral would celebrate Will and did, but the aching fresh devastation of his loss was beyond expression, striking us dumb as every parent bled for his bleeding parents. The awful silence has stayed with me, the absence of sound in such a crowd on a summer's evening under the tumbling crimson bougainvillea of the colonnades.

Schools and death – schools where we were formed more than we knew at the time. And in a boarding school where you did most of your growing up, bonds formed to carry through to death.

When asked why we sent our sons to Riverview, I would joke that it was the necessity of supporting blue-and-white football jumpers, Nudgee's colours. There was more, of course. There was the hope this expensive, privileged school would have the breadth to cater for the differing talents and aspirations of four sons, that my sons would enjoy the space and spirit that had been available to me. There was the hope that the Jesuits would encourage a sense of service, social justice, the *magis* – the more. The elitism that came with expensive fees was a worry, the danger of being a rich kids' ghetto, but the boarding house and the many families who genuinely sacrificed to pay helped keep the place grounded, while the bursary program – not a sports or academic scholarship program but based on need and justice – provided the school's soul.

Nudgee was different. Whatever those who didn't know might have thought, the school was not elitist, though a degree of elitism was inevitably conferred upon it by the paucity of the period's education. Fewer than a third of Australians finished Year 12 in the early 1970s, a lower percentage again in Queensland. In the 1950s, when my eldest brother won a secondary scholarship, only two state schools in Brisbane offered the Senior matriculation exam. If you were in the country and your parents valued education – the education they were denied – there were few choices.

We were a diverse bunch, with little to be pretentious about and few outlets for pretension for any who aspired to it. Dunlop Volleys were about the flashest sandshoes available and many of us didn't have them. The first 'fancy' football boots –

Adidas with screw-in studs – were only starting to appear on schoolboys' feet and seemed ridiculously expensive. The main outward sign of relative wealth in the car park when parents dropped us off was the age of the car, not the marque. A mass of Holdens and Falcons, a European car very rare indeed. Some boys came from well-off families, many did not. Some – mine – went without more than a child realised.

There was a less obvious reason for Riverview: an inherited responsibility, a duty not to backslide from my parents' achievement, giving their six children long, golden summers of childhood and as much opportunity as they could grasp. Nudgee was possible through sacrifice and fees forgiven and scholarships.

We boys didn't care who was wearing a second-hand uniform and who was not, in the unlikely event we even noticed. We were bonded by the sport-based tribalism that sustained us, by pride in our success, believing in 'the Nudgee spirit' that gave advantage over the enemy, and by our shared experience of surviving the bad elements within the Christian Brothers.

'That's what being in the working class is all about, getting out of it.'

Nudgee, at a time when education was the great class breaker, was largely about Catholic ascendancy. And playing rugby union. Not necessarily in that order.

Now, the Riverview Year 12 car park is a study in North Shore sociology. Cars like that girl's Nissan and shiny new Europeans and everything in between. Plenty of 'safe' cars – older Mercedes and Volvos, tanks without much acceleration. The equivalent money would buy a younger Commodore,

Falcon or Magna with more power than a 17-year-old might wisely handle, or a neat little Corolla whose impact with a big four-wheel drive is the stuff of parental nightmares.

I saw a crash test comparison of an older Volvo with one of the better new compacts – the Volvo lost. What do people know?

Old Brian Doyle story: I want to die peacefully in my sleep, like my uncle Patrick, not screamin' and yellin' like the passengers in his car.

The land beneath

Turramurra. Like the cars in the Year 12 car park, there are gradations to the upper North Shore. It's not the homogenous white-bread middle-class the rest of Sydney disparages.

There are gradations to every suburb if you know them well enough, let alone whole regions of this sprawling city. It's part of Sydney's appeal that it is a dozen or more cities with different lifestyles for the choosing, if you can afford to choose. The North Shore's role is to be staid and leafy – the adjective 'leafy' is nearly part of the name. The Leafy North Shore – abundant trees and gardens on generously sized blocks of the established middle and upper-middle class. Nothing much exciting happens up here, but they do a good suburban tree which the local council protects with unreasoning passion, trees before people. Get a decent storm through Turramurra every few years and down come massive gums onto houses and cars and people, if they're unlucky. That's exciting. But don't try to clear a threatening tree or the Ku-ring-gai Council will hang you from it before a cheering audience of local flora fanatics. That's very exciting.

Turramurra, Sydney's wettest suburb. A little higher than the surrounds, it has a microclimate that specialises in rain, and the trees respond. If you're awake to it, awake to the land that continues to live beneath a city, waiting for us to pass, you can feel that gradation, leaving Gordon, crossing the Mona Vale Road intersection into Pymble. Get clear of this curve into the Pymble shops and the road seems a little wider through to the freeway, the trees taller and thicker, more established and solid, like the inhabitants, until they're blown over.

This is the heartwood of the federal seat of Bradfield, which is the heartwood of the Liberal Party, a stronghold since there has been a Liberal Party, the safest seat in New South Wales, the safest metropolitan seat in the nation. When it was established in 1949, its first member was Billy Hughes in his dotage, the final sinecure for the World War 1 prime minister, the Little Digger, the little urger. He was in his late eighties but that didn't worry the dutiful citizens of Bradfield.

Billy Hughes. The nation has proven better than its masters three times in referenda, defeating Menzies' attempt to ban the Communist Party in 1951 and both of Hughes' conscription plebiscites. We gave proportionately more blood than anyone in the first war but Hughes wanted to send yet more men and boys into the Western Front killing machine. Most diggers voted no, did not want conscription to their hell.

Another kind of death, death on another scale. Slaughter by governments, by ambition, by ideology, by politics, by delusion, by men well removed from the blood of ruptured and blasted bodies. There's no forgiveness possible for those who cause it, who pursue and use it. And our old battles never end, festering on in history wars as we try to know ourselves or defend our mythology.

The threat of conscription must have worried young Bob Menzies. His brothers volunteered so it was 'agreed' that he would not, became very busy getting connected and comfortable instead. He failed as wartime prime minister in 1941 but grabbed it again in 1949 with Billy Hughes in Bradfield and didn't let go until 1966, until he had introduced conscription to send boys to kill and be killed in Vietnam. The sanctimonious face of conservative certainty, conscripting other mothers' sons for a lost war we had no business fighting. And the great appeaser thought Hitler wasn't all bad in 1938.

A very white Australia then, bipartisan racism. 'We didn't really have a racial problem so we don't want to import one,' a Labor politician said of desperate Jews prewar. Jewish refugees were 'slinking rat-faced men' who might want to 'bring here their own undernourished and undeveloped women and breed a race within a race', said Sir Frank Clarke, for 20 years the president of Victoria's Legislative Council. He was the member for Monash from 1937 to 1955, his electorate named after our greatest general, a Jew.

The solid burghers of Bradfield wouldn't know that about their Liberal Party, Menzies long since airbrushed, his myth tailored to serve each iteration of politics, his speeches and letters reimagined along party lines, like ugly and inconvenient scripture reinterpreted by church/temple/mosque scholars to make it swallowable by the faithful. At least Billy Hughes was no appeaser of the unappeasable, a rare conservative voice at a time when it seemed only the local communists were concerned, when the Catholic hierarchy was backing Mussolini in Abyssinia, Franco in Spain and Hitler in Sudetenland.

The land waiting underneath doesn't care. After the custodians were killed and scattered, the waves of interfering migrants rolled through, the settler farmers clearing the bush, urbanisation as the city spread, bringing foreign trees, autumn colours. The land breathes on beneath them all. Now more unit towers are growing where large houses stood, where livestock grazed, where the bush was thick, where the Guringai people lived for millennia. And in time the land will absorb them all, our history forgotten. Somewhere, another virus, a much worse virus, ourselves, an asteroid. 'In the long run, we're all dead.' In the long run, we're irrelevant.

Years after Jim declared comfort in his irrelevance, Barack Obama published his memoir recalling visiting Egypt and seeing a face that resembled his etched into an ancient wall. He had his own Ozymandias moment, realising everything he had done, everything he had said, would be forgotten. Dust to dust.

Nothing beside remains. Round the decay
Of that colossal wreck, boundless and bare
The lone and level sands stretch far away.[4]

Get me out of Bradfield, out of old wars and old politicians empowered to kill, and here's Wahroonga and the right-hand turn at the lights to save me, to spill me onto the M1 heading north, to start this drive a second time with the promise of the road opening up.

August 13, 2.11 pm

G'day again Michael

I am noticeably losing weight from my face and arms ... Catherine said I should write quickly ... A sense of urgency is settling upon the flock.

I will answer your questions ... But firstly let me say no acknowledgements are required for my input.

I will take anonymity over acknowledgement in your work of faction ... If my reflections are the catalyst for you to begin to write something, it is fine by me. If your writings manage to help someone else, then that is even better.

As to the years 17 to 30:

I cover 2 queries here, one covering my interpretation on what happened and the other youth suicide.

I am not at this point a religious person, but am fairly convinced that it was only the deeply held religious beliefs that I had at the time which stopped me being a statistic ... Two reasons helped me survive: the fear of eternal damnation and the belief I had to face my demons in this lifetime.

And secondly, I didn't want to shame my family. I had enough empathy for those that I would have left behind to know it wasn't fair to them. I had shamed them enough.

You know the start of the story. I left school with some athletic success, running, a member of the First XV, a Commonwealth Scholarship, big and strong and fit, and generally I thought reasonably well regarded.

On the exterior, calm and strong, maybe even appearing self-assured ... But beneath the facade lay a lot of turmoil, a troubled soul. I know this most probably could have been said about many of us ... How do we measure each other's pain, suffering, anxiety ... I can only talk of mine.

I still am a highly anxious person, beneath the exterior. I like you have carved a life to suit the person I am (not saying our lives have similarities) ... I avoid, I retreat, and in some areas I simply haven't done.

I would love to have spoken at Tom's wedding, I would love to have spoken Tom's eulogy, but I could not and did not. I have no regrets about not doing so ... I have learned to accept myself for who and what I am, and am extremely grateful to have broken down as many barriers as I have.

Alcohol was my medicine ... We didn't combine very well ... You would have seen many people who cannot or should not drink ... I am one of those. The fall from grace for someone with what I thought was a fairly respectable profile was swift and painful ... It hurt. I could not drink, and I needed to drink ... Not a pretty dilemma ... No more need be said, it's done, it's dusted, it is part of who I am.

As for cancer diaries, reformed drinkers' stories etc ... It's all been said, it's all been done.

I liked your chook and the pig story ... So true it gave me a laugh.

I was diagnosed with stage 3B prostate cancer in August 2010 ... They could have operated, but at 54 years old I was going to be left totally incontinent, and totally impotent, and still they would not have got the cancer ... Next stage androgen deprivation therapy (chemical castration) ... and I said no to that too ... I did extensive radiation therapy ... HDR brachytherapy and EBR radiation.

As to death, we are on the same wavelength. Like cancer, there is cancer and cancer ... And there is death and death.

The death of a child is too cruel to contemplate, the death of an 80 or 90 year-old is a blessing of the highest order. Cancer in a child is too cruel to contemplate, cancer in the elderly is a way out.

Obviously opinions such as these are potentially very upsetting to people, and need to be phrased a little more gently than I may do.

I will have a think and maybe write some more.

Thursday

Had a sleep on that and I will leave it at that for the time being.

I see the medical oncologist next Wednesday for the first time in 5 weeks or so, so I might have more to say after that.

Hope this email finds you and family in good health … Ask away any questions you have … I can always choose not to answer …

Stay well, young fellow.

Jim

The Black Dog

Jim raising the Black Dog coincided with the first anniversary of Robin Williams' death. As a p.s. I sent him a link to a piece I had written questioning the sentiment of some in the immediate response to that great artist's suicide. I hold a grudge against Peter Weir for what he didn't have Williams say in *Dead Poets Society* – a missing speech that flawed an otherwise inspirational film, Academy Award nominations and all.

Williams' character should have had one final declamation – empathetic, moving, brilliant, sad, quietly but forcefully impassioned as Williams could be. It should have been a speech decrying Neil's suicide as a betrayal of *carpe diem*, of all the Dead Poets Society stood for, of surrendering rather than seizing the day.

Instead, Neil's death was allowed to lie there as an unanswered dramatic statement, the convenient theatrical denouement.

It annoyed me at the time and annoys me still as it left a film with enormous youth appeal and much joy apparently accepting suicide as a big statement, as a comprehensible way out of difficulty for a teenager. In Neil's case, it could be construed as something like revenge on controlling parents, parents who still didn't subsequently understand their son.

An opportunity was missed to rail against the plague that youth suicide has become. For all our sorrow for the afflicted individual and, hopefully, our care for the depressed, the dreadful ending of a precious, loved, young life cannot be treated as anything less than the most misguided and total mistake, as horrific waste, as utterly unnecessary and ignoble.

Dead Poets Society didn't do that. The fear of copycat deaths that stalks parents and schools after a suicide may have been assuaged just a little by the Williams speech that wasn't there. It angered me.

I was one more irrelevant fan along with everyone else who valued his gifts, whose life was made richer, happier at times thanks to his great talent, his art. The phenomenon of modern fame creates the illusion that we knew Williams better than we possibly could have, while we're left with sympathy for people we don't know at all, those who did know him closely and loved him.

Before we had any knowledge of the particular torture Williams was suffering, that he died by suicide saddened me further, and the mass outpouring of sympathy for a suicide worried me.

The silence of parents bleeding for bleeding parents. Crimson bougainvillea tumbling down the colonnades.

I copped a little stick for the article in some quarters, some appreciation in others. The stick was overshadowed by an email from an American father who lost his son not long after he watched *Dead Poets Society*. We never know what influences, good and bad, we can have, how we help and harm.

Somehow it came up in conversation with a woman I barely knew. I went further than criticising *Dead Poets Society* and said Williams' suicide was a similar disappointment. I didn't know he had extreme Lewy body disease, didn't know what that was, didn't know his mind was terminally torturing him, that he was suffering a slow, terrifying death. She told me. Her brother-in-law had it.

August 14, 11.17 am

Dear Jim

It's a cliché to say 'I don't shock easily' after a life in journalism – being a professional observer of people, businesses, nations, including my share of the grittier side of the job in the early years – but if this email didn't shock me, it certainly gave me one hell of a surprise.

No, it was more than surprise – it was a shock to find out you had such demons, that you of all people were anxious under your strong bush exterior. I think you've just taught me another lesson: to assume nothing. (I've long tried to do that about people's relationships. You never know what's really going on in other people's marriages, for example; you're lucky to have a rough idea of your own sometimes. So whenever I've heard of someone breaking up, I've tried to never buy into whose 'fault' it was.)

I would like to understand much better, if it's a question you're prepared to answer. Just telling me that you were anxious under that calm, tough exterior doesn't go far enough. A fear of public speaking, that's common, and shouldn't be that big an issue – more of a symptom than a cause?

How wry – I never had the courage to be much good in defence when we played, I envied you that ability and fearlessness, and now I find out you would have liked to let your chops flap as easily as mine. If only we could have traded some of each back then.

What else was happening to you then, old mate? What troubled you? I took off from Brisbane as soon as I could after finishing my cadetship and lost contact with pretty much everyone. You went back to where and did what? And at what point and why and how did you quit alcohol? When you say you were a bad drinker, what do you mean – destructive?

70

The cancer part of your emails is sobering but doesn't shock me. It's part of our journey, just the timing varies. I would like to know how a man who tells me he has always been anxious has been able to shoulder this so well. I suppose that's the nub of what you'd like to share with people, that and the quality-of-life decision. I'm guessing your wife and girls have a lot to do with that, as well as Tom. Your empathy as well, in a different context.

I don't know if I have said it but I look at much of what I'm trying to do with my work now as attempting to get people to keep perspective about our country and the economy, to look through the politics and the daily noise at what really counts. Maybe that's what we're trying to do for people in this conversation.

As for losing weight, that's a funny thing about our age: you meet someone you haven't seen in a while and they've lost some weight, you don't know whether to congratulate them on getting fitter or worry that they're sick. I managed to drop 5 kgs with a variation of the trendy 5:2 diet (well, I hope it was the diet!) and saw people have that reaction. It's like asking a large woman when the baby is due only to find out she isn't pregnant – sometimes no comment at all is definitely the right comment.

Over to you, mate.

Michael

Temptation

It was cruel, but I sort of did that in reverse once. They were friends and I should have been kinder.

It was early in the chemo process, before my hair disappeared, at dinner with two couples, one lot knowing, the other not.

'You're looking fit – have you lost weight?' asked David. A compliment, being accused of losing weight.

I catch a quick glance from Glenda, who knew. 'Oh,' her eyebrows said. And there was the temptation for mischief lying on the table, waiting to be picked up or ignored.

Before class in Year 10, for no good reason I wrote the nickname 'BASIL' across the width of the blackboard. He was our English, Religion, Maths 1 and Maths 2 teacher and dorm master. That was too much of Basil in a schoolboy's day. We were in the first stream but the brutal second stream maths teacher was belting his class into getting better marks. Basil responded by abandoning half his English classes to maths as well. Our English results suffered. It didn't make any difference to our maths.

Someone dared me to leave BASIL there – good chance it was Kev Carmody – so I did.

'Have you ever thought how dangerous it is to ask someone of our age if they've lost weight? Wouldn't you feel bad if it was really cancer?' I smiled.

Glenda's eyebrows tried to leave the table.

'Yep, a dose of cancer can do that for you.'

His face sagged – a terrible thing to do to a friend, but I laughed and apologised and explained the temptation was just too great. How often does someone with cancer get to pull a line like that?

I think David, a fellow Queenslander, a scientist, forgave me. His wife, Annie, also a scientist, immediately wanted all the details.

Basil's jaws clenched and unclenched. He was a great one for jaw clenching in front of the class and for large smiles outside.

Owned up on that occasion, copped it, carried on. Worth it as part of a year-long feud with him, a feud I won when he lost it and gave me six of the best for something he knew I did not do – Kev did it, Kev told him. Kev. We had started Year 10 at the back of the room together. Basil moved us to the front row soon enough.

We tortured some of the teachers, some of the teachers tortured us – and worse.

Then some of us end up torturing ourselves.

21 million Beetles

You start this drive three times, maybe four. There's getting going in Sydney, the halting traffic-light-ruled effort until the M1, and then you're off at last, starting again, the speed limit 80 with the promise of 100 soon enough and on to 110, with some faith in an unwritten New South Wales law that a driver can add another eight per cent.

It's a different drive on the M1, enough traffic to not threaten the speed limit but moving, picking up momentum as we sort ourselves out, driving without traffic lights and pedestrians and cars parking or turning. The freeway is undemanding without those impediments and while held in place around the speed limit. Find a stalking horse, a fellow traveller who would also like to go just a little faster, settle in behind him – nearly always a him – and set the adaptive cruise control to let the car do the thinking for this leg.

Adaptive cruise control, the Giulia using radar to accelerate and brake itself to remain a constant distance from the vehicle in front. A slight warning vibration in the steering wheel if I stray over a line without indicating. Next, active lane holding, the car steering itself, only asking the touch of a hand on the wheel. How far might the brain wander then?

For most people who spend most of their motoring time

74

sitting in a commuter traffic jam, the new Rolls-Royce and the new Corolla both have comfortable seats, air conditioning and sound systems, which are all that count in that situation, but the Toyota is more reliable and vastly cheaper, so the Corolla is the better car. Or something like that is what the gentle and sophisticated Peter Burden used to say back when he wrote the motoring section of the *Financial Review*.

But we're not sitting in a traffic jam now and I'm Alfisti – an Alfista. The Italians design cars and breathe souls into them, souls that have been known to whisper 'go faster' to you. An Alfa is for driving, the Germans merely for transport. Or so Alfaholics pretend, claiming in our prejudice that all German vehicles are mere variations on the *volks wagen* – and that perhaps stolen by Ferdinand Porsche from Ganz and Ledwinka.

Josef Ganz and Hans Ledwinka – unlikely names to stick with me on a freeway when easier things don't, the men with claim to be the real fathers of the Beetle years before Porsche. Random things remembered and others forgotten and time to get lost down rabbit holes searching for them.

In kitchen table conversation I went to mention a shop in, in … the suburb between Wollstonecraft and Northwood. 'Greenslopes,' I thought, and knew it wasn't – a suburb in Brisbane, where the repat hospital was. 'Greensleeves,' I joked to myself. As I searched for the word, I said Greensleeves out loud as a joke, as if we'd always called it that, like 'casting nasturtiums'. But we hadn't. A quizzical look.

'What?'

'You know, John Howard used to go to the fish shop there …'

'Greenwich.'

'Yes, Greenwich, Greensleeves, whatever.'

Greenslopes. My uncle Emmett worked there as an orderly. Came back from the war, tried a few things, got married, got divorced, got a job at the repat hospital pushing diggers' beds around and stayed there. Emmett – only family called him Emmett, he was Jerry to everyone else, strange name for a digger driving trucks in North Africa to adopt – would sometimes go out on prawn trawlers, bring us a sugarbag of Moreton Bay bugs, back when they were considered trash. And he was known to pour his little nephew a shandy on the quiet.

Jim said he found himself thinking much more about the past. He thought it was part of the effect of his steady, certain dying. Said he found himself finding disproportionate joy on encountering people from his past. Someone he hadn't seen since his wild drinking days turned up and Jim couldn't get over how happy he was to see him, to reconnect. Reviewing, remembering, a time of reminiscing.

Driving with Emmett and Jim and Ganz and Ledwinka and Beetles while the Giulia nearly drives itself. Volkswagen made 21 million Beetles – the real ones, not the retro fashion statements – each one carrying a little of Ganz's and Ledwinka's design DNA. And I share about a quarter of my DNA with Emmett, with each of my uncles, those men of the war, of the Depression. My sons share an eighth, their children a sixteenth. We branch out, blow away, but the roots remain, physical and otherwise.

August 15, 9.09 am

Hello again Michael

I shocked you … journalist of 40 plus years, and I still manage to shock … Shocking in itself … part of my story is I think that people misread the beast.

I'm pleased that the grieving father wrote to you for your article on Robin Williams and suicide … that's when we know we have done well. I am heartened that your ambition and intention in your work is to try and get us to focus on the big picture … you're a good person, most probably much better off in a holistic sense to be free of the restrictions that come with being attached to one media organisation … and that one in particular.

I thought about that today … relating it to myself. I most probably didn't do what I would have chosen in life. I negotiated the maze (within myself) and lived a life determined by the hurdles that were placed in front of me … but looking back now I am pleased with the outcome … I sometimes feel I could not have asked for a better life.

On another point, Michael … my three girls have joined in this conversation … as silent partners. I hope it won't inhibit the back and forth … They wanted to know what I was saying, so I said look.

Now Sue knows more about me than I know about myself … but the 2 girls less so … and they should know … they see me as a big fearless lump, and I don't want them to think after I die … 'I wish I had known'.

I can choose to share with you (and I find it healthy and helpful), but the people I really deeply want to protect and help could have been left on the sidelines … Their presence won't inhibit me, and hopefully not you.

I said to Gary O'Rourke once to tell Serg anything … I said he could have a family slide show night with my scans … just for fun … I'm pretty

77

much an open book. That's the case with you and Serg (or anyone else) and anything I might say … It's not a confessional and you're not sworn to secrecy.

Next subject … Fear/anxiety and courage.

It does NOT take courage to be fearless, but it takes great courage to function in the face of fear, real or imagined … an agoraphobic has to summon up enormous courage to open the front door.

My experience suggests to me that the fears within (imagined is a poor description) are far more formidable than the actual physical fear … hence the lack of fear on a football field, or the lack of fear in death/dying.

And once again, how do you measure fear? … What level of fear did you experience on the football field? … What level did I experience? … How much courage did it take for you to jump in those lineouts against BGS, BSHS, TGS? … A lot, I imagine … they were big boys.

Some have said I'm strong or courageous in my attitude to dying (to this point at least) … but I strongly disagree. At this point I simply have no fear of death.

After much effort to face, trace and eradicate my anxiety problem, I still don't understand why I have anxiety or where it came from … my guess based on my little knowledge is that they were inherited … I was simply born as such … I identified strongly with agoraphobia … and not because I wanted a label.

I just don't know … I suppose if I did, I would have had to have been blessed with some form of enlightenment.

I agree with you that fear of public speaking or the like are but symptoms of some greater malady, but there is a great difference between an uncomfortable feeling of anxiety (which can be channelled into some positive force), and an overpowering, crippling sense of dread and fear.

I never actually identified with being depressed … a psychologist once told me you can't have one without the other, but I'm not sure on that.

As for stopping drinking alcohol … From 21 on I stopped many a time, sometimes for 12 or 18 months … My life was so crap off the booze, riddled with fear and anxiety, that I always started again. Alcohol was again just a part of a greater issue.

Eventually in late 1986/early 1987 I found my way into AA, which I went to regularly for 10 years until 1997 ... never been back since ... it helped me and I haven't had a drink since around January 1986.

I never lost much sleep over the word alcoholic ... I did know my life would be much simpler and better if I didn't drink.

'You can never trust a man who doesn't drink' ... I've had that one levelled at me now and again ... now others can think what they want, but my personal experience was that I was much more honourable and trustworthy sober than drunk.

I worried about medication as this cancer progressed ... I've got morphine, Endone, Targin to name a few at home now, and have had so for 12 months ... all I take, some very regularly, some just occasionally, and it has never been a problem for me ... I feel very comfortable with them, which is a relief, and I definitely have no sign of addiction or mood or personality change ... It was a genuine fear of mine.

Bad drinker? ... Well, I don't know, it was 30 years ago, and I have no desire to check or see how I would handle it now. I love being of a sober mind, I love being away from a drinking culture. Who knows if it was just all the unresolved turmoil bubbling to the surface, who cares? It does seem pretty obvious I didn't drink well, never sure if I would laugh, cry or fight ... You and Serg and such just tend to become a little mellow when you drink, and I didn't do that.

In a lot of cases I still don't like being around people who are drunk ... I enjoy and appreciate the shyness and reserve that comes with sobriety ... but I am no anti-drinking zealot ... I will sit around a table with you and Serg and let you partake in a fine red wine for as long as you like ... just so long as you can handle me on coffee.

Those years 17 to 30 were not all bad ... Personally they were, but work-wise and financially I was reasonably successful. Managed the family farm, which was sold when I was 23 ... and I think I did it very well for a young fellow ... Worked harder and better being a recluse.

From 1979 when we left the farm until 1986/7, I worked oil and gas or just out bush and built up a substantial holding in residential rental flats along with a sizeable share portfolio ... Adjusted for inflation, I would have been better off then than I am now, the last few years being rather harsh for this old cowboy. My financial success did in some way compensate for my personal struggles, but I always knew deep within that I couldn't run forever ... One day I would have to face my demons.

Just rereading your email ... What happened?

I don't think I successfully made the transition from schoolboy to adult ... Once I had to stand alone, without the protection of parents or teachers, personally I was found wanting ... I stumbled and fell, it took me a long while to recover ... a delayed adolescence?? ... once again, who knows.

I struggled with human nature, I still do ... The world is a hard and harsh place ... I just need to focus on the beauty and the beautiful people. Mankind's inhumanity to their fellow man is beyond my ability to comprehend ... I'm a candle in the wind sort of fellow.

Well, Michael, there is a lot about me in these emails ... I hope you are comfortable with that? ... It might just be the nature of the discourse at this point.

You were going to share my dying experience with me, and maybe we just need to get some of the life experience out of the road first ... get the foundations in place for the last hurrah.

I'm a bit lost as to where to go from here, which is another way of saying 'that's it for now'.

Thanks again for your love, interest and support ... it's a little out of the blue situation, but it's good for me. It is interesting how you have cut it and cut it so well in the rough and tumble world of journalism ... you're the tough one, Michael, not me.

So until next time, stay well and healthy ... Have you visited the coffee shop in your pyjamas yet? ... It would never do at the Ascot Gentlemen's Club ... Actually, we should make it the Gentlepersons' Club ... On Thursday we had 3 old boys and 2 fine women ... I like the company of women, and rather sensitive men ... I don't fit in the man's man world.

So, Michael, that's it for now ...

Kind regards

Jim (and his loving and loyal support crew) ... That's not a joke ... I don't know what this old cowboy did to deserve the love and support that I am surrounded with ... Starts with the girls, then the friends, and finally at least 5 extraordinary doctors.

Veloce

We're moving well enough. Some geese overtaking slowly in the fast lane and not quick about getting back where they belong, but fast enough. Kill the cruise control, accelerate past them, touch the pedal for the instant surge. The Alfa likes that. If you are attuned to it, you feel the Giulia crouch a little under acceleration, settle tighter, wanting to go faster and keep going, what she was built to do. And that's in the 'normal' setting of the suspension and transmission options. Twiddle the DNA knob to D, dynamic, and there is a little more growl, the gears hold higher revs longer, change down more willingly, the suspension firms. Find a curvy road, flick to manual and drive hard again, be allowed to drive for the pleasure of driving again.

It is an indulgence. Not a complete indulgence – I test-drove the marvellous and ridiculous Quadrifoglio version for that. An hour on Sydney roads, a hoon for an hour in the world's fastest petrol-powered four-door production sedan, the gear changes barking, so fast, so balanced, so much tight endless power under your foot and in your fingers. My licence would be lucky to last a month.

So I bought the mid-range Veloce; not the Quadrifoglio rocket but faster than the more-than-adequately-fast base model. An indulgence. Unnecessary. But if not now, when? This could be my last car. 'A car that will see me out.' A legion of boomer retirees tapping a lump sum from their superannuation for a new car to see them out. Camrys and Hondas and the odd European indulgence like mine. And big four-wheel drives in which to become grey nomads. Or SADs, a Tim Winton character called them – See Australia and Die. Buy and drive the Alfa now while hips and knees can get down and into it. And, a touch harder, up and out of it. Before Dupuytren's makes the wheel uncomfortable in your claw and a hip's bursitis takes the pleasure out of a long drive. Buy and drive a fine internal combustion engine before the silent electrics take over. A generation soon enough that will never feel a thoroughbred snort and roar on an aggressive downshift into a bend. Poor bastards.

The Veloce is more than enough with a fine stretch ahead. Coming down from the ridge to the Hawkesbury River promises the curves up the other side through the sandstone cuttings where they've dropped the speed limit to 100, 90 if raining, but it's the best stretch of the M1, as long as you remember the fixed speed camera traps, and you'd be a fool not to. You wouldn't be driving, enjoying driving, if you missed the warning signs ahead of the cameras. Fines here are for being inattentive, not for speeding.

And you're moving through the walls of sandstone. I first drove this road – it was called the F3 then – in 1979 when we honeymooned on Lake Macquarie in my brother Terry's house. Such a length of fast road seemed a feat of engineering. The cuttings were fresh, almost bleeding colour, Hawkesbury sandstone's rich ochres glowing. If you could stop and touch it – and you would like to, to place your hand on that stone the way you lay your palm on fresh-cut wood – the stone looked like it could be warm with a life. Good enough to lick.

I tell people I'm good and I am – all good, mate. More likely the lymphoma is beaten every day, for sure. Left me with a desire to touch wood and stone and a 10-centimetre scar down my belly from the hemicolectomy that found the lump hiding behind the ulcer, the ulcer that the Korean–Australian gastroenterologist and the Egyptian–Kiwi surgeon thought just wasn't 'right' despite a score of negative biopsies.

I don't notice the scar across my bellybutton – swimsuit modelling wasn't working out as a career anyway – but I'm aware of the increased desire to touch beauty, to absorb the wonder of it, to imprint it, to remember it.

A big eucalypt by the path down to my local park, its skin freshly shed, calls my hand to rest on its smooth curve, to feel the cool strength of that tree, to draw from its depth and connect with its soaring splendour and the asymmetrical art of its limbs above, search for birds in the canopy, whistle back to any magpie warble.

On the way south, Berowra turn-off, there is a sandstone impression of the Flatiron Building, a stepped red prow dividing the road. It's blackening with the years, no longer the bright red when it was freshly cut, but still grand. You see it, register the majesty of that stone, and it's gone. If I could have stopped there, could reverse time to stand against the stone when it was fresh, to absorb the turn-off like the path leading down to Petra, I would.

The red, the yellow, all the ochre shades, the honey gold. Arthur Streeton called Sydney 'the golden city' when he returned to Australia – the rich, bright sandstone public buildings under the Australian sun.

Few of the freeway's cuttings are fresh now, sections smudged and greyed by exhaust and weather, the lichen taking hold in the shadows where the sandstone feeds it.

I have a photograph of lichen on old blackened sandstone down by Berrys Bay – I've started photographing surfaces, shadows, flowers and, of course, snow gums. That cutting through the Berrys Bay rock is, I don't know, way more than one hundred years old. A hundred years of city smoke and smog and dirt, scores of years when Sydney was sulphurous with coal fires, when the North Shore Gas Company made town gas by burning coal in adjoining Waverton, when there was a coalmine in the middle of Balmain across the harbour. Now lichen and moss are bringing life and colour back to it, the land beneath stirring, given half a chance. Sombre greens and beige, splattered and globbed, but infinitely variable up close. It invites the eye but not the touch, like the skin on the back of a bushie's sun-blotched hands. My father's hands. Jim's hands.

They see me as a big fearless lump, and I don't want them to think after I die … 'I wish I had known'.

We five surviving siblings gathered to mark what would have been our parents' 100th birthdays, to salute them and acknowledge our debt. Both times we were mainly trying to know them, to learn more about them from each other, trying to patch together a three-dimensional picture from the snaps in our different scrapbooks. The young father for my older brother and sister in simpler Australia, the older father for me and my younger sister – Dad's first grandchild and youngest child the same age. Our mother forever seeking for us what the Depression denied her, forever hungry for opportunity on behalf of her children.

Sometimes I look at my hands and don't recognise them. They are old or older hands. A man's hands, big enough, with veins and sunspots and a little thickening of joints, perhaps a bit thinner for a while after the chemo. Even before that, though, they were not my father's hands when he was my age. They've never been as strong and honestly worked as his.

It strikes me driving now, my hands before me on the wheel, speeding up and away from the Hawkesbury through curving halls of sandstone and up into weather-tossed eucalypts, a little obvious pop psychology: I've judged manhood all my life by my father. To be him, to survive his childhood, to grow, to be strong, to be brave, to father, to work, to swim through the dark forces of police work and corruption and remain a gentle man, to serve, to not complain, to remain. Without knowing, I've marked my weaknesses and those of others against his benchmark. My idealised father I could never know, who mostly kept his own counsel.

Jim's hands were like my father's. Both bush born, both bush worked as boys, young men, both running farms when little more than boys, Jim his family's, Dad for a squatter who favoured him, trusted him, who imprinted adages. 'If you can't be on time, Richard, be five minutes early.' The squatter's own sons sent far away to Geelong Grammar for school. Dad not even a teenager when he was sent to work on a station as a rouseabout. A year out beyond Longreach before a few days 'home' at Christmas. Dad and Jim both fine horsemen. Dad became a mounted policeman during the Depression when police were still mounted as their means of transport in parts of the bush, not for ceremonial purposes. As a young constable he would do the rounds of the McPherson Range ridges on horseback, from Beaudesert up to O'Reilly's Guest House before Bernard O'Reilly made the place famous with his own solo bushmanship, finding the crashed Stinson and its two survivors. And ride an Indian motorcycle on the track of a road back to Brisbane whenever he could to court my mother.

'I'm wasting away, Michael.'

We were sitting at the kitchen table on his little farm. Jim held out his arm to show me, opened and closed his hand, made a fist and the tendons of his wide forearm still rippled. Jim, dying of cancer, wasting away, with arms still stronger than mine.

'Well, if this is wasting, you must've been a fat bastard to start with.'

Show no pain

I felt nothing much at all when I was told I had cancer. I thought I should be feeling something, at least a little panic, a little horror. Instead I remember observing myself looking for a reaction, for any drama, and found none. My heartbeat didn't change. 'That's cool,' I thought.

The first time I left Australia was for a holiday in Fiji. I was 19, Judy and I flying off together back when international travel, even to Fiji, was an event. Friends came to the airport 'to see you off'. I wore a tie. Snorkelling by myself around the coral atoll we were staying on, maybe 50 metres from shore, I was joined by a shark about the same size as me, the better part of two metres. 'This is interesting,' I thought.

I had been as fascinated by sharks and snakes as any boy, maybe more so. Watched all the Ben Cropp documentaries, read *Life* magazine special features. I knew he or she – I've always thought of him as a he – was probably a well-fed shark in the rich tropical waters, that he wouldn't be one of the more notorious species, that he wasn't too big. I knew the thing to do was to swim calmly and steadily back to shore, which I began to do, no splashing or haste. And the shark started swimming beside me, a little more than a body length away, keeping me company, slow sweeps of its tail wagging its body through the water, his pale yellow eye on me.

'I'm calm,' I thought. 'I'm OK with a shark swimming beside me. This is cool.' I was impressing myself.

As a two-metre shark wags through the water not far away from you, its head moves side to side. On a wag towards you, you get a glance at his mouth. A two-metre shark is not a monster, but it still has quite a wide mouth – and you can think how much of a leg or arm such a mouth could grab, which is indeed an interesting thought.

After an eternity, probably all of 10 seconds, the shark lost interest and lazed away into the sea haze. I continued steadily swimming. A couple of Fijians were sitting on the beach.

'Bula.'

'Bula.'

'I don't know if you can do anything, but there's a shark out there on the reef.'

'Oh! How big?'

'About as big as me.'

'Oh! You try to catch 'im?'

So much for being brave with a shark. Stay calm and swim on.

Being told I had cancer was a bit like that. I observed myself staying rational, not reacting, showing no fear, might have thought 'bugger' but kept it to myself.

It was what we were trained to do, what was inculcated as boys back in the day. Show no pain. Get up quickly from the tackle. Don't flinch under the strap. Keep your head up. Of course you don't cry. You're harder than they are. Fuck 'em.

Maybe we all are, or most of us. An evolutionary mechanism that gives the cognisant dying an acceptance of death. How else could the second wave go over the top at Lone Pine? How else could Alison, friend and sometime dog-walking companion, so calmly discuss the unheralded discovery of grade IV glioblastoma? (An aggressive and terminal brain cancer, for the uninitiated.)

It was surreal, she said. 'But I'm OK with it, really.'

A very young and fit 60, a doting husband, three daughters, an 18-month-old grandson, another grandchild due in three months, a sharp 90-year-old mother. She was initially given the prognosis of a median survival time of 12 months. How many YPLL is that?

A seizure without any prior symptoms, an immediate operation, the tumour was shallow, her mind unaffected. Radio and chemo ahead, if she wanted it, the choice hers to discontinue.

'Really, I'm OK with it – I wouldn't want to hang around, I wouldn't want to be a drag on the girls getting on with their lives.'

And within a week, an extension.

Best news, she texted. The tumour is methylated, only 30 per cent are, and they respond to treatment the best. 3 to 5 years or longer.

I'm a fraud.

Not really. I do have brain cancer, but the best kind, perhaps.

So now I drive with Jim's ghost and Alison's present reality, can look forward to dog walks with her as her future unfolds the way I corresponded with Jim, if she wants. Boomers lending each other shoulders as the YPLL roll up.

Emails are easier.

August 21, 1.24 am

Jim

I have been pondering your last letter. (I'm old enough to want to dignify as 'letters' emails that are sent with thought, as opposed to the mere memos and waves most emails are.)

I welcome the larger audience to this correspondence and hope it is good for them as it for us. I'm not sure how relevant it is, but my mother would have been 100 this year, so my four surviving siblings and I had a dinner to celebrate her birthday, as we did our Dad's, and spent much of the time trying to understand the people that they were, putting them in the context of their times and challenges. It was a good thing, helped a great deal by my brother Terry having sat down with Mum and Dad one Christmas and interviewing them on tape about their lives, some of it down to a fairly intimate level. I hope your girls know and appreciate you more for this 'interview'.

Jim, I hope you take this as a compliment, but in some ways you remind me of my father. He was from the bush and never lost that heritage. A strong man, a hard but fair man when he had to be as a copper, who tended to hide a gentle soul. He swam in dark currents – being a policeman in as corrupt an institution as the Queensland police force in those bad old pre-Fitzgerald days would have been soul-destroying, never mind the grind of police work exposed to some of the worst of human nature – but he remained a gentle man despite it all.

As you know, I'm rarely lost for words, but seared into my memory is a brief exchange we had that left me wanting to tell him so much more than I did at the time. He was retired (and retired from the security job at Myer Indooroopilly he took after retiring from the police force) and wondered why I was leaving Hong Kong when I seemed to be doing well there and he sort of obliquely said that he hadn't achieved much with

91

his life. I couldn't get words out. I think I said something like, 'Dad, that's not true,' but couldn't explain. I did much later, before he died, in a letter, but I still so wish I had been able to tell him right then how much he had achieved, how much he had given his children, but I couldn't. It tears me up now recalling it. Maybe it was the shock of his statement at the time, as I certainly saw him as 'a strong lump' in many ways. I loved him dearly, but we did not communicate easily, conversation did not flow beyond the obvious.

(Another aside: I remember some comedian's line about conversations with his father when he rang home: 'How's work? How's your car going? I'll put your mother on ...')

So that's too much about me when this is about you and your journey and your girls and the greater understanding of you that they might gain. I think it's normal that we would like to be able to travel back in time and see our parents as they were when they were young, to understand them as people instead of as parents. Suspect that was part of the appeal of the idea of the *Back to the Future* movies.

Which leads to some obvious questions from your last dispatch.

What was the life you would have chosen? The sale of the family farm, was that a shock at the time? But running the farm didn't seem to be doing anything positive for your anxiety. What brought you out of the suicide danger zone? Was there anything in particular that made it possible to manage anxiety? And having done that, having learned to contain something as hard as extreme anxiety, is something as natural as death less of a problem?

I can only agree with your observation about it taking courage to overcome fear, not to simply be fearless from the outset. Those rare types merely incapable of fear don't earn any points for effort – and are possibly insane. There is a decision to consciously put fear behind, which is quietly heroic. At a minor but instructive level, I've seen it in some of the kids I've coached on the rugby field. I've seen it in my oldest son on two particular occasions in primary school that made me very proud and that I will tell you about when I next visit the Ascot Gentlepersons' Coffee Club if you ask.

(Re those lineouts, I knew they were the reason I was in the team so I had to give whatever I could in them. Because I mostly could jump, certainly when Wagner coached us and taught us the Japanese style of jumping first ahead of the throw, there was no physical fear in it, only fear of failure – though that BGS mob were dirty cheating shits in U16s. When I was simply up against bigger, better jumpers, it was utterly, completely, screamingly frustrating, but that was the game in those pre-lifting days.)

Another track – and tell me if I'm on the wrong one – but do you think part of your strength now is from a life closer to nature than most of us in the urbanised tribe have? I don't want to lead the witness on this, but I want to understand your feelings.

Terry stayed with us last night – his first visit to our new house – and in conversation it came up that a neighbour of his is dying from prostate cancer. Must be going around, I said, and told him a mate of mine was too and talked about that and my admiration of your grace and style. Terry in turn said that it seemed most people given a death sentence came to be, more or less, at peace with it.

I could only sort of agree with that. In my limited experience, I haven't come across people who've carried on like total chooks, but there are degrees of strength and insight. My little sister's husband died young from melanoma with one year's notice – another regret, that I didn't know him better at that time, us in Sydney, them in Brisbane, just a visit here and there. Tracy told me Gavin was very prepared for his death and not frightened by it, relished every day and its beauty. Tracy-Ann with five children, the oldest just 15. My oldest brother, Brian, was in denial until very close to the end – he kept thinking he'd be able to do things that could not be done, which of course left his family affairs in a bit more of a mess than they should have been. My old TV mate Ian Ross died well (if that's not a stupid term) but I felt there might have been a brave front involved rather than inner peace.

What you say about feeling the naturalness of death, if I'm not misinterpreting, is what I would hope for and what I would hope my family would see in me.

I thought of you earlier today and the drug cocktails you're now on when a story popped up in the daily headlines I get from Bloomberg about using ketamine to treat depression.

Understanding our minds remains our greatest frontier. It's crazy that we can have the Hadron Collider playing with the bits that make up the bits that make atoms, on the edge of dark matter, but don't really know what pushes people over the edge. The Bloomberg story sounds like ketamine has great potential, but it's the way of the world that, because it can't be patented, there's no incentive for the drug companies to push it.

So I wonder if the sensitivity you disclose to the harshness of many lives is part of what made you fragile. That sensitivity is what I see in good people and totally lacking in those who are not. We were raised in a time when it wasn't done to show much sensitivity, weren't we? When cowboys were just supposed to get back on the horse and boys playing rugby were meant to not show any pain. Is there something here about the need to suppress feelings then compared with your ability to be open now and the difference that it makes?

Yes, it's another question. That's what you get with journalist types – there always are more questions. But just to set you straight on something, I haven't had to be tough to do fairly well in my racket. My parents and God gave me talents and a brain that were suited to the trade and then I was lucky on a number of occasions with the opportunities that came along. I have been very lucky to be able to do what I enjoy for a living. I don't know how many people are able to do that.

Take care, you old cowboy, you. I am very comfortable with finding out as much as you care to tell me about you, since you ask. I just wish I had been able to sooner, that I had been able to appreciate your depth as well as your strength.

Your lucky mate

Michael

Annette

It's not hard to do what you enjoy and have some talent for. The slings and arrows require a thickening of the skin, but any child on social media suffers that now. The occasional abusive physical letter back in the day now seems quaint.

My big sister Annette was with me in the car once when I had to drop into Channel 9 for some brief purpose. She was visiting from Brisbane and I pointed out the large studio where Kerri-Anne Kennerley was fronting *The Midday Show* at the time. Annette said something to the effect of how hard that had to be, 90 minutes of live television a day, Kerri-Anne had to be amazing. She was serious.

Annette ran the hospital side of the Brisbane Mater's child protection unit. She spent vastly longer than rostered hours dealing with and caring for battered, bashed, poisoned, sexually abused and neglected babies and children. She was the hospital side of a team of medicos, police and social workers developing a co-ordinated approach to abused children, a Churchill Fellowship recipient. She saw things that would break any heart, things I couldn't deal with, and she did it on a nurse's salary without payment for the overtime when there was always a child who needed help and protection. And she thought a highly paid performer before a camera and adoring audience for 90 minutes did it hard.

For decades part of my job was interviewing the nation's chief executive officers. And not just Australia's – some of the global giants of the age, masters of the universe. The good, the bad and the ugly, but mostly the average, by the nature of averages. And the average CEO, like the average in any role, is pretty average. Often enough I conducted their first television interview in the top job and their last, observing their careers and personas expand, watching the less grounded be seduced by their dependent underlings forever smiling up at them, coming to believe they were worth the millions they were being paid, that they had superior opinions about everything when they were as likely to be narrowed by their job focus.

There were exceptions, but not many, who could admit they were overpaid, who could keep what they did in context, who realised theirs was not the most vital tier of the enterprise.

Most thought they worked terribly hard in their many meetings and first-class travel and nights in comfortable hotel suites as they logged long hours, deserving the reverence they were shown. I thought they were not much chop at delegating and were wary of undertaking what should have been a vital goal: finding someone better than they were to replace them.

The air is sweeter in the C-suite, the food and wine better, life more civilised closer to power and influence, removed many levels from the coalface of surviving, of making ends meet. The reality of health care workers during plague, of the Karuna nurses tending the terminally ill, of the people on little more than the basic wage to whom we outsource the care for our elderly, all the caring, protecting and serving workers – the people we reach for when our needs are greatest – is humanity over money, entanglement in life rather than power. They end up being among your most important people – the people you die with.

August 24, 2.33 pm

Jim

Serge told me you had to have an operation – I hope it's gone well and is making you more comfortable.

I seem to be on a roll with people in hospital at the moment – my mother-in-law has had a fall and is in a rehab hospital with a cracked tailbone and my third son, Dominic, smashed his shoulder on Saturday while playing the last rugby game of the season in what was probably going to be his last season and now definitely will be. He's seeing a specialist today to book in for a shoulder reconstruction.

Neither of which hold a candle to you, of course, but I wish my 91-year-old ma-in-law had some of your spirit and perspective. Like a line in 'Ol' Man River', she's sick of living but scared of dying and mostly miserable about both.

Anyway, the Ascot-or-wherever Gentlepersons' Coffee Club is a movable feast. Let me know how you're going and what you feel like doing.

Keep strong

Michael

The brothers

I'm coming up quickly on a W124 E-Class Merc, the sedan version of Tim's Million Dollar Mercedes coupe. We helped each of the boys with their first car, and when Tim was about to start Year 12 we needed a car with a tow bar for the runabout after downsizing from the Chrysler Voyager. Tim for some reason wanted a car with a big grille – of all the prerequisites one might have – and a maroon 1988 Mercedes 300CE, the pillarless coupe, turned up on eBay for $8500 from a Melbourne dealer. For a Merc, it wasn't too ugly. It seemed a good price for that model, it had a tow bar, allegedly not too many kilometres, and there was some sort of warranty. I had a job in Narrandera so I flew to Melbourne and drove it back, taking a chance buying a car without seeing it and immediately driving from Melbourne to Sydney via the priest poet John O'Brien's old town and parish, the scene of 'Said Hanrahan'. 'We'll all be rooned.' But we weren't, there was nothing that another grand didn't put to rights with the car.

I'm not sure what my parents would have thought, a Mercedes for a first car, even a 20-year-old Mercedes.

The sedan I'm passing looks in good nick, older couple taking care of it, driving at the speed limit, keeping left. They seem as common now as when they were new. The Mercs, not old couples. OK, the Mercs and the old couples. And when they were new, the Mercs, they were worth a fortune. I mentioned we'd bought a 300CE to friends who were Mercophiles and they knew it and loved it, had one themselves once. Did I know what the Mercedes-Benz 300CE coupe cost in 1988? It was the top of the line, a bit over $130,000 on the road.

A lot of money, $130,000. 'Depreciating Assets!' in flashing multicoloured lights above the car yard. In 1988 it was a vast amount. It was enough to buy a better-than-average Sydney house, a house that would be worth $2 million today. 'Appreciating Asset' a handwritten sign hung over a fence post. So I claimed Tim drove a million-dollar car to school.

Expensive car choices, relationship choices, time choices, health choices – it takes discipline to see the counterfactual. 'Opportunity Cost' a scribbled sticky note lucky to be noticed somewhere down the side of the package.

But Alfas are different, I tell myself. They have souls. Or buy a classic and they don't depreciate. I sold my 105 series GTV, the 1975 two-litre, last of the breed, for what I paid for it and it's now worth seven times that. Should never have sold it. Christ, you really felt you were driving, connected to the car, sharing the momentum. No power steering, no aircon, the seats a little thin, the deep-dish steering wheel a 'safety' feature – the steering column would have further to travel before spearing you through the chest – but driving at the speed limit felt like driving.

And I know I was captured by my childhood like everyone else, hankering as old men after the cars we loved from afar as boys. The 105 Alfa coupes were the most exotic vehicles a Petrie boy saw, well before Dustin Hoffman and *The Graduate* popularised the Spider. Kevin Bartlett and John French in their GTAs battling the Fords and Holdens and Mini Coopers and imported American muscle cars – the Mustangs – around the Lakeside circuit in the 60s. Dad would be on duty there and sometimes a big brother or sister would take me. The muscle cars were faster but something beyond that in the Alfas' subtle curves subconsciously grabbed and held me. Wealthy-enough old men create expensive classics by having the money to acquire and preserve boyhood fantasies. Rosebud. A bit pathetic, really, but I don't care. There's no logo more beautiful, more evocative, than Alfa Romeo's – Milan's red cross and the Visconti serpent. Stuff your pseudo-psychology and the art of motorcycle maintenance. I should never have sold the GTV.

But there was a near-new GT that seduced me: the 3.2-litre V6. They'll do that. And they'll say 'drive me, don't fly, drive me faster, overtake and move through and beyond the mere cars and trucks, make fast choices, take your chances'.

This is a good stretch of the M1 for that, the best of its 127 kilometres. From Mooney Mooney up along the ridges and down again to the Woy Woy turn-off. It would be better without the Central Coast traffic but the road itself is grand, its run, the sandstone, the views at times out over the bush rolling away in further valleys and ridges. Thick bush over steep ground. Hard to imagine travelling it the first time, on horseback, on foot, slashing through scrub, blind under the canopy, the cliffs, not knowing what was next, where was next.

I specifically remember this section of Jim's drive, willing myself to remember it, wanting to recall the feel of the weather on that ridge. A grey watercolour wash across the skies, shades of grey layered above the dark green of the gums, a green made darker and slicker by squalls. Wind in the treetops, chop and movement above the deeper rolling of the land. These live, lithe, wet trees are not the 'drab green and desolate grey' of A.D. Hope's bitterness.

> In the field uniform of modern wars,
> Darkens her hills, those endless, outstretched paws
> Of Sphinx demolished or stone lion worn away.[5]

The school text memory remains. We were to know his nation of trees, but certainly not his love poetry.

> My cunny, my cracker-jack, my cantrip, my kissing-crust,
> Rock-rump and wring-rib in wrestle of randy-bout,
> Lithe-lier, limber-leg, column of counter-thrust,
> My heave-horn, my hyphener, dew-dealer in-and-out;

'What's the rhyme scheme, boys? It's ABAB, isn't it? Four-line stanza, ABAB. Note the alliteration, boys.'

> My soft-sigher, snuggle-snake, sleeper and slaker,
> My dandler, my deft-dear, dreamer of double-deal,
> And, oh, my wry-writher, my worker and waker,
> Stirrer and stander now, fledge to my feel;

'Yes, Brother.'

Yes, Brother, adolescent boys would scan that one for new vocabulary given the chance.

The Brothers. Some were good men. Some were not. Some were sadistic bullies, tiny despots ruling a fiefdom of children. Some were simply out of their depth and could be bullied by boys. Oh, we could bully a weak teacher all right. Some were gentle, somewhat lost souls. My history teacher and high-jump coach seemed to be forever amazed at the madness around him. I heard he retired early from teaching to spend time painting watercolours.

We had Brother Proctor in Year 9, my first year at Nudgee. My parents couldn't afford the fees in Year 8, did not have the money, and I cried at the thought of not going. What a little shit I was, inflicting that pain on my mother and father, not understanding their sacrifices to educate six children, to give their sons and daughters what they had been denied. The school couldn't help until Year 9. Half fees for Years 9 and 10 on the condition that I win an academic scholarship for the final two years. It was still hard for my parents, and I get to Nudgee and there's Brother Proctor.

They called him 'Poofter Proctor'. I didn't believe it – born a sceptic – wouldn't believe it unless I saw it. And then I did. In our dormitory of double-bunks, three deep in a dozen rows. Proctor would sit on a lower bed after lights out, as all those 13 and 14-year-old boys settled – shuffling, whispering here and there, a loud fart with resultant catcalls. Proctor would silently shine a torch in the direction of noise or movement. Shout 'settle down!' after too much. And he would be running a hand over the body of the boy in the bed, over chest and stomach and up and down his thighs. That's what I saw, what I knew happened after he sat on the bunk beneath mine one night. Some told worse stories about Proctor when he was headmaster of Nudgee Junior, a boarding primary school, when he bashed Sergio, when he bashed many boys who are now old men.

Proctor could fly into a rage over nothing in front of a primary school class, tip over his own desk, throw whatever was to hand at boys, primary school boys. And in another breath he'd be laughing, shouting soft drinks at the tuckshop for all.

Serge said how glad his group was to leave Nudgee Junior for Nudgee Senior – whatever happened, at least there wouldn't be Proctor. And Proctor was transferred to Nudgee Senior.

He never touched me. I told myself I wouldn't let him, that I would speak out. I don't know. He didn't touch Jim either, but he called him into his room once, called out from behind a part-opened door.

'I go in and there's Proctor lying back on his bed, his pants off, and a bloody great erection,' Jim recounts in the Ascot coffee shop. 'He says, "Look at that! Want to touch it?" I say, "No" and walk out. Jesus.'

August 24, 9.35 pm

Hi Michael

Sue here. Jim asked me to let you know he is having trouble sending and receiving emails at the hospital, something to do with his iPad, so he is not sure when he will be able to write.

He wanted me to tell you he was very sorry to hear about your son. He remembers you saying it was going to soon be his last game and you were not unpleased about it. Such bad luck.

Jim of course didn't ask me to tell you about his troubles but thought I would just tell you a little.

The surgeon saw him this morning and has a concern about the stoma and is considering a further operation this Thursday. We are all desperately hoping that he won't need it.

Jim is coping with the colostomy with his usual courage, openness and humour while all of us around him mostly just cry.

It has been very tough on him physically and a lot to adjust to mentally but he has such an extraordinary capacity to accept things and to quickly adjust. I think he always thinks of others, never wants to burden anyone and just never feels sorry for himself. He is a miracle to watch in hospital. No matter what state he is in, he always gets the nurses' names, always asks how they are, always thanks them and just never ever ever complains.

Anyway, Michael, I better stop, hopefully Jim will be back writing to you himself very soon. I hope your son will be OK. Such a worry for you.

Take care

Sue

August 24, 11.52 pm

Sue

Jim obviously continues to demonstrate why I've always thought if I was picking company for a trench … And I knew that instinctively as a schoolboy.

I don't know what Jim has told you about our schooldays – beyond the Brother Proctor horror stories – but we weren't especially close friends then. We played in the same rugby team for three years, shared our infamous Enmore digs on the Under 16 tour, were in GPS athletics together (Jim with success as a runner, me as a middle-order high jumper), always got on well and I like to think we had mutual respect, but we didn't hang around together outside school. Nevertheless, the bonding that happened at Nudgee, I think especially if you were in the same rugby team, if you pulled on that jumper and worked together and relied on each other, along with that respect, it forges a kind of brotherhood. You know a good person when you lived with them for four years.

Thank you for telling me what's what. I'll take your advice on whether he'd like a visitor on Sunday. At least I don't think I'll cry – instead I might ask him if he's already been told the old line: What's the biggest problem with a colostomy bag? Finding shoes to match. (My father was to have a cystectomy, but he beat the system by dying of a heart attack the day before the operation. I guess that shoe problem got to him.)

Sue, you also must be made of strong stuff – a kindred spirit with Jim and so obviously good for each other. Not that I'm sure of anything being obvious anymore, not since Jim told me his apparent strength was a cover for such terrible anxiety.

I'm travelling again this week, but I'll try ringing 'the old cowboy' before hitting the road.

Love
Michael

Trust

A conversation with an economist friend, Frank Campbell, turned to memory, specifically how financial markets forget and repeat their follies, but also how memory forms, and the tricks of memory we play on ourselves as we select and discard, consciously and otherwise.

My mother-in-law tells the same stories over and over as her dementia gathers pace. Every time we drive over the Harbour Bridge, it's about how her family would visit Sydney each year and what a big deal it was to drive over the bridge, how the girls at her school all wanted to know what it was like. 'It was like a bridge.' As Maureen keeps on keeping on, the bridge litany evolves a little – there's less detail about her great anticipation of the annual Sydney trip. Sometimes she says 'we'd come every weekend'. Sometimes she doesn't know she lives in Sydney. And now that story is fading away altogether. She wants to be driven home, to her parents' Brisbane house, thinking they are still alive.

Frank told of a retired academic in child psychology who said one of the earliest skills a baby learns within the first six months is the capacity to trust. Some babies learn this skill better than others. If you learn it badly, you're storing up trouble for the rest of your life. Frank wondered if learning to trust continues at relatively high but maybe diminishing rates right through to our adolescence, a period dominated by school, if it's the first flush of discovery that you can trust your mates, as a semi-autonomous individual, that can bind you through life, however intermittent the later contact is.

It's commonplace to have old friends not seen for many years but able to pick up where you left off. If Frank's suspicion is right, boarding school back in the day would reinforce the effect, especially with a hostile element as a common enemy. We were only schoolboys, turned men by haphazard chance.

August 25, 3.04 pm

58 million people die each year … according to a Q&A program I am watching courtesy of the Wesley Hospital … am I being singled out?

I don't know, Michael, me and 57,999,999 other people.

I am back in print … I had ground to a halt.

Sorry to hear about Dominic … Poor bugger … Wish him well from me.

You told me of the courage your son showed on several occasions. I want you to tell me of these.

We have lost track of our conversation, which may not be such a bad thing … a fresh start.

What sort of life would I have chosen?

Well, originally I just wanted to be a busted arse old ringer with 10,000 sheep, a few dogs and a few horses. To make that happen I needed a good old girl by my side with a couple of kids at foot.

Maybe later I had thoughts of a life in the share market, which I did anyway, in a very reclusive way. My self and the personality I was blessed with have always been a key factor in the course of my life.

4 pm

Have been sidetracked by visitors and the hospital day. To have more surgery tomorrow to do running repairs on stoma and am about to start the bowel prep for that any time … it will be very messy, 2 litres of bowel prep and a stoma bag of about 200 ml.

Back to what I wanted to do … Whoops, it's bowel prep time.

The texture of colour

Jim propped up, tubed up, in a hospital bed with his iPad companion. Those solid fingers, apostrophes not worth the effort without a proper keyboard, his life with two fingers across the screen, my schoolboy mate, as the cascading catastrophe of a failing body befalls him.

Kev Carmody, transferred home to his Gold Coast townhouse with a drip in his arm the morning I call on him, a detour on another drive north when the Queensland border December window opened in 2020. We laugh about the trouble he got me into, he talks of the importance of imagination to stay sane in school, we don't talk about the purple blotches over his body or the finality of cancer in both kidneys, we talk about Jim.

'Tractor,' says Kev. I had forgotten. Jim's occasional nickname. I don't think I ever called him that.

With a 50/50 decision, the odds are 80/20 you'll make the wrong one.

No, it just seems like that sometimes. We're programmed to fear loss more than valuing gain, we remember our failures more vividly than our successes. There are people who believe – or at least say – the times are so bad it would be irresponsible to bring a child into the world. The reality is that the times have never been so good for our species, more promising for the average human baby.

Climate change threatens but we have the technology to deal with it, if we care to. As far as plagues go, this is nothing. Small comfort for the dead and damaged, but plagues of one kind or many others were a constant for all but the most recent decades of our existence. We've forgotten as we thought we'd tamed them with science undreamt of by our parents. We boomers had measles and mumps. My former *Financial Review* colleague Colleen walks with a limp from polio. Our parents' time – it wasn't until 1944 at the Commonwealth Serum Laboratories that Australia became the first country to manufacture penicillin for the domestic market. Alexander Fleming got the credit for discovering it, but it took an Australian and a German Jewish refugee, Howard Florey and Ernst Chain, to seize the potential and make it work, to make antibiotics. Until then, cuts and scratches could kill through blood poisoning, everything from strep throat to syphilis finished us, pneumonia and tuberculosis wiped out millions, infections in childbirth slaughtered, battlefield and hospital infections killed as many as bullets. Life expectancy for a male born in the 1890s was 51 years, 55 for a female.

Mammals are all granted about the same number of heartbeats in their average life – one billion, barring misadventure. A hopping mouse races through them at machine-gun speed in three years, 634 beats a minute, feral cats permitting. An elephant's heart will pound 30 times a minute for sixty-something years, absent hunters. But not quite all mammals – we're pushing our hearts out to two-and-a-half billion beats.

We manage to live so long now we've changed the ways we die. Deaths from dementia increased by 67 per cent in the 10 years from 2010 to 2019 to become our second-biggest killer, albeit with the equal highest median age of death, 89.1 years, with the number-one cause, ischaemic heart disease. As the nation ages, dementia will soon enough be number one. It already is for women.

Ischaemic heart disease took 10.8 per cent of us – the coronaries clogging, the heart muscle not getting enough blood and oxygen. Dementia, the brain fatally failing, for 8.9 per cent. The third-biggest killer, cerebrovascular disease, 5.85 per cent, median age 86.3 years – the brain's clots and strokes and stenosis and such. Those three causes accounted for just over a quarter of deaths, half of that figure being people aged 88.5 years and above.

Tragedies when any of those strike the relatively young. Approaching 90 … something has to do the job, to be the ticket out. More women died in their hundreds in 2019 than in their 20s and 30s combined, 1533 to 1389.

Of the top 20 causes of death, the youngest median age was 43.9 years, suicide in 13th place, pipping accidental falls in 14th.

The cancers are spread through the top 20, lung cancer and its close brothers the most popular in fourth place, median age 74.3 years, 5.2 per cent of deaths. Cancers of colon, sigmoid, rectum and anus came sixth, 77.6 years. 'Malignant neoplasms of lymphoid, haematopoietic and related tissue' – lymphoma and friends – eighth, 2.8 per cent of deaths, median age 78.5, one rank below diabetes, one above the flu and pneumonia.

That was 2019, the last 'normal' year. In 2022, our year of letting it rip, COVID deaths soared to overtake dementia as our second-biggest killer, median age 83.

We adapt quickly, humans. We moved in days from masks and locking down cities to freely inhaling the virus and quietly accepting more than a thousand Australians a month dying from it. Well, we were over it. Well, they're mostly old. Well, half of them, anyway. Take your chances.

There are decisions we take that predispose our means of exit. There are types of decisions we take as we face the possibilities, take our place among the statistics. Try not to think about the statistics, about the odds. Concentrate on beauty, watch closely the flight of birds, the bullet rainbow lorikeets, bin chickens granted grace in the sky, black cockatoos' slow, deep wing beats trailing long tails. Listen for bird call, stop for however long the magpie might bless you with warble, the country's anthem. I try to learn their language, try to warble back. Judy thinks it's crazy. Maybe it is. Discover the depth of flowers, the texture of colour, embrace weather, laugh. I'm all right.

Get your check-up, wait for your results.

The Hunter

There's a decision to be made near the top of the M1, the third time the drive starts: at the end, turn right for the coast road, the Pacific Highway, or turn off a little earlier on the M15, the Hunter Expressway that heads inland up the Hunter Valley to join the New England Highway.

The New England is mostly two lanes, curlier, the land drier. It used to be the quicker when the coast road was also mostly two meandering lanes. After three decades of roadworks, the Pacific Highway is finally all four-lane motorway. The Kempsey bus crash in 1989 – two coaches head-on, 35 people dead, more injured – provided the political heft to commit to that. It is straighter, the scenery lush in parts, beautiful over the fat and lazy northern rivers with the rich green mountains beyond, walls of thicker eucalypt forest with its own charm at times but less changing, less open. There is more traffic, more caravans, and still the better part of two hours faster than the New England. Safer with its divided road. Yet, if there's time, I prefer the New England, the more engaging drive. On this particular drive, for and with Jim, it has to be over the tableland.

If there was a little more time, if I had started earlier, there's the Bucketts Way variation, cutting back inland from the coast at Stroud, through Gloucester, the Barrington Tops, Bucketts Way through Walcha, Thunderbolts Way to join the New England south of Uralla. Before the M15 it was quicker than driving up the Hunter Valley. It's still the prettier way, the twisty way, the narrower, quieter road through bush and mountains and valleys and mist. Timeless country arches away into the distance of the national park, deep valleys stretch back millennia into this old land of patient trees. The land, the forest, at one with the sky. Eternity opening up a touch, a swerve, beyond the road.

The Alfa would love it. You'd have the selector in D for dynamic and it would stay thus into the mountains and up into the rich land of the coastal plateau, thick grass, fat cattle.

But I did not leave early on Jim's drive, not that it mattered. A little discombobulated perhaps by the intent of the drive, getting ahead of myself in the inertia of purpose, anticipating the New England, the prettier road a distraction from the leaner country in my mind and not the route most driven all these decades. So it's the Hunter Valley, not the Barrington Tops.

Much of the M15 is concrete. I can't explain how that surface somehow diminishes it. A glare to it, a hardness that makes no sense. A perfunctory section, a memory perhaps of boring American freeways.

It ends at Singleton and from there to Muswellbrook coal dominates the road and towns. The massive dark wounds of open-cut mines not always screened by saplings, the flat-top hills of overburden unnatural in their symmetry. Endless coal trains run on the parallel railway line to Newcastle. The scale of the venture is hard to grasp, that insignificant people could conceive and execute such valley creation and mountain moving for humble black rock. Monster draglines gouging the earth, loading giant trucks to build coal mountains to feed the trains to run to port to another mountain to be scooped by toothed Ferris wheels onto conveyor belts to pour into ships, convoys of them, a coal armada across oceans to be unloaded and railed and barged and trucked again into furnaces to create steam. Impressive and absurd, wealth and destruction.

Our own power stations loom ahead. If you lift your eyes from the road and tell your mind the car is stationary, it is the industrial might of the power station that is moving, marching across the land, the beige concrete cooling towers rising up as they approach, hyperboloid structures of an otherworldly religion, trailing vapour clouds as they move.

Ozymandias echoes. The scarred land waits.

Muswellbrook. Breakfast pancakes at McDonald's. Don't know why they call them hotcakes. A road-trip tradition – only visit the Golden Arches on a drive. Harsh experience has taught the utter unreliability of coffee in country towns. Remember pulling over outside Nyngan – the trip the 159 collected the speeding ticket – to tip out a cup of anonymous hot liquid. Unless you know, best not to go. The Macca's mid-size flat white with an extra shot a safe if unremarkable alternative throughout the land. Even in the US now – even a truck stop Macca's in Nowhere, Idaho had an acceptable flat white. The kid behind the machine thought it was an English drink.

There is a new bypass at Scone, the town skirted, its statue of a mare and foal now unseen. You are officially in the Upper Hunter, the roadside thick with fennel, the hills beyond beckoning with their consolation for missing the Barrington Tops. The road starts to twist and roll with the land from Wingen, still feels the land, rides the contours instead of imposing passageway through it, a road that does not let you see very far ahead, that opens pages with its turns, that communicates through the car. You're driving.

Murrurundi vignette. There's a boy feeding a lamb with a bottle over a fence a little on from the grand Emirates Park horse stud. Other side of the road, a modest house. A memory is jogged of feeding poddy calves at the Ryans' farm and the biggest holiday of my young life the year when guinea fowl chickens hatched and Terry and Patrick shaved Kate's cat's tail and old Bob so slowly died in the home yard. An enormous gentle draught horse, he could carry all the kids on his back at once. So quiet, so peaceful. Snake bite, they said. We were sent out to touch his eye to ensure he was dead.

Some years later, Kate was the first girl I kissed. Kissed and fumbled and fondled and exchanged letters from our respective boarding schools. And then hurt her. Moved on and did not see her when she moved to Brisbane for university. We were only kids but now that failure hurts me as much as any of my regrets. Promises made or expectations raised, believed at the time, then dissipated for one reason or another, those sins of omission.

The boy with the lamb and the bottle are gone and you leave the millionaires' precise horse studs behind – Emirates Park, the billionaire's horse stud – and accelerate up through the Murrurundi Gap over the Liverpool Range to arrive on the tableland. Open land. Open skies. Farmland still, not bush, but a sense of width, of country, of real farms rather than the cossetted vineyards and horse studs and hobby farms of the Hunter Valley.

That's the fourth time the drive starts, outside Murrurundi, the drive you've been imagining, the one you imagine and want to remember, that you can lose yourself in and not think about too much at all.

The nuns

I managed to get lost on the way from the airport to Wesley Hospital, taking the wrong turn with one of Brisbane's tunnels, the Clem7. Is Brisbane a sister city of Yokohama? Uses Nissan's nomenclature department, anyway – a tunnel called Clem.

Clem Jones, the long-time lord mayor whose main achievement was rolling out sewerage through Brisbane's suburbs. The dunny cart men gone. The dead Clem remembered with a giant tunnel. Fitting enough.

Clem flushes me out in Stones Corner, the wrong side of the brown snake river. I had rung Sergio from the airport. He rings to check what happened to my suggested arrival time. 'Stones Corner? What are you doing in bloody Stones Corner?' My navigation skills will delight the Ascot Gentlepersons' Coffee Club.

Serge and Mark Harrison are there with Jim, sitting around a low coffee table laden with old magazines in an alcove outside his room. Jim is attached to a drip hanging from a stainless-steel trolley. He's wearing a green hospital gown and fluoro pink socks, the ones with rubber nodules underneath for grip on hospital floors.

'Love your socks. Where can I get a pair?'

'Very exclusive. I think they're a bit too groovy for you, Michael.'

He goes to stand up to shake my hand but I get to him first and Mark gives me his seat beside Jim. It's awkward somehow. The alcove is public. Somebody else in not great shape is down one end of it. The usual constant noise and movement of a hospital.

The four of us, old schoolmates. Cue the 20-something Simon and Garfunkel singing 'Old Friends'. All that's missing is a park bench. Nothing strange for them now about being 70.

Paul McCartney was 15 when he wrote 'When I'm Sixty-Four'. John Lennon only made 40. Last time I was in New York, the fans were still coming to Strawberry Fields opposite the Dakota, taking their selfies around the Imagine mosaic. A cold, clear January day, snowy patches in Central Park's shadows. A busker off to the side singing 'Strawberry Fields Forever' forever.

The park benches have small donors' plaques.

IN MEMORY OF BEN GOULD, A FEATHERWEIGHT
CHAMP WHO RAN, WALKED, PUSHED BABY
CARRIAGES AND FINALLY SAT IN CENTRAL PARK.
FROM HIS WIFE, DAUGHTER AND GRANDSONS.

HENRY BURNS, 1928–1996
A GOOD MAN WHO ALWAYS LIKED
A GOOD PARK BENCH
IN HIS MEMORY

And thus remembered.

How do you make small talk with a man about his stoma?

We do. Mark has to leave after a time. A tea trolley comes around. Younger members of the Royal Family smile up at us from the magazines. Somehow, I can't remember how, we talk about belief. It might have been from my brother Dick, a priest, having visited. When Tom was dying, Jim had asked Serge if he knew a priest who might talk to him. Dick helped Tom die, stood with the family through it, sharing, absorbing some of their pain, conducted the final service. In turn, Jim and Sue asked to have a conversation with Dick.

Jim's none too sure about belief but remains a cultural Catholic like the rest of us. The institutional church had not endeared itself to him from the beginning. Before Nudgee, he was sent to board at a convent school in Mitchell when he was five years old. He was abused and belted.

The nuns were worse than the brothers, much worse, Jim had said. It was before we started our conversation, after one of the dinners Serge would organise. He said it with a quiet intensity that surprised, with a sharp edge of uncharacteristic bitterness. I think I asked him what he meant but he didn't want to go further, the old Jim before we opened up, just said it was brutal for a little fella.

A little boy away from his family and animals and the unlimited farm.

Another time somewhere, perhaps towards the end of an evening when contemplation comes closer: 'What could scare me on a rugby field, Michael? I'd survived the nuns!'

Sue told me. A particular nun took a deep dislike to little Jim. Jim, sweet Jim in a tough body. Maybe she thought he had looked insolent, or just unattractive, his silence mistaken for contempt. He was belted and worse. He was scared of the dark, perhaps anxious about things even then, but his punishment would be to sit alone in the dark outside the dormitory through the night. He was certainly anxious after.

Never mind the church, there is something this man – matter-of-fact about life and death the way farmers are, the rationalist – can't explain. Sitting in that hospital alcove, Jim tells me of a dream unlike any he's ever had, a dream he woke up remembering clearly, a dream he felt and could not disbelieve.

John Bryant, an older brother of a mate of Jim and Tom's from a neighbouring property, had died suddenly of a heart attack.

John Bryant came up to Jim and said, 'You know I'm dead.'

Jim said, 'Yes, but that doesn't matter.'

They were standing in what seemed to be a changing room, like they have at swimming pools. John Bryant kissed Jim on the face. John's lips were cold, icy cold.

Jim turned to see Tom lying on a bench, Tom looking sick and shrivelled.

Jim woke up. He could still feel the cold lips on his skin. He understood it was the kiss of death but knew from that moment that Tom would die before him.

Jim had already been diagnosed with prostate cancer, but Tom's lung cancer had not yet been detected.

Tom certainly fought the cancer, took years dying, years longer than the months the doctors predicted, hanging on, refusing to die. Jim said he was little more than a skeleton at the end, shrivelled up.

Tom's funeral ceremony pamphlet is among the papers in my desk drawer.

Tom McCormack 16.07.52 – 05.11.13

I didn't know him – he finished at Nudgee the year before I started – but I flew up for the funeral, respect for the living. Tom looks out from that page in his prime, like he's a model for bush manhood. There's a grin with a touch of cheek to it, a straight gaze out from under a well-shaped Akubra. His forearm with a rolled-up sleeve is propped almost under the square chin. Without being able to know, you think he's at a cattle yard, resting on the top rail. He could be the Marlborough man.

There's no explaining the dream. It was real.

Speed

Murrurundi. It's a good word to say out loud, Murrurundi. And there's better to come: Wallabadah. Wallabadah. Wallabadaaahhh. Say it long, a little high and wide, stretch the last syllable and it can be the start of song, Wallabadaaaahhh. Kamilaroi land. Clap sticks and feet pounding dust.

That's up the range, up the curves. Divided road here. How often do you see police cars waiting, hiding, off the side of the road going up a mountain? Not often, but you're aware of the risk and keep an eye out but floor it anyway, feel the kick-down, the grip and power, the g-force grab through the seat, tear past trucks in the slow lane.

The Veloce has 206 kW of power and 400 Nm of torque. That means it's quick, this light body slipping through the air. The Quadrifoglio has 375 kW and 600 Nm – 505 brake horsepower in the old money. That means it's outrageous. From zero to 100 in 5.7 seconds for the Veloce – the Quadrifoglio less than 4, top speed more than 300. The Veloce more than enough, a top I haven't tested of 240. Need a road good enough, clear enough and definitely clear of police, an autobahn. And I'd need the nerve, acknowledging reflexes aren't as quick.

The speed cops can get you on the move now, coming towards you – sit behind a truck, snick out a little with the radar and nab you a kilometre away. Did that to the Giulietta QV outside Stanthorpe at night. Did that to the 159 wagon between Broken Hill and Brewarrina – a bright orange highway patrol Commodore that was camouflage in that country.

Driving to Broken Hill, the bush finishes at Nyngan and the outback starts, dark soil gives way to red and rocks and endlessness. A deeper eternity again. And beyond Broken Hill, Silverton, the setting for the first *Mad Max* movies, brutal beauty, beautifully brutal at times.

The Veloce rips without effort to 160 – the old 'ton', 100 miles per hour – and beyond. I've done 185 and climbing on an empty stretch of the Monaro Highway heading towards the snow before seeing a car on the horizon that might or might not be a cop and taking my foot off. It wasn't, but I feel a little fear at those levels, adrenalin and fear. Not about the car – it sits and holds like it was only 80 – but it's fast and stuff happens. One night outside Canberra when I first had the GT, I cruised the length of Lake George to check for police, turned around and gunned it to 200. Effortless. Stupid, I suppose – could have been a roo, a wombat.

Stupid taking such a risk and we all take them. A ridiculous proportion of us still smoke. It's a worse bet than speeding. We know alcohol is carcinogenic, among other things, but most of us don't care. Doctors automatically add a number to however many glasses a week we declare when asked. We get our scares, our lesser heart attacks, and cut back, maybe, but en masse we embrace and take our risks with less honesty than pushing the speedo.

The GT was black, tan seats, the 3.2-litre Alfa V6, the ultimate refinement of the 156 series, the manual stick a large silver ball in your hand through the gates. A risk. Life's a risk, taking chances.

In the COVID-fuelled consumption surge for those of us who were fortunate, I bought another black 3.2-litre GT, told myself it was an investment, that they are going up in value. That silver ball and the engine's rumble. After my brother Brian died, I think for a while I took more casual risks, silly little risks, lived a little faster because he was dead shy of 58. And now, buy and drive a manual GT while you can. A little more carefully, more sensibly. Losing your driver's licence a risk too.

That's out there anyway, if you live long enough – get tested every year and maybe lose your licence. Or you have the sense left to surrender it when uncertainty and failing reflexes bedevil driving. Or surrender it out of fear of failing the test, the indignity of that. Then the road's gone, the freedom to go gone. Dependent on other people. The pleasure of the machine moving, of guiding and driving it, gone. Before you can vote, before you can drink (legally), your driver's licence is a coming of age. Your wheels. To collect a girl for a date. To get to work how it suits you. To go wherever you want without asking, without arranging, without explaining. The weekends unlimited. The potential to throw a bag in the back and clear out. Gone.

Said unsaid

September 2, 11.10 pm

Jim

The anonymous wisdom of the internet:

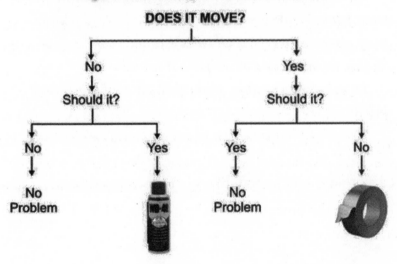

A laugh. Or at least a smile, you hope. The jokes and memes and videos Serge and I send around the AGCC members hope to achieve that. A distraction, a lightening.

But more than that, if subconsciously as much as intended. An emailed joke can also say:

'Hello, old mate, how are you going? I thought of you when I saw this, thought it might give you a chuckle, thought "you're a wry old bastard yourself" along these lines. For half a second, in some part of my brain — without thinking it, without actually seeing it — there would be an image of you smiling, you being warmed a little by this flicker of humour, which in turn warms me.

'I'm running around doing stuff in a different world, haven't spoken to you in a while, but I haven't forgotten you, I won't forget you. I'm travelling with you, here if you need me.

'Us blokes, turns out we are capable of having a heart-to-heart, but we're also comfortable not to. Good to see a friend's name appear among the usual inbox detritus, another way of slipping the calling card on the table, if you want to pick it up.

'Or not — doesn't matter. It's all good. No need to overthink it at all.

'Hey, some of these jokes are bloody funny! Go well, old son.'

And all that is said unsaid, like so many conversations.

September 3, 11.15 am

That's exactly how I run the farm, Michael.

    Home from hospital yesterday … All good.

    Thanks for your visit.

    Hope Dominic and all the family well.

Jim

September 3, 12.48 pm

Jim

I thought that, being old school, there might be a bit of baling wire involved as well, or at least the odd bent coathanger. (Which reminds me that it's been a long time since I've seen a coathanger being used for a car aerial – technology marches on. Kids don't know the basic skills they're missing out on.)

It was indeed good to see you and I'm glad to hear you're home – however good they are, however nice the nurses, a hospital is still a hospital.

I suppose there's a fair chance you've seen the Julia Baird article that's been everywhere the last 24 hours. Her outcome obviously has been better, but reading it again had me wondering about what you were thinking when you were first told the C word. I asked about that on Sunday but somehow forgot to come back to it after your amazing dream story. It must have been another important step in understanding your journey.

Like you, I really can't begin to understand the dream. I'm not big on organised religion anymore, I'm over the cant, the dress-ups, the dogma invented by a self-perpetuating club of old men, but I'm still a believer and have a sense of more. I'm also a bit into ancestor worship – not really, no sacrificing lambs to the ancient Pascoes – but I continue to have what some might call a prayerful relationship with my parents. And after your dream, you're in no position to think that's odd!

Twice I have heard my parents' voices as clearly as I can hear anything, both times they were offering brief but welcome advice, not anything really useful like the Powerball numbers. I know there's a perfectly rational explanation for that somewhere, but I'm happy to take it as part of feeling looked after.

They weren't looking after me this morning when I unwittingly turned into a bus lane after doing *Sunrise* and copped a $319 fine and lost one point. I'll have words with Dad about that.

Love
Michael

Faith

Julia Baird wrote powerfully in the *New York Times* of her dance with cancer, reprinted locally in the *Sydney Morning Herald* and subsequently in her book, *Phosphorescence*.

> *It's a peculiar, lonely kind of impotence, a cancer diagnosis. If you ran a thousand miles, aced a billion exams, hit a dozen home runs, nothing could reverse or erase the fact of cancer.*[6]

A gloomy prognosis with advanced suspected ovarian cancer, large tumours, a long and difficult operation, eight days in intensive care, but then a better prognosis – not ovarian but a rarer form of the beast, not aggressive and with a higher survival rate.

> *My prognosis is good, but like others, I will need to live with the fear of return. This week, my blood tests came back clear of cancer. But my scar runs the length of my torso; I feel permanently altered. It will feel strange returning to normal life.*

The journalist and author found strength in prayer and stillness, the love and support of family and close friends.

My doctor asked me a few days ago how I became so calm
before the surgery. I told her: I prayed, I locked out negativity
and drama and drew my family and tribe – all big-hearted,
pragmatic people – near. I tried to live deliberately.

'Can I just say,' she said, 'you should do that for the rest of
your life.'

And how long is the rest of your life? How long before those
fine intentions fade, like so many fitness regimes, so many
diets, so many loves? How long before other fears and problems
overshadow your hard-won inner calm? Or the old fear returns.

But I pray anyway, a 'cultural Catholic' if nothing else.
Not sure to whom. Or to Whom. Not as often. Sometimes I
think not as often as I should. Having looked at the religions,
Christianity seems the most reasonable, the least unreasonable as
long as you ignore what the empire builders and dogmatists and
hucksters monetising crowd emotion have done to it. There's no
room for dogma – faith can only be a matter of faith.

There is much to pray about, to thank Her for, to
acknowledge. I give thanks for beauty. I used to give thanks
for the ability to do the work I did. I'm a father of four boys.
I prayed for them every night. Visited their rooms when they
were little and asleep and prayed for them, prayed for them
to be happy, healthy, intelligent and wise. To have a sense of
humour and a sense of justice. To be good brothers, to grow
old happily together. I prayed to my parents to watch over
them, to intercede for them, to hold their grandsons in their
care as they held me. I prayed for all my family. I prayed to
be a good father, to somehow give my sons something like the
upbringing I was given. I apologised too. I apologised for not

being a better son, for not loving more when I should have. I'm not sure it makes sense but that doesn't matter.

Funny, maybe, that I don't remember specifically praying for the cure of my own cancer – I'd let my brother the priest do so on my behalf. He'd have better channels. I left it vague for my mother and father to consider, that it might all work out for the best.

And as months passed and became a year and more from the end of chemo, it all was. My memory at the time of diagnosis was being told that if you remained in remission for five years, you were considered cured, you were back with your cohort's longevity. I was living with the expectation of being cured, of dying from something else one day, while Jim lived and Alison lives with the certainty that they wouldn't.

COVID and the desire to escape to Sunshine Beach when the border windows opened interfered with the six-monthly check-ups, the 18-month appointment slipped back to 21 months. The blood work was all good at first reading. If you think you might be a little more tired, have an echocardiogram to check the heart. Wait for the results. It's all looking good.

September 4, 11.00 am

Well, I'm back after another lengthy break ... Thanks for your email last night and the Julia Baird article ... an extraordinarily fine piece of writing. She nailed it.

I think I might try to pray more, to make contact with God, whoever or whatever that may be ... We can search the heavens, we can search the universe and the worlds that are within, but eventually I suspect the kingdom of God lies within us all.

I really enjoyed the link you forwarded ... surprisingly. It quite lifted my spirits. I crave quietness, stillness and love, I think. The world and its affairs no longer interest me much. I was very taken with the story of your current relationship with your parents, I am pleased that you remembered the story of the dream I had. I crave simplicity.

The surgeon, David Taylor, nearly broke me up the other day. I said to him to forward the accounts for the surgeries to home. He said, 'No accounts, I did it for the scheduled fee' ... A simple act of kindness and generosity from a stranger was almost too much for this old cowboy to bear.

NSW traffic police seem to take a dim view of people driving in bus lanes ... The state shows little mercy.

I've lost my way in this exchange, Michael, but I think your last question was 'what was I thinking when the cancer word was first mentioned' ... Well, that was 2010, so a fair while ago, but I do remember it as a very confronting time, especially when we were trying to decide on treatment options. Indecision and the variety of options caused great conflict within.

When cancer was first mentioned, I remember Sue crying as she spoke to the receptionist after the doctor's visit ... I felt like these events belonged to the movies, not real life. Straight up the urologist/surgeon said it was a very aggressive cancer which may or may not respond to treatment, and then he gave all the treatment options.

The first person I rang was Tom and I told him I had advanced prostate cancer. I felt quite matter-of-fact about it, maybe numb ... disbelief.

Cancer of the prostate and its threat to my masculinity ran uppermost in my thoughts ... I would rather have any cancer than that. Then the treatment options seemed (or are) worse than the disease. My first response was not to treat at all and let the cancer do its job, with the doctor saying this was not really an option. I was 54 years old, with impotence and incontinence staring me in the face ...

I'm editing you, Jim, the details of your initial chemo, the false hopes it raised, the rollercoaster, the side effects you hated, the total numbness like a spinal block, some medicos insensitive, contradictory.

I suppose it's like being on a train ... it depends who is travelling with you.

That was 2010 and now there are more support groups, better treatment, greater understanding. Or I hope there is. Alison's doctors tell her she is lucky to have her cancer now and not 10 years ago, much better treatment available and she's glad of that. I suggest she should ask for the cancer to be postponed another 10 years for further improvement, but that seems not to be an option. Luck is a relative thing.

It was at this stage that I ran into Sergio at Toombul ... both Sue and I were in bad need of a friend and Serg filled the bill ... I started walking with Serg 3 or 4 mornings a week ... talking and walking, walking and talking ... They were not easy times.

The treatment, the chemo, became better, easier to handle. Jim tuned it himself. There was remission.

I remember thinking about 12 months out, life had pretty much returned to normal and it all seemed little more than a bad dream ... It was all over, we had survived the storm ...

Strangely the return (actually, it never went away, it was just undetectable for a while) of the cancer was less traumatic than the initial diagnosis ... Maybe because deep down we suspected it had never gone away, maybe time helps us all adjust, or maybe what seemed unbelievable and unacceptable 5 years ago just seems the new norm.

It did hit us hard when the PSA began to rise, when the metastatic bone cancer became detectable, and finally with the spread to the soft tissue and the obstructive nature of the disease became apparent ... but none of it was as bad as those early stages.

Why? ... Maybe because I choose to accept and not to fight ... I did not give up and I still haven't ... I don't think it makes any difference to the final outcome, it just makes the journey easier if one goes with the flow.

The other is, do we accept whatever it is as the new normal?

I will leave it at that for the time being, Michael ... This email a bit of a ramble ... I hope it finds you and your family well, Dominic's shoulder on the mend and definitely no more traffic offences.

Next question?

Jim

The odds

There was that, too – a numbness when the word 'cancer' was said. I also had the excuse of a little fog, awakening from the colonoscopy ordered to check for bleeding to explain the anaemia. Quite anaemic with no symptoms other than there being a shortage of iron in my blood. Felt fine.

There's a large ulcer, Doctor Sandra said. I've taken biopsies but I'm 99 per cent sure it's cancer. I could be wrong, but I don't think so.

Then she was gone, leaving me to the post-colonoscopy restorative cup of milky coffee and a biscuit. It could have been worse – it could have been milky tea.

Told Judy they had taken biopsies to see what was what and there was fear in her eyes. Don't worry, I said, we'll find out. No point worrying.

We were into a good news/bad news routine. Nearly sure it's cancer. (Boo!) The biopsies were all negative. (Hurray!) She said she wanted to do another colonoscopy to be sure. (Boo!) Took 19 samples this time – all negative. (Hurray!) Stop taking aspirin and we'll keep an eye on it. (Whatevs.) I've discussed your case with a surgeon, she said. I've made an appointment for you to talk to him. (Uh-oh.) Look, Yasser said, the biopsies were all negative, but we're trained to believe what we see.

Where your ulcer is, high up at the start of your colon, is a little unusual. Sandra wasn't happy with it. I'm not either. You have a choice to make …

And it's one of those discussions with a doctor where you're given the options but there's really only one rational option.

What would you do if it was you, Yasser?

I'd have it out.

Rightio, let's get it out.

He's there with bright red photographs as I surface from the anaesthetic. The ulcer is a bloody mess, pulled apart a bit on a length of colon turned inside out. There, he says, see behind the ulcer, see the lump in the colon wall? A slight, smooth bulge in the shiny tube.

Better out than in, eh? Good doctoring, good to be uneasy, good to trust eyes. Thank you, Sandra, thank you, Yasser.

It takes a few days for the results of the lump's analysis to land, lymphoma, a couple of weeks for the stomach wound to heal, then off to the haematologists.

No point worrying. Whatever it is, it is. Whatever, there's time.

We're treating it with the expectation of a cure, Luke says. When pressed, on some American score chart, 80 per cent. Pretty good odds.

I'm OK.

Sequent toil

The weather cleared during the drive up the Hunter Valley, not reaching this far inland, stopped at the range.

So it's clear driving now over the New England Tableland. Topped up the tank in Murrurundi and no need to otherwise stop unless I want to. Have a stretch beside the road. Feel the hip, bend over to release the lower back and a soft grunt in the process. I recognise that little 'uh'. The first time I spotted it was on a plane. I had dropped something and as I bent to pick it up, an involuntary intake-hold-release of breath. An old man's noise, the sound of a no-longer-young man bending. I wondered how long I had been doing it.

I'm 190 centimetres tall – six foot three in the old money. Sometimes it's a lot to bend and raise. It's a lot to park in an economy airline seat. How much longer would they let me sit in the exit row with the leg room? And how would that be handled? A quiet word, an unexplained reassignment of seating.

I've placed my phone with the QR code under the boarding pass reader. A failure buzzer and the light went red.

In red on the reader, 'seating assignment issue'. 'Seating assignment issue,' repeats the young woman and directs you back to the desk from the queue of passengers.

'Oh, it's an exit row,' another young woman says and quickly looks at you again, the briefest pause, but a pause. 'Are you happy to assist?' she asks.

'Certainly. I'll do anything for leg room,' you smile. She smiles back. You pass. This time.

There's time, plenty of time. I could have gone Bucketts Way. Don't know why I thought there was a rush other than the desire to be gone. I hadn't settled into the drive, behind and ahead of myself.

Time.

Like as the waves make towards the pebbled shore,
So do our minutes hasten to their end;
Each changing place with that which goes before,
In sequent toil all forwards do contend.[7]

Jim

I'm sorry to hear that you had to go back for another operation – unless it's just the desire to wear those groovy socks, in which case there is clearly no hope for you.

Thanks for continuing to write and to be willing to go over old ground that may be painful. You continue to educate me in a number of ways, with the medical journey just part of it. Your decision to not give up but also not to fight it fits with something I have a half-memory of reading somewhere in the past, something along the lines of the journey being made better by attitude, but the outcome statistically not changing. Quality improves, quantity doesn't much change. Unless I've misinterpreted you, unless you mean fight the way Tom must have.

A sense of peace is what we're all after, I suppose. All those poor bastards dominating the headlines now, the millions in all sorts of refugee camps elsewhere in the world, all most of them really wanted was a peaceful life in their village. The village might not have been too flash, but in a world of war and terror and death, peace is a reasonable goal to have. And the level of dissatisfaction among so many who have absolutely everything seems to come from a lack of inner peace with their lives. Someone wrote that peace is only boring for those who haven't suffered war.

And so endeth the sermon.

You ask me to tell about my sons showing courage. (Dom is doing fine by the way – had lunch with him on Father's Day.) Two quick stories about my eldest, Nick.

One came to mind when you told me of your anxiety about public speaking – Nick's first debate. It was in primary school, just Grade 4, the year before he started at Riverview. As I watched him waiting for

141

his turn, it was obvious to me that he was nervous as all hell, pale and worried. My fatherly instinct was to want to tell him that, hey, it's OK, it doesn't matter, but you can't do that in a school room. Anyway, when his turn came – he must have been the second or third speaker – I have a clear memory of this little boy almost physically putting the fear behind him, swallowing hard and getting up and speaking well. That was the first of many debates – he debated all through school, including winning a GPS seconds premiership for Riverview. He was very good.

The second was in his first year at Riverview, which back then had a very small primary school contingent of one Year 5 and two Year 6s. They combined them for sport against other primary schools. Nick was and is a very smart fella, but he hasn't been gifted with superior sports skills. In his first term at Riverview, he had to choose a summer sport and put down cricket. (It should have been basketball, a game he only came to in his last two years at school and which he enjoyed.) Anyway, Nick was batting at the bottom of the batting order in the B team (there were only two) that wasn't going very well. The way little boys' cricket worked was that bowlers were limited to a couple of overs, so for their last game, the coach thought he'd be smart and play his worst batsmen against the opposition's best bowlers, with the theory that the better batsmen would score easily against weak bowlers.

The plan was dubious and was made worse than dubious by a scheduling blunder. Up against St Pat's Strathfield (which had a much bigger primary school), somehow their A team turned up against our B team. It was a mismatch like a Nudgee As taking on a Terrace Cs. But Nick and another sacrificial lamb had to open the batting. Again, I could see the same understandable fear, but with much the same act of determination as in the debating room, he went out there anyway – he had no choice, I suppose. His job was to absorb as much punishment as possible for as long as possible, to put his body between the ball and the wicket – which he did. I would not have – I would have waved the bat at the ball from a safe distance. Nick was struck twice, connected bat to ball for a face-saving run and the bowler missed both boy and wicket a couple of times before finally putting him out of my misery. I have never been so pleased to see someone bowled out.

I have watched all my sons play their sports when I could and coached two of them for several years in club rugby. Dom was a firsts basketballer, Tim was seconds, Chris stuck with cricket and all did their bits on the rugby field, winning much more often than losing – but I have never had more pride in any of their performances than I had in Nick scoring one run against St Pat's. I thought it was a little boy showing great courage, literally taking a couple for the team, at an age when you'd wish your child didn't have concerns.

I mentioned Nick was intelligent – he switched to tennis the next summer. That was his last game of cricket, if you don't count backyard stuff with a tennis ball.

The first Riverview headmaster we came across wasn't a big fan of sport, more into the arts than sport, once said something like: 'People say sport develops character. I'm not so sure of that, but it certainly displays character.'

As a coach I tried – and often failed – to have as much joy and celebration for the kid who has a crack as the star who scores.

And now I'm raving on. It's hardly the stuff of Victoria Crosses, or facing cancer, but you did ask me.

And my next question for you as I try to understand more of my old schoolmate is for you to give me the context of the family farm being sold. You've explained that it was heart-tearing, but how did it come about – the place wasn't viable/a price that couldn't be refused/bad seasons/what?

What came to me as part of this thinking about what we don't appreciate about different lives at school is Tommy Ng – remember how serious he was about practising kung fu and how generally he was a very serious individual for most of his time there, maybe only loosening towards the end? Well, did any of us appreciate what happened in Malaysia in 1969, when the Malays were indulging in their one gift to the English language – running amok, killing Chinese? We just thought Thomas Ng was a bit weird. We were in our own quite peaceful world, the odd Christian Brother notwithstanding.

Keep strong, old mate. I thought my little Nick was 'old school' in that cricket game. I was proud of that. At one time or another I've seen that in all my boys. I think you're 'old school' too, in the best of ways, not in the insensitive way it sometimes seems, but in strength of character, a man in full prepared to be sensitive as well as strong. Like my father.

Love
Michael

Quiet Australian

We mostly continue to live in our own little world, have for a couple of centuries, the odd world war notwithstanding. We sally forth occasionally, join dubious wars for dubious reasons, but we try not to invite the world in, prefer to not see what we don't want to think about. A wilful ignorance rather than schoolboy innocence. Born into our island of privilege, a rich crop grown from our roots in stolen wealth, we do enough to tell ourselves we do enough.

Catching up with a Volkswagen Amarok now, not the most common ute inland. Amaroks wear a large VW badge, the circle sitting bold, nearly a third of the tailgate's height, as the Alfa closes and overtakes with a surge from quick downshifts for the joy of it. Ganz and Ledwinka back into my cabin, summonsed by wondering what they would make of Volkswagen making utes in Argentina for Australia, make vehicles everywhere from Mexico to Russia, Sweden to China, with brands from Britain's Bentley to the Czech Republic's Škoda.

They were men ahead of their times but perhaps couldn't see ahead of their times. Ledwinka was head designer for Czechoslovakia's Tatra. Menzies in 1938 thought the Czechs were troublemakers, getting in the way of peace. Tatra's patents

145

were not an issue after 1939 and Ledwinka adapted – he was jailed for five years after the war for collaborating and then retired to Munich.

As a Jew in Nazi Germany, Ganz was easier to deal with. There are vastly worse things than car crashes, than a virus, than cancer, than getting old and dying, than our nightmares, than a sane person should be able to imagine. And we didn't want to imagine until we were forced to look. As the terror began in Germany, even after Kristallnacht, Australia capped its refugee intake at 5000 a year. We have long form with boat people, buried within us like the DNA fragments left by a virus.

We prefer to avoid an accounting, the 'black armband view of history' a pejorative. Airbrush history to suit the purpose of the times. Better to concentrate on brave explorers than First Nations genocide, on hero diggers than our betrayals of humanity.

A.A. Gill once wrote an unusually kind piece about Australia – unusually kind for him, anyway. Said he loved the place, loved its innocence and that nothing ever happened here. That's why we are so fixated with sport – it's nothing happening at speed, the illusion of something happening. And Ganz finished up here where nothing happens. Perhaps the first man to talk of a *volks wagen*, he escaped Germany in 1934 and emigrated from Switzerland in 1951, had a job at Holden. The Americans got Einstein and Fermi and we got Josef Ganz. By the look of that period's Holdens, nobody listened to him, anyway. He died in 1967 forgotten, a life lost in time, raindrops in an ocean. A young Dutchman discovered his story 40 years later and wrote *The Extraordinary Life of Josef Ganz*.

We fight old wars and then create new wars out of the old. I've been getting crankier about it – par for the course.

Old man shouting at TV. Old man shouts at cloud. Jim, tough country Jim, turns out to be soft, saddened and depressed by the suffering of others.

Stay sane by making the effort to enjoy irony and still find the beauty. The outrage of youth easily slides into curmudgeonly crankiness, the adrenalin that would foment revolution distils into bile. There's more to be sorry about, to regret, and seemingly less that can be done and perhaps less energy to do it. Having time can do that, time to reopen the old wounds, dig up forgotten bones and worry them anew. I don't know if it is being compromised in the shade of the virus or just getting older or the combination thereof, but my mistakes haunt me more now, my sins. The summing up years.

And as if our own are not enough, we revisit the sins of our fathers and call them down upon us, try to show we've learned something as we continue to bumble blindly on. It's easier to cross-examine the past. We ask the big questions of the dead when they can't answer and the questions are out of the context of their times, but they're still fair questions. What did you do in the war, Daddy? What did you do before the war?

A Berliner friend says that was what 1968 was about in West Germany, the young asking the questions of their parents; it was where the subsequent terrorism came from. That and a little help from the Stasi. The formal de-Nazification didn't answer those questions. The new Germany couldn't exist, there couldn't be pride again without those questions being answered from within. And Germany now owns its past better than any country, acknowledges it humbly, truthfully, freeing it to move on while the rest of the world maintains degrees of denial.

The weight of history sits more heavily in Berlin than anywhere I've visited. You can stroll the poetic ruins of ancient Rome and breathe Angkor Wat's humidity and enjoy the pyramids' pretty *son et lumière*, but that is picture-book history, viewed from outside. They could be on different planets. Berlin lives a history that shaped and still shapes my world. The centre of the 20th century, the front line of our greatest cataclysms, the ghosts still visible, relics warm to the touch, again the centre of Europe.

The Neues Museum, housing reconstructed ruins of Meso-potamia in the reconstructed ruins of Berlin, the bust of Nefertiti framed by soaring granite columns acne-scarred by bullets and shrapnel.

And what will our children and grandchildren ask us? What did you do about climate change, Poppy? Why did you have a fossil fuel car? What did you do as inequality spread? Did you try to prepare for the decline of our mineral wealth, Poppy? Were you a fighter for broader and better education? Did you tolerate the misogyny, Poppy? Were you sexist? Did you fall for the culture wars? Were you a Quiet Australian?

September 9, 8.22 am

'A sense of peace is what we're all after, I suppose' … and then you remind me of all those poor bastards who have lost their peace, families, lives and everything else, through the horror, injustice and absolute stupidity of war.

Then I think I don't want millions of war refugees resettled in Australia, and I feel ashamed of myself … this is not our land, I don't think it belongs to the Aboriginal people … it certainly doesn't belong to me … I simply have the advantage of possession, and as we say, possession is nine tenths of the law … a Syrian refugee has as much right to live in Australia as I have, but then I don't open my house or my farm as an enclave for the poor bastards.

It is a complex situation … and then I think if there is a 'judgement day', mine is getting rather close … how do I explain my thoughts and actions to my creator (if there is one) … self and the desire to protect and nurture that self are God-given instinctive desires.

Will that get me off the hook, Michael? … The world is far too complex for me to understand.

I remember Thomas Ng … compared to my sheltered little world … whatever happened to Thomas?

I do know that you raising the subject of an international refugee crisis (and its cause) certainly makes me reflect on the situation that confronts myself … I feel quite a lucky man upon that reflection.

Fighting cancer … we fight cancer, drugs, crime, wars etc. … do we ever win?

We are born to fight, we love to fight … I think we would rather fight than love.

So yes, I think Tom like most others fought cancer, and fought to stay alive … admirable in a way, but my instinct is not to fight. The question of course is can I hold that line?

As an aside ... I had an old mate in AA ... he said to me that Good (God) always reigns supreme over Bad (Devil) ... you have one look at the refugee crisis and you have to question that.

I think in my own life, I find it easier to be bad than good ... Good takes a bit of effort.

Your sons and courage ... It takes courage to survive in this world ... Your kids are like ours, they are lucky to have parents who care ... but then as a parent it takes enormous courage to let our children free in a world so full of danger ... watching your son Nick go out to face the bowling that was above and beyond him ... you just want to race out and protect him ... it's debatable who shows the most courage, the father or the son.

I feel so many emotions when I look at my grandson, Victor ... 17 months old ... we are weaker and more vulnerable as we get older.

'And my next question for you as I try to understand more of my old schoolmate is for you to give me the context of the family farm being sold ...'

Well, selling the farm ...

The one comment I would like to make, which overrides everything I might say about the farm, is that selling the farm enabled me to ultimately live the life I have lived ... and given the choice I would not swap that for any other life ... of course, there are things I would like to change, right up to the point of dying ... like leaving the girls with more money, it's an immediate and upfront wish and desire, but I am grateful for the life I've been given.

It wasn't what I would have planned.

By the time I left Nudgee in 1972, we were virtually insolvent, living and surviving on the kindness of family, banks and creditors. People paid school fees, one person forgave a substantial loan ... We had purchased his property 'Lingard', which adjoined 'Glenalba', in 1966 ... Wal was an old man and he and my father were old and solid friends ... Wal continued to live on 'Lingard' after we purchased it from him. Dad became very ill in 1972, and remained so until his death in 1981 ... He died aged 66 years.

Wool and sheep began a slow decline in the 1950s ... by 1970 they had hit rock bottom ... Our property ran about 7500 sheep and 120 head of cattle. Cattle prices collapsed in the early 1970s ... Cattle were only a sideline for us.

Sheep and wool began to recover sometime in the 70s, cattle around 1979.

Tom was 20 years old when I got home in 1972 and had been working the place with Dad and a station hand ... By December 1972, Dad was in Greenslopes Hospital ... he would spend a lot of time there and eventually died there in January 1981.

Tom and I worked the property on our own from 1972, not replacing the station hand when he left. This remained as such until maybe 1977 when Tom started doing some oil and gas work. I worked the place on my own with casual labour and Tom's help in between jobs. Tom's frustration began to surface in the mid-70s, but I will come back to that.

For a couple of young fellows who liked a drink, we didn't do too badly ... We had one mission and that was to spend as little as possible and get the debt paid off.

In 1979 we sold our 100-odd head of cattle into a quickly rising market ... We had the property fully stocked with 7500 sheep and no debt ... a pretty solid effort for an operation that was down and out only seven years previous.

We sold the property and the sheep in March and April 1979.

Why did we sell when we had just achieved a debt-free status? Well, discontent began to surface ... Tom and I started on $25 a week and continued to work for around about that sort of money.

There were 5 children ... My older sister had some sort of handicap, so that left Tom and I and two younger siblings. We were a good Country Party (you will like this, Michael) voting family, so one would have thought we were Capitalist by nature.

Sadly, when it came to succession planning and business, we were Socialist.

The property had to be split equally among the four siblings ... Tom and I quickly worked out the harder we worked and the more we saved, the more we were going to owe to our siblings and parents.

Many parents were also content to retire to Mitchell or whatever the nearest local town was ... my parents wanted to retire to Brisbane, so every dollar we made was to provide for their retirement.

Hence once it became clear to Thomas he was on a flogging to nothing, he wisely wanted out. I didn't think too much, just hanging in there doing the job at hand. It was no reflection on generosity or loyalty, it was simply who we were as people.

Tom quickly adapted to changing circumstances, I just kept on.

Tom's love of 'Glenalba' grew as he got older ... He went back out 12 months before he died just to be there. I loved it dearly, it broke my heart to leave it, it was a physical and emotional parting ... It seems a ridiculous thing for a grown man to say.

I think it's growing up there, the isolation ... I don't know, but I do know it was far more than property ... it was part of me, body and soul.

Strangely I moved on from it maybe more so than Tom ... I have no desire to go back to it now ... as an old uncle said to me, 'Only a dog goes back to its vomit.'

I think buying the farm in 2008 finally cleansed me of any lingering attachment to the place ... I hope so, anyway, because it was nearly 30 years later.

Pricewise, we sold just as the market began to turn ... Property prices had been on a downward spiral since the early 1960s ... 1978/9 was the beginning of the upturn which continued until today ... Rural property prices today are so overvalued it is a joke, not dissimilar to residential house and unit prices.

As an interesting aside ... we sold in 1979 ... I made pretty good money on some gold shares late 1979/80 and could have bought the place in 1980 for the price we sold at in March 1979 ... such is life though ... I did lose something I loved, but even now it seems hard to believe that it was for the best, for me especially.

September 11

Morning Michael

Hope this email finds you fit and well.

Whole email has been written over a couple of days ... Wrote as I thought, so if some sounds a little depressive, it is just how I was thinking at that moment.

Material for your book ... fiction, faction or comedy ... not sure what category we would fit into.

I have never before written down some of the memories which I have here ... you would think it could be good for an old man.

Maybe you should do the same for your life? ... Not to me, but there is something different about having random thoughts filtering through one's mind and writing it all down. It is an interesting experience.

I was surprised I could put down some of that history in some sort of order, and for me some sort of clarity.

As is always the case, it is the author's view of history ... I didn't run it by any other family members ... do we want to open that can of worms? ... I think not.

Thanks, Michael, you're a good man, I believe.

Love Jim

The earth

Oh Jim. You're dying and I'm picking away at you.

A scrap of memory comes to me: a short story, Doris Lessing I think, about the widow of a hallowed war poet. He had kept carbon copies of everything he had ever written to her.

Am I using you, old mate? Working you for what I can't feel, don't have ownership of, wasn't born to, can only fake? I'm sucking at your marrow for an epiphany, mining you for something about manhood and the land that's in you. Was in Dad, but he never had the means to do much about it. When he was posted to Goomeri, the quiet country town I was born in – you've heard of one-horse towns, this was just a one-pub town – he leased a dairy farm. Brian, the scholarship winner, had ideas about wanting to work the land after Year 10. It was agreed he could take a year off school and he and Richard and Dad worked the little dairy farm to save the money for Richard's school fees. Gap years aren't what they used to be.

The hard dawn-to-dusk life of dairy farming taught Brian to go back to school, disabused him of thoughts of the bush until he was dying and bought acreage outside Beaudesert, the town he was born in. We were a country copper's kids, one born at every station. Brian never spent a night there.

It was my mother who pushed education, who took so much overt pride in her children's achievements. Dad's was quieter, but there. It was Mum who craved for her children what she was denied, especially for my three older siblings when going to Year 12 was a particular rarity and expensive. Mum was pulled out of school to work during the Depression; a cheap female junior could find a job when her brothers and father could not. Her father walked to Darwin on the rumour there was work at a new abattoir. There wasn't. In a moment of bitterness once, she dismissed Dad as not caring about our future, said we all could have left school at Year 10 as far as he was concerned. Yet it was Dad doing jobs on the side to pay fees, shearing, cleaning the hall.

I don't know how much of that Goomeri dairy farm was about school fees or Dad wanting to work with animals and land.

When we were at Petrie, there was an old bloke Dad had helped, Tom Martin – unlicensed driving, unregistered vehicle or some such. I don't think Tom was big on documentation. With hindsight, he was probably illiterate. Old Tom lived in a tumbling down house on a few acres of scrub out back of Narangba. He worked at the Redcliffe rubbish dump and fossicked there for scrap metal and junk of all descriptions, bringing it home on the flatbed of an ancient truck, making his place an Aladdin's Cave for a boy. He kept pigs and ducks and chooks with scraps from the dump. Tom gave Dad a piglet as thanks and Dad told him to keep it for him. It grew and bred and Dad had pigs and soon some ducks and chooks among Tom's. There became regular trips out to Tom's, for a chook or duck or to help fix a fence. There were feral cats I was welcome to shoot with a .22 and, later, an old car – a Morris – I was allowed to drive in first gear, bush-bashing around the paddock. A couple of times it was to slaughter a pig. A curved butcher's knife into the squealing, screaming throat and down hard to find the heart. You get used to death early on farms, life and death, headless chooks and all, but not the scream of a pig about to die.

Old Tom died when I was at Nudgee, at the end of Year 9 coming up to Christmas. His property was undocumented – he was a poor version of a squatter all that time. The land went to the government, acres of hard scrub that would now be comfortable suburbia. And we moved into Brisbane and Dad retired. He grew a few strawberries and tomatoes in the backyard, a place he would escape to, perhaps for purpose, perhaps for peace, perhaps to feel the earth.

September 13, 11.18 pm

Dear Jim

So you've taught me a new word, 'lymphoedema' – and a right little charmer it turns out not to be. The power of Google to educate the blissfully ignorant.

Re writing some of your history: I am biased – being a person who has always loved the written word and who has found that writing forces you to order your thoughts, as well as enjoying the challenge of trying to order them well – but I would think your girls will appreciate the greater knowledge of you that comes from it. I know I do. For me, it is a way to catch up with you, to catch up with the long time between cups of coffee, so to speak, as we've led our different lives but happily enjoy being back in communication, albeit in dreadful circumstances.

And reading that garbled paragraph back, it doesn't speak well for my writing! But I think you know what I mean.

It does me good to hear you talk of your love of the land itself, the space. It does not surprise me at all. Your girls should be proud of your achievement in turning Glenalba around. Again, Jim, your strength in all sorts of ways is a very fine thing. I have a half-arsed theory about how much of ourselves we attach to things that are dear to us, attach enough and we can give them their own lives and personalities that feed back into us. And when the thing is living to start with, the land, it's all the more powerful.

I could never work that hard to live the farm life and I love the city, but I find my soul refreshed whenever I get into the bush, even if it's just the drive from Canberra to the snow across the high country. (I managed to sneak away at the start of this past week for two days' skiing, an indulgence of mine – couldn't believe the number of dead roos beside the road between Canberra and Cooma, mainly the bit close to Canberra;

maybe we should give the place back to them.) It's part of our great good fortune to have this country to fall back on, or fall into when we chose.

The choices we make and the twists and turns that just happen to us seem to be equal parts of the journey. It would be a rare and probably boring sort of person who set out from childhood with a plan and stuck to it. A friend of mine liked to quote someone who said, 'Life is what happens while you're waiting for it,' or something like that. But that's another avenue altogether for rumination.

Please keep your thoughts coming when you will. The grandchildren thing is an unknown for me so far. It was interesting that you said at the AGCC that you feel more protective of your grandchild than your children, whether that's a greater caution that comes with years or not, or something about the children of your children. I don't know. Another generation – that is a little scary itself.

Love
Michael

Life's lottery

The Australian Bureau of Statistics used to feature a population clock ticking away on the front page of its website. It's been banished from such a prime position now, perhaps a victim of COVID uncertainties or sensitivities with borders closed. It still exists if you search for it, though, netting out our births and deaths, people arriving to live in Australia, Australian residents leaving to live overseas.

In April 2013 the clock forecast that someone would step off a plane or a baby would be born to become the 23 millionth Australian at 9.57 pm on Tuesday the twenty-third.

Back then Australia was gaining an extra person every 83 seconds. Net overseas migration was providing 60 per cent of our population growth but the predicted hour and most international flights arriving during the day made it more likely the nominal first of the new million would be a newborn. I took it upon myself to welcome and congratulate the first one-in-23-million Australians. There was good cause for congratulations. I told Baby 23,000,000 he or she had won life's lottery just by being born here – a phrase I subsequently noticed a politician repeatedly using, somehow diminishing it.

With all the optimism of 2013, though, it was easy to be optimistic. It still is if you keep the world in perspective. So I told Baby 23,000,000: If your mother is an unmarried teenager reliant on our social welfare system, you are still much better off than most babies born on April 23, 2013. Odds are that you will have better housing, better health and much longer life expectancy than your mewing peers.

You have a universal free health care system serving your immediate needs when the world's richest nation still can't organise such a thing. You have doctors and nurses concerned for your welfare and the start of an immunisation program that gives you a world-leading chance of making it to primary school – unless you are unfortunate enough to score a ditzy anti-vaxxer mum.

And talking of school, you have the promise of 13 years of free education if you want it and have the ability and common sense to grab the opportunity when much of the world is lucky to finish primary school. Thereafter, we have a student debt system that offers you the chance of tertiary education without your parents being rich and/or apprenticeships in very valuable trades.

You strike it particularly lucky in being born in a country that enjoys the rule of law – more so if you're rich and white, less so if you are not, but it's still there. You'll get to decide which bunch of politicians is less worse than the other on a regular basis and make your way in a society that is relatively free of corruption. (Everything is relative.)

Yours is a society that, while not as financially egalitarian as it was a little while back, remains one with a bridgeable gap between its rich and poor. There is luck involved, but it at least remains possible for you to do anything that your talent, drive and dedication is capable of. You can even end a sentence with a preposition.

If you're a girl, you'll be able to wear as little or as much clothing as you wish and you'll have the same rights as a boy to the education and career of your choice. At our present rate of evolution, that right will be taken for granted by the time you get to exercise it and you'll be legally able to marry the person of your choice, regardless of race, religion, social strata or sex.

Religion? It's your call to believe or not believe in whatever god or gods you like, as long as you peaceably extend that right to everyone else because faith is, well, a matter of faith.

You might not guess it with all the whingeing and whining you'll hear but you've been born in a champion economy. Your fellow citizens are convinced they are highly taxed, although they're in the bottom third of rich nations on that score, and, ironically, that the government doesn't do enough for them, although they're in the top third when it comes to social safety nets.

If you're really, really lucky you'll be born a Queenslander and therefore inherit ownership of the nation's greatest rugby union and league teams but have the freedom – if you can afford it – to live in Sydney, the world's most beautiful city despite what its citizens try to do and not do to it.

But you don't have to. You'll have freedom of movement to enjoy the whole Dorothea Mackellar panorama – sweeping plains, rugged mountain ranges, jungles, deserts, drought and flooding rains. You can go troppo in the build-up and cuddle around a Tasmanian fireplace, worship vast, empty surf beaches and embrace the blizzard-tortured sculpture of snow gums.

You can open your heart to the endless openness of the outback, absorb that red dust and character into your soul, or thrive in a tiny inner-city apartment with the sound of sirens and aroma of coffee, spilt wine and stale beer as constant companions.

We have cities and country towns and bush, Baby 23,000,000, where you can find your life's meaning, or lose it if you're careless. It's up to you – and that is the most wonderful privilege of all.

And you get all that just by being born here. Beyond such extraordinary fortune, it's a matter of wishing you well, hoping that you are born into a family that loves and strengthens you, that gives you what you need rather than what you want, that encourages you to adopt the best of the national character – believing in a fair go, supporting the underdog, being prepared to stand up for a principle against the odds.

John Menadue wrote an Australia Day reflection on what is different about being Australian. For him, it came down to redemption, to giving people a second chance. He quoted his friend Ian McAuley as saying that while the British sent the puritans to America, they sent convicts to Australia and that we got the better of the deal. The underprivileged and the outcasts in Australia got a second chance.

For you, Baby 23,000,000, it's a first chance. Please enjoy your incredible good fortune and privilege and welcome the responsibilities that come with it, instead of taking it for granted, whingeing and demanding to be given more while offering less. Maybe you'll make it even better. I hope so.

Another generation, a new life with everything ahead. Victor is snowy-haired and happy and confident and into everything he can get his hands on, as a toddler should be. Jim said he wasn't sure that he wanted Victor riding horses, was wary of the idea of teaching him, Jim who was born in the saddle, who taught his daughters to ride. We took risks we wouldn't want our children to take, but they find others soon enough. Chris flying solo when he was in Air Cadets, jumping out of a plane to mark a birthday; Chris and Tim solo travellers in some of the more foreign, riskier lands; Dominic running with the bulls and, worse, telling his mother beforehand that he was going to do it. All four of them when they started to drive, when they would take the ball up on the rugby field. And they were only physical risks – there are the risks of their hopes and dreams that torture a parent. The risks of their relationships and all the cycle of fears and hopes and prayers start over again with grandchildren.

Jim didn't say it, I didn't ask him, but I think he didn't like the idea of Victor riding because he wouldn't be there to keep him safe, to minimise the risks.

I understand now, four grandchildren later, the frustration of separation during COVID. Chris and Bianca's twincesses, Aria and Bella, stuck in Dubai; Dom and Carmen's Harriet and Xavier in Brisbane, another expected. The sugar cane curtain parts, we rush north – the coast road. Duty of one sort or another, Judy's mother, calls us back to Sydney and the border shuts again and the virus rolls in and out.

Threenager Harriet climbs like a monkey, up and through ropes at various parks. We hover closer than we did with our own children – an extra responsibility, an extra pressure if she was hurt on our watch.

There's a spongy little rugby ball among the Brisbane crew's toys. 'Rugby ball!' Xavier exclaims with glee when he brandishes it. He announced he wants a 'big rugby ball' and I've bought him one for his second birthday – but I don't think I'd like him to play our game beyond school.

I'm getting soft. White paintball splatter on an intersection not far from home leads your eyes up to a jumble of sticks seven metres above. It looks like random flotsam caught in a tree after a flood until you notice the pair of white-faced herons poking at it. The elegance of the birds a contrast with their untidy small mess of a nest.

I cross that intersection once or twice a day with the dog. Checking the nest becomes a habit; a glimpse of fine blue-grey plumage, sometimes a cool stare back from on high. One day, a parent standing on the edge, bending her long neck up and down, perhaps feeding a chick. Another day, one, two little heads just visible. Another day, you make out there are three chicks. It's not clear how they can all possibly fit as they grow through November, getting bolder, standing on the edge of the nest to preen. You share nods with other walkers who pause to look up and see the birds stretching their wings.

A southerly buster tears through in the early evening, a howler, rain heavy on the roof, against the windows, trees frantic. There will be branches down. And there are in the morning, windfalls on the footpath and road.

I'm searching the ground from afar as I approach the intersection. The birds' droppings have been washed away. There's a woman looking up and another dog walker approaching from the other side. We've never spoken. She turns, grinning. 'They're all right.' We three strangers stand there, exchanging happy inanities about the storm, the wind, wondering how those sticks hung together through the tempest. The fledglings look down with something like disdain. It will be a good day.

I must be getting soft. There's no way the council would grant a DA for a construction that flimsy.

Dispersal

Wallabadah, the southern end of the New England Tableland, the eastern edge of the Liverpool Plains. After coming up the range from Murrurundi, the first town, the first slowdown, is little Willow Tree, but then quickly on, ignore the turn-off to Quirindi on the Kamilaroi Highway to the left and keep on to Wallabadah.

That's unusual, when you think of it – a highway named after the original custodians. It's normally a colonial explorer or prosaic geography. The Hume Highway, the Oxley. The Pacific Highway. The New England. The vast Kamilaroi Nation covered most of the tableland and out to the west, stretching from the top of the Hunter Valley into Queensland, yielding the eastern strip to the Anaiwan from around the Moonbi Range and Uralla up to Tingha.

We're evolving. Signs now along New South Wales highways announcing whose land it was and is and will ever be, blood that cannot be washed away. Open yourself to the land and you can't cross it without feeling the pain.

The squatters moved north from Sydney and the Hunter into the tableland in the 1830s. Watch dry ground closely when a sprinkler is turned on. The water builds at the edge of the spray's reach, not sinking in, steadily gaining mass at the level of grains of dirt until it starts to roll over it, pushed by the weight of water behind. It creeps rather than flows, to begin with; fits and starts, insignificant victories over tiny exposed roots, a crystal lick around a blade of grass, a quick tumble into a hollow. It keeps spreading, branching out until the earth is inundated and then starts to sink in, absorbing and being absorbed by the earth until it covers it all, the dust gone to mud. The later water flows easily out over it, beyond, further out.

'Guns, germs and steel,' as the man wrote. A massacre here, smallpox there. An understanding made early – Governor Lachlan Macquarie's diary, April 10, 1816:

> *In pursuance of this resolution, and on the grounds of the most imperious necessity, arising from their own hostile, daring, outrageous, and sanguinary Proceedings, I have this Day ordered three Separate Military Detachments to march into the Interior and remote parts of the Colony, for the purpose of Punishing the Hostile Natives, by clearing the Country of them entirely, and driving them across the mountains; as well as if possible to apprehend the Natives who have committed the late murders and outrages, with the view of their being made dreadful and severe examples of, if taken alive. – I have directed as many Natives as possible to be made Prisoners, with the view of keeping them as Hostages until the real guilty ones have surrendered themselves, or have been given up by their Tribes to summary Justice. – In the event of the Natives making the smallest show of resistance – or refusing to surrender when called upon so to do – the officers Commanding the Military Parties have been authorized to fire on them to compel them to*

surrender; hanging up on Trees the Bodies of such Natives as may be killed on such occasions, in order to strike the greater terror into the Survivors.

I acknowledge the Kamilaroi people, the traditional custodians of this land, and all the First Nations whose land I will pass through. I pay my respects to the Elders, past and present, and extend that respect to other Aboriginal and Torres Strait Islander peoples.

A few words, no biggie. If we grasped the extent of the crime, we'd begrudge the survivors nothing. The word 'custodians' is preferred to 'owners', this land that is never owned but ends up inhabiting the people who are of it.

There were survivors, are survivors, some more, some less. History airbrushed. We were not told about the resistance or the genuine sanguinary proceedings. 'Aborigines were employed as stockmen on the stations' is about all most local and enterprise histories might record, if that. Wallabadah Station, Goonoo Goonoo Station further north – 600,000 acres, the best of the Liverpool Plains, selected by the Australian Agricultural Company in 1834 as a swap with the government for half of the AAC's one million acres at Port Stephens. The dispossessed barely a footnote while a fortune was made from wool.

'Dispersal' was the euphemism of choice in Queensland. Native police units called in from the south to hunt down and massacre those that the local settlers and disease did not. The Queensland frontier wars were fierce in the north and lasted decades. It took nearly 20 years to kill more than 1000 Yuwibara around Mackay, a district that was proudly represented in federal parliament by a coal-hugging buffoon dedicated to 'mobilising support for our nation's history and heritage against black armband revisionism'.

If you can feel the land, you can feel the blood in it. Cross the First Custodians' land and feel it. Wonder into what eternity all our actions might dissolve. Every other country town has a historical society. Not many dare dig too deeply in their history lest their hands come up red. Memorials to our first war are very rare indeed.

My brother Richard, the priest, has spent a large part of his life trying to help Aboriginal and Torres Strait Islander people, a cause for him when he was still a seminarian, back when the issue was barely acknowledged, well before the referendum that granted the real Australians citizenship. I asked him why he had become so active and he told me it was because of Dad. As a country policeman, my father was the local Protector of Aborigines, a position that granted enormous power, total power, over human beings. Richard said he did protect when others did not. He was at ease with the people when others were not, he did not assume the worst when others did, he did his duty and helped people. It was what he did. People were people to Dad.

When Petrie was a one- and then a two-man police station, the lock-up was in the house yard. A high-roofed square, a sheet of iron between hardwood walls, a small barred and glassless window high on the rear wall, the door inches thick with a bolt the size of a boy's arm. I remember the occasional prisoner, more often a pay-day drunk sleeping it off than anyone sinister, Dad cooking and serving a plate of bacon and eggs and toast and an enamel mug of tea, giving them the dignity of cleaning up in the laundry under the house before taking or sending them away.

Single boyhood events can form us, can shape a life. Richard was back in Goomeri from Nudgee for the holidays, a blackfella with a torn and dirty shirt was at the police station, about to face some official business. A magistrate might have been involved. Dad told Richard to go bring one of his white shirts.

I had two white shirts, my brother told me, a good new one and another well worn. (I'd guess a hand-me-down from Brian.) I took the old one to Dad and he threw it back at me. Don't you try to give this man an old shirt. You've got better than that.

Richard has spent his life giving away possessions and time and care, sometimes not judiciously, frequently uneconomically, but always generously.

In the detritus of family belongings is a newspaper cutting about three 'coloured youths' going on a tear from Cherbourg. They'd stolen a car, broken into a shop in Kingaroy and another in Goomeri, stolen clothing, guns and ammunition. Country Queensland, 1955. A degree of hysteria. Search parties organised, posses. There would have been men whose fathers had cleared blacks from the land, one way or another, who had inherited the culture of justification undiluted. They knew about the blacks in old Queensland – you had to separate them from their country to end resistance. The Wakka Wakka people in the Burnett had resisted, fought a guerrilla war against the early squatters, killed 28 invaders, and were nearly wiped out in the reprisal raids and by the native police. Throughout the state the remaining resistance was broken by 'removing' those who weren't killed, the original custodians rounded up from all over Queensland and sentenced to reserves away from their land – Palm Island and Cherbourg among them. Cherbourg, a death camp in its early days, a history of deprivation not spoken about, not acknowledged. By 1934 there were 900 people there from 28 different tribes.

Country Queensland, 1955. The Coniston massacre across the Territory border was only 27 years before – scores of Aboriginal men, women and children shot and hacked to death in 1928 and the perpetrators cleared of any wrongdoing. Not the last, but the last 'official' massacre. Constable Murray, the leader, praised in the press. Constable Murray was alive and well and living in Adelaide.

Dad said his biggest worry was the whitefellas with guns. He received a phone call, a suspicion that somebody was camping in the scrub near Kilkivan. He went in front of a search party, creeping through the bush, worried about being shot by someone behind him, not the boys in front. The boys, two 17, one 18, around a fire. 'Drop 'em or I'll shoot,' he said. The boys arrested. No harm done. And the family subsequently teased Dad about watching too much John Wayne.

There are two photographs. The three youths – two Aboriginal, one 'South Sea Islander' – standing in thigh-high grass, not handcuffed, not bound, two of them holding hats, one wearing a neat wool vest and tie. They had stolen clothing as well as guns. Behind them, stark ironbarks, an FJ Holden and a Ford Zephyr. And a fading picture of a policeman standing beside the stolen goods. Five rifles, a pile of suitcases and overnight bags. The policeman's posture is not great, he's leaning back a little, not pulling his stomach in or puffing his chest out. He is not looking at the camera but off at 45 degrees, stiff. He's lean, as working people were then, his trousers baggy, high-waisted. But you can notice his left hand by his side, broad, thick, worked, strong. He's my father, the year I was born, aged 47 but younger than I could ever remember him beneath the country cop's broad hat, a man I could never know.

There's another family story passed down. A call one night, something about someone in the pub with a gun. Dad walked up, unarmed, of course, opened the door and there's a man standing at the bar with a handgun and the patrons back against the wall. Dad kept walking towards him, heart racing, talking, adrenalin pumping, telling the man to let him have the gun, not to do anything silly. He took the gun with his left hand from the man's right, taking it away from his body, looked down at it and realised it was a fake. So he flattened him with his right.

I knew Dad kept a handgun in the glove box of the police car. I think he only ever used it to put down injured livestock. I was young, not even a schoolboy, but I knew the gun was there and wanted to examine it. Very early one morning, everyone else asleep, pale grey light, I snuck down to the car parked on the driveway. I remember this very, very clearly. The car and the glove box never locked. The heavy silver pistol, dark grip, pointing it at the floor of the car and pulling the trigger. Nothing happening. Looking down into the barrel of the gun with my hands around the grip and trigger. I somehow cocked the thing and put a bullet through the floor of the police car. Looking up to the side veranda of the house, the louvres snapping open, Dad.

I wondered how Dad would have explained that hole, but the hole allegedly was an evolved embellishment of memory. Terry and Annette assure me I only put a good dint in the side of the footwell, the slug ricocheting wherever.

I don't remember what happened after seeing Dad's face through the louvres. I can imagine a father's fear and relief, my mother's scolding. Suspect a little more firearm security was practised thereafter.

I see a police car outside a country police station house and think of that. And a very early memory: in the car, just the two of us, a toddler sitting on his father's lap and being allowed to 'drive', to hold the steering wheel along the street from Cooks Corner, years before seatbelts, decades before child seats, the small boy's thrill of it. Doing that more than once for the final short stretch home, but then not permitted anymore. Possibly a bad look for a policeman.

You watch the speed driving into Wallabadah, coming around the corner, a straight stretch to the old hotel. A police car sometimes sits just beyond it. The Marshall Macmahon Hotel, built 1867, the same year Captain Thunderbolt robbed the Northern Mail coach there. It's the New England Highway but the address of this bit is Coach Street. The verandas around the sandstone walls always well shaded. The corrugated iron roof always a little haphazard. And down the end of the main drag as the road curves to go over the Quirindi Creek, the First Fleet Memorial Gardens, this small town's other claim to fame. Here, up on the tableland, hundreds of kilometres from Sydney Cove, a memorial to the first convicts and redcoats to invade the land. The many times I've driven this road, I've never stopped there. This time there's time.

Headstones, shade cloth in the shape of ships' sails and rigging over picnic tables. Storyboards with paintings of slicker ships than ever carried convicts. And with a charming touch of self-awareness, a sign with the headline 'Why Wallabadah?'.

This Memorial is for the descendants of those who sailed on the First Fleet. Many of the descendants now regularly use this area for family reunions and for quiet reflection. There is no other Memorial in Australia that lists all the names of the people who sailed on the First Fleet.

The Memorial's physical location is not that important as the descendants come from all parts of Australia and from overseas. Liverpool Plains Shire Council supported the vision of Ray Collins, a descendant, who built this Memorial. The rejection of this vision by other locales within New South Wales is why it is here today.

It's quiet. The sun pleasantly warming the tableland air. Still a little fresh. The gardens are empty except for me and a couple setting out an early lunch at a picnic table. An older couple, another old couple, grey nomads. You can see they're in the routine of this, come prepared with all the picnic utensils, even a ... a ... the word for the cloth you put down over a table before you set it. I think 'bedspread' and know it's not. Maybe that's all right – as long as I know the word is not right, I'm OK. When I start calling a tablecloth a bedspread it will be too late for me. A tablecloth. See, it was there.

And you're back in the car, the car that was sitting beautifully in isolation, a machine of beauty. And you push the big start button on the steering wheel and you're over the creek and out of Wallabadah and away from towns. This drive isn't about the towns, anyway. Not about the places but the sense of place in between them.

September 21, 7.43 pm

Jim

You've gone quiet on me – and that's a worry when you've been back in hospital.

Is the AGCC in session tomorrow, or is it the WGCC instead?

Hope to see you soon

Michael

September 21, 7.59 pm

Hello Michael

I have gone a little quiet ... but I did write to you this morning ... I have cut and pasted it below.

Maybe my email was lost in the pile of correspondence you would get.

AGCC in session tomorrow. Be good, old mate.

Jim

G'day Michael

Hope all is well with you and family.

Sue and I down to the farm Thursday 17th ... a month to the day since we left on August 17th. It bought up a lot of emotion and issues, just being back here. Mainly the impracticality of trying to hold on to the farm after I die, and the fear of leaving Sue with all these unresolved issues ... the horses, the finances, the trinkets I have collected over a lifetime. I wish I could just clear the decks. We are going back to Brisbane this morning.

Not writing anything down at present. I know we started this as sharing the dying process, but then we veered off into some sort of autobiography.

I'm struggling a bit at the moment, and the novelty of writing it down doesn't seem quite as appealing. The theory versus the reality?

Emotionally much more fragile, and easily brought to tears. I think, what is the point of writing down a diary of a lot of depressing negative crap? It's normal, it happens to anyone in a palliative situation ... It is no big deal, so just get on with it, old boy.

So we will see what happens.

Serg said you were interested in coming down to the farm. You are very welcome if we can find a time that fits both of us. It's no big deal, the main thing is you know you're welcome.

Mark Harrison called in on Saturday for a quick cuppa ... Smoko, he said, now there is a word we have lost.

So, Michael, I might leave it at that for the present ... If I feel the need or desire to write I will. We will catch up for coffee soon.

Love Jim

Unintended

We catch up at the AGCC, Jim and Sue and Victor clambering merrily over them, their delight in him tangible. We don't talk of dying as such but there's a current of sensitivity below the sparkle of old friends over coffee in spring sunlight. We speak of the rise of Uber, Sue a strong advocate in those early days. A story of Sue upset after a hospital visit, an Uber driver stopping the car at her home, waiting for her to gather herself, talking with her. Sue and the girls feel safer with Uber drivers.

For me, the long and successful inveigling of parliaments by the taxi companies – not the drivers – was a tapeworm of structural corruption that needed unwinding. Some sympathy for the most recent buyers of taxi plates, the state governments complicit in the racket, but a structure that had been exploited to the point of needing to be broken. Soon enough Uber and its peers were exploiting their drivers, their riders. Kids on poorly lit bikes riding off into wild nights on wet city streets to deliver food, a job we wouldn't want our own children to risk but happy to risk someone else's child. That Law of Unintended Consequences.

And Jim leads me down another road.

October 1, 8.50 am

Jim

The joys of government licences and perverted markets – we left that hanging at the Club.

As I think I mentioned, as a boy I spent many holidays on a dairy farm outside Rosewood. Loved it. The parents were good friends of my parents from an earlier country town, the father a mechanic before taking up the dairy farm. His wife was in many ways my second mother, a former schoolteacher with a great sense of fun. She was very encouraging, very positive. I think she had a role in trying to make me think both by talking about politics to a child and asking why I thought whatever it was I thought. Or thought I thought. I can conjure her up now, Myrtle Ryan, laughing in her farmhouse kitchen, tanned, weathered, a little nicotine-stained.

Of course, I didn't appreciate it at the time, but the Ryans were living in rural poverty, kept poor by the milk quota system – effectively indentured to the milk marketing board or co-op or whatever the thing was. They only survived by the father working for the council slashing roadsides and the usual farm thing of child labour. (They had three children of similar ages to my brother Terry and me – the daughter was the first girl I kissed and I was not a good friend, or any friend at all, after we left school. Something that embarrasses me still.) I also didn't understand the undercurrents of the family – the dad had a bit of mad Irish in him. The marriage became unhappy. Looking back, revisiting childhood eyes, I can see all that now. It has left me angry with systems that try to keep people locked in their place, trapped. While many people strive to maintain the status quo, it tends to be strangling plenty of others.

Which is quite a diversion from the idea of a degree of compensation for taxi-plate owners. I think you're right – state governments have been accomplices and therefore should bear some of the costs. But individuals still have to take some responsibility for their own mistakes or it turns very National Party indeed: privatising the profits, socialising the losses!

Keep the AGCC jumping and save me a seat there on October 23.

Love
Michael

October 1, 11.57 am

Thanks for your email, Michael, and thanks for sharing some of your experiences. It is interesting how as 60 year olds we reflect back on the lives of those who were adults when we were children or boys ... be they Christian Brothers or the parents of others, or just our own.

I often reflect on some of the families that worked at home ... as a child I knew them very well, especially because of the isolation ... I think the adults would all be dead now. They would have gone through the same experiences as I am currently going through. I didn't know it hurt so much.

The older I get and the closer death is, I become more forgiving and much less definite ... I suppose we differ on that point, and that is ok ... you need to be definite in your business. Not much of a market for someone who writes and says they have no idea anymore ... wouldn't have a bloody clue, is about all I could put down on paper ... NFI.

My fucking left leg and my genitals continue to swell ... oedema ... what's in a name ... death by a thousand cuts ... the only comforting thought I have is that this is as good as it is going to be ... but then I think of all those adults I knew or observed as a child, and almost without exception they are either dead or dying. Some would have died horrible deaths, so who am I to complain. Yet I do complain, and it really upsets me at times, most of the time, I suppose.

Returning to the subject of reflection, we tend to roundly condemn the behaviour of past generations, when in fact they did the best they could according to the beliefs or ideologies that reigned at the time ... future generations will roundly condemn our society and the things we hold dear.

Those Nudgee days seem but weeks ago sometimes ... Yet it is all over, no matter I die this year and some may live another 30 ... it is still just a speck in time. Yet we seemed ruled from within according to religious,

181

moral or political beliefs ... most seem to defy logic, and at the very best seem extraordinarily inadequate when put in context with the enormity of the whole.

I think too much sometimes ... which is a frustrating pursuit for someone who comes from the point of view of knowing nothing.

What more can come from dying slowly than doubt ... Only a fool wouldn't be riddled with doubt ... doubt about everything.

I have been told by several good doctors that as things stand, I should without intervention die of kidney failure (6 to 12 month timeframe) ... a fairly pleasant and peaceful way to die, I am led to believe.

The closer it gets, the more I doubt my courage to let this happen ... It is what I want to happen, but I still doubt myself. The other options of a way to die are not pretty ... my kidneys are my salvation.

Thanks again for your email, Michael ... I didn't think I could write again, I didn't know what to write about ... the well of words had disappeared. I find myself in a strange place ... I can't believe I'm dying, I can't believe I'm getting sick ... but I most definitely would appear to be. My body is disintegrating before my eyes. It must be of some use to me to write it down, even if it be confused gibberish.

Hope this email finds you and yours in good health and spirits.

Love Jim

October 9, 1.16 am

Dear Jim

Sorry I went silent for a while – been running around the country again and running away from mess and mayhem on the home front. Nothing that an organised person couldn't fix. And I'm nothing like an organised person.

Writing now from Broome – yes, it's a tough life, but someone had to speak at a regional development conference so it might as well be me. I left home at 8.30 am yesterday for a 10 am flight to Perth, had to spend a couple of hours at the airport before the connection to Broome and checked into the hotel here at 9.30 pm Sydney time – 13 hours' travel and I didn't leave Australia. Good to be reminded sometimes just how large it is. I've been here once before as a tourist so it's been good to come back working and having to find out more about the region. The Kimberley is rich in many ways, but 45% of the population is Indigenous and way behind the other 55%. Blackfellas around the park and the pub, but no sign of them employed in Broome. Caught up with Pat Dodson – a former priest, a national and local Aboriginal leader and old mate of Richard's – who is working on all sorts of good things, but the reality on the ground here seems to be a different world. There are no easy answers, the way it has gone and remains.

Which is all an aside.

Thanks for another very thoughtful email. I'm actually a big fan of doubt, especially when it comes to religion. I'd like to make it compulsory for all religions to include some doubt among their dogma, to remind people that we are not capable of knowing all the answers and that all religions are someone's best guess. A bit of doubt might hold back the fanatics from doing terrible things. Richard sent me something many years ago that included a line that stuck, something from a Sufi poet along the lines of: 'No man can know the mind of God. Those who claim to are just troublemakers.' That said, I personally find Christianity the least unreasonable of the faiths, as long as you pick and choose the bits that make sense and disregard the rest.

God, a god, helps me make some sense of the universe. It works for me but I don't expect it should for anyone else. It doesn't make sense to me, or I don't want it to make sense, that this extraordinary world of such diversity and beauty is all there is, and a random event at that. Maybe the 'spirit' is what we make ourselves, the love and understanding we generate, the miracles of life we share, the goodwill that people of goodwill create. I feel that with you. For all the doubt and worry you profess, I somehow still feel the strength in you I recognised 46 years ago.

And while we are but specks in time, we are all in the journey together, part of that greater contemplation. We are what the many people of our childhoods made, but we also make and influence along the way. And we never know many of the influences we have.

Example: The latest terrible American school shooting precipitated some thoughts about the US gun craziness that had been building for a while, so I was presumptuous enough to write them in a way that seemed to strike a chord with many but also annoyed some – the way things do. Within that piece, you influenced me to include an oblique reference to rural youth suicide. It would have been easy not to, but it was thinking of your disclosure about anxiety that make me include it. The story was read by a lot of people – more than 100,000 according to the website on the day – and maybe it had an influence on some of them. And so it goes.

I made the mistake of replying to an American right-wing gun nut on Twitter (politely, logically) but was then swamped by a wave of tweets from the nutjobs, people absolutely certain about their right to bear arms. They're beyond logic, off in their own religion of certainty. I won't make the mistake again of answering such people, but I was tempted to send them all a link to the next horrific American gun story – the 11-year-old boy who shot and killed the 8-year-old girl next door because she wouldn't let him play with her dog. There would be no point. Maybe we feel such senseless suffering more as we get older because we do get a little wiser. I remember shooting birds as a boy and now feel embarrassed about that. Just casual slaughter of whatever had feathers because we could, not for food. Aside from feral vermin, I couldn't do that now and wouldn't like my sons to do so. Yes, we change.

I'm also sorry to hear that various bits of you are playing up. Your contemplation of your preferred means of death does seem eerie – and I'm just reading what you tell me about it. You're breaking our usual social taboos about death, acknowledging it when most people try to deny its existence for themselves.

See you in two weeks.

Love
Michael

Fantasies

The nature of a machine – its purpose, its soul – will out.

Buy a fast car, a powerful, tight, grippy, toey, connected, fast machine – it doesn't even have to be so powerful, just feel quick – odds are you will have the fantasy of driving it fast, to experience the speed and ability of the thing, the hug of g-forces under acceleration and cornering. And at some stage, you will.

Buy and hold a double-barrelled shotgun and you'll be imagining clay targets disappearing in a puff of colour or game birds falling from the sky. You'll put the machine to your shoulder, feel it snug against your cheek and move it through the imagined arc of your target. Trigger. You can nearly feel the recoil.

Buy a semi-automatic assault rifle and hundreds of rounds of ammunition, you're imagining … what they're designed to do, what they're good for, the only thing they're good for.

Assault rifles are rubbish for target shooting. A 'sporting' shooter after deer or a professional harvesting kangaroos wouldn't want one.

They're the weapons of survivalists believing they need to defend perimeters from marauding gangs, of militia preparing for war, of vigilantes confronting protesters. And they are the weapons of mass killers, the weapons of choice for most American mass murderers. They are machines for killing people.

Fantasies are fanned by investing in them – by purchasing the rifles and high-capacity magazines and stockpiling ammunition, never mind the 'bump stock' adaption to create a machine gun, the thing made famous in Las Vegas and quickly sold out in the US. An individual's desire to buy a military assault rifle, let alone high-capacity magazines, is all the mental assessment necessary to forbid such a purchase. Or it would be in a rational nation. A beneficial catch 22.

Supercar owners may legally explore their fantasy's limits by investing in track days and closed-road events, ripping up hill climbs. The owner of machines specifically good for killing people, what do they want to do?

I was good with the Bren gun in cadets at Nudgee – that beautiful light machine gun whose major fault was that it was too accurate. In the mass-killing business, you want your machine gun to spray fire, not concentrate it. I knew the fault and used it on the firing range at our final cadet camp in 1970. Top score by not giving in to the temptation for the allocated rapid-fire rounds, only squeezing off a couple at a time. The pistol grip, the quaintly curved magazine to take the same rimmed .303 ammo as the old rifle dragged through two world wars and Korea. Follow the curve to snap the magazine in, pull the cocking handle back, slap it closed, the little round window of the sight offset to the left, the target, fire. I could do it. I imagined doing it. Setting an ambush against an anonymous invader, hidden off a track, waiting for a full section to be in view. Contact. Fire. Fire into bodies. A magazine, two. Pull back, melt away.

Nudgee abandoned the cadet corps at the end of 1970, the Christian Brothers in this case reading a little ahead of the changing mood of the times. I had volunteered/been chosen to condense the sergeant and cadet underofficer courses at the end of sub-junior, Year 9. The CUO course was an intense week over the December holidays, taught by regs back from Vietnam, contact demonstrations with the targets in 'black pyjamas'. I could do it. Most others on the course were going into Year 12.

We generally control our fantasies, live with them harmlessly enough, the lives and deeds unlived, not done, let pass. But a few will not.

An industry feeds the ratbaggery and feeds off it, echo chambers echoing here now. Conspiracies and outrage fanning the febrile, poisoning. How's your fantasy? A fantasy of death. Not all of us evolve much.

The farm

The farm is 220 acres, a lifestyle place, Jim says. Breaks even most years, a few thousand up and there are the deductions.

'So how much are we subsidising you with our taxes, Jim?'

'Subsidise isn't a very nice word, Michael.'

Sergio collects me from the airport in late October and does the driving. We had exchanged badinage about Serge not being much of a cowboy – no RM Williams in his wardrobe – but he metaphorically dons his chaps and spurs and saddles up for his friends. Jim's latest email sounds like he could do with a distraction.

Rode a couple of horses this morning and thought, my days of riding are drawing to a close …

I am at the stage of letting go … I don't drive in the city, my sex life is done and dusted, my days of horseriding are nearing an end, my rectum is permanently decommissioned, I'm letting go of the farm … My whole life is being gradually decommissioned, and it is ok.

Warrill View is a speck on the Cunningham Highway between Warwick and Amberley. I've driven through it scores of times and it never registered. It didn't rate a 60-k speed limit then, just 70. It has since been reduced to 60. There's a fresh blue crucifix on the northern approach.

A shop, a school, a handful of houses on the highway, a sign for the turn-off.

ROSEWOOD WARRILL VIEW RD
Coleyville Rosevale Mt Walker
3 Historic Site Cunningham Lookout

Jim's place is technically Rosevale, but Rosevale is an area, no longer a place. The farm is down a narrow gravel road, wending its way through country that is beautiful, but few would call pretty. At times there are views of the Great Dividing Range, back towards Cunninghams Gap – the 'Scenic Rim' as attempts to encourage tourism call it – and the dark blue hues through the gums are grand. Later, having driven the farm Toyota up a winding track to the hill at the back of the property, amid a mob of pretty-faced wallabies, the gap itself is hidden by a darker blue Mount Fraser. Clouds are starting to build up over the range, blue-greys against the infinite blue, the mountains darker shades again beneath them.

'The colours are always changing,' Jim says. There might be a half note of wonder, maybe pride in his voice. This is his country now. I can feel his ownership, his custodianship, a thing that is not a piece of paper or computer record. I know it's not Glenalba, paradise lost, the Maranoa station he grew up on. It's not the 24,000 acres brought back from the brink, nursed and loved and then gone. 'I knew every inch of that property,' he tells you, and you believe it. It's not Glenalba, his soul's lost love, but this is land the way people with land in their blood know it. Land that requires work and care. Land that responds to care, love that moves at the speed of grass growing, a universe of 220 acres that encompasses all the sky and the weather it brings for the land and all the life that grows and moves upon it. Paradise enow.

I guess there would be very few hobby farms this size that more than pay their way. The land needs knowledge and work, work even when your legs and testicles swell. Sue tells us quietly when he's out of the room that it's getting harder for Jim, that it frustrates him that he can't do more.

Some of the paddocks had been slashed – Jim on a tractor despite the lymphoedema that makes him move stiffly.

I ask if he improves the pasture. No, you don't spend a dollar you don't have to. If you spend a dollar you have to get it back. I begin to recall two characters in an Annie Proulx novel, one the very model of the modern scientific rancher, the other a mean penny pincher, both finishing up with much the same bottom line. Jim's not mean – his cattle are prime, the fences all good – but he knows where a dollar goes on a farm.

'I'm a bit of a conservationist,' Jim says, guessing there might be a wallaby for every acre as they hop away. He says 'conservationist' as if it might be a foreign word, but it's a little act, a tiny understood joke between us. Of course he is. Doesn't like killing things anymore. Even a superfluous rooster to eat, the axe doesn't swing as easily. Brown snakes, that's different. Shoots them. Another schoolmate, another whose family property was lost to debt, might lease the property after he's gone. That would be good. He is a good man. You could trust him 100 per cent. He'd take care of it, Jim says. If you said only run 30 head, he would. Someone else, they might suddenly buy 60.

The grove of grass trees is superb, a line of them, the biggest I've seen, tall and straight along the side of the hill, hidden until you're upon them. 'You can't call them blackboys anymore.' And again, it's an understood joke, a wink without malice at political correctness. They're ancient, silent, slow-growing trees, hundreds of years old, the crown of long green blades cascading down to the skirt of dead leaves around the knobbly trunk. Trees that survive bushfires to flower. As tough as the land and as prey to whitefellas. They would be worth serious money to sell, a protected species requiring a licence to harvest. Inevitably there's a black market. Jim wouldn't sell them. 'If you want one, if you or Sergio want one, you can have it, but I wouldn't sell them,' says Jim simply. I don't want one – have nowhere for it anyway, and it's the grove that is spectacular in the quiet bush, not an individual plunked in a suburban rockery. If giant grass trees exist in a secret grove and nobody sees them, they are still magnificent.

It's not a long drive in the ute to gently cover the extent of the property, stopping for the view, the grass trees, to let the wallabies hop away, the farmer automatically pausing when in sight of a steer, eyes quickly checking its condition.

What to do with the farm continues to worry Jim, whether he should sell it now or leave it for the girls to sort out, how unfair that would be, concerned he hadn't prepared them for this. Maybe lease it for a while, see what happens. And while he's saying that, you're seeing the pleasure and peace he's drawing from the place. You don't say it but you know it would not be possible for him to sell. It will be Sue's problem.

And the four of us sat on the veranda and talked and laughed about old times, retelling the bigger stories, sensing an urge to reclaim those years, all the years while Jim can, happily settling into our anecdotage a little early.

We tell Sue about the 1971 Nudgee football tour to Sydney, or she wants my version of those events she would have heard before. The First XV and 16As billeted out with Waverley College families – random outcomes, none more so than Jim and me. While the rest of the team was clustered in the Eastern Suburbs, Sergio in luxury accommodation at that, Jim and I scored a room in an Enmore boarding house. Pre-gentrification. Pre-pre-gentrification. The owner, a woman by herself, might have thought a couple of Nudgee boys would be a good influence on her quiet, non-rugby son. It was a strange set-up, breakfast with the landlady and son, but armed with our own key to come and go thereafter. I had just turned 16, Jim still 15.

The drinking age in Queensland was still 21 then. The other Waverley boys told their guests it was under 18 in Sydney and took them off to the Watsons Bay Hotel. The other boys partying, Jim and I, somewhat isolated, thought we needed to do something, should have a drink. How? Jim suggested rum and Coke was a good thing. I was taller – a tall, skinny, fresh-faced kid – so it was me who fronted the bottle-shop window of the nearest pub.

'Whaddya want, son?'

'A half bottle of rum, please.' In my deepest voice.

'OP?'

'Sorry?'

'Overproof or underproof?'

Well, absolutely no idea, but hey, what sort of sook did he take me for? I was a Nudgee boy, a Queenslander! Rum was mother's milk!

'Overproof.'

Of course! And make it snappy, my good man, a chap could die of thirst in these parts.

He didn't even bother to ask about the brand. A bottle in a brown paper bag, a label I've forgotten that didn't mean anything to me and that I never saw again. Captain Bloodnock's Rot Gut. Paint Stripper & Hospital-Grade Steriliser. Pirate's Death. Or some such.

We bought a bottle of Coke and mixed measures in our little room at the front of the terrace house. We tried to drink it and I've not touched rum and Coke since – almost a sin for a Queenslander.

'Rum and milk's a good drink,' said Jim, possibly remembering a sip of some winter's weak medicine.

We bought a bottle of milk. The Original Demon's Rum curdled the milk. We tried. We tipped it out. So much for the wild Nudgee boys' tour of Enmore.

Waverley had two teams: the team that took Nudgee boys drinking and the one we played. It didn't matter. We 16As got the job done as the curtain-raiser. Queenslanders were typically 17 when they finished Year 12, New South Welsh folk 18, so the firsts had a one-year handicap against southern teams, the southerners two years of open-age cattle to choose from. It didn't matter. Future Wallabies, Mark Loane and Paul McLean were in the Nudgee firsts that year. We were supposed to play Joeys after Waverley, but Joeys cancelled when they saw the result.

On our last night in Sydney, the Enmore outliers weren't going to miss out. It was agreed to meet up in Kings Cross. We invited our host's son but he told us it wasn't safe to go to the Cross and he wouldn't. It was 1971. Vietnam R&R was still a thing. The boy was probably right.

The lights, big Coca-Cola sign, the hustling and the hustle of the Cross, the prostitutes and strip clubs and bars and we children from Brisbane and the bush.

Barry Kennedy, our year but two years older than the rest of us, in the firsts, a bush publican's son, bold enough to find out on our behalf what everyone was wondering, approached a streetwalker and asked how much, was told and exclaimed, 'Christ! I don't want to buy it, I just want to hire it!', and then had to run when she turned to get her pimp to teach him a lesson. The one certainty, they wouldn't be able to catch Barry, athletics captain 1972. Near the end of Year 12, his mother was killed in a car crash 10 days before GPS athletics. Barry went home to Boggabilla, came back silent and sullen, ran his fastest ever and never smiled.

The spruiker outside the Pink Pussycat, 'Come in, boys, come in!' And they took our money and we did and could almost afford a beer each, wondering about the taxi fare back to Enmore. As your eyes adjusted to the gloom, you could make out most of the Nudgee First XV and 16As in that room, getting a more rounded education from the women on the stage.

Barry's response and the Pink Pussycat spruiker forever etched in our folklore, our shared experience retold, polished. And four decades later, Jim's daughter Catherine was renting a bedsit in Enmore, at the front of a big old terrace in the lane around the corner from a pub. We worked out it had been our room.

And Barry Kennedy, captain of athletics 1972, three years in the First XV, two GPS premierships, started 2021 with a heart attack that stopped his brain but not his heart. Palliative care until his body ran down and stopped on January 21.

Later, on the veranda while Sue was inside. 'I can't believe I'm dying,' Jim said. 'It's unreal to me.' Even as he monitored his body betraying him.

October 30, 6.06 am

Oct 29

G'day Michael

Back down to the farm today for another stint.

A bit of rain since I've been away, 33 mm, which is better than none. Sounding a little like a National Party man here ... so I will stop quickly.

Had a nice talk with Dick the other night ... I don't know him that well, but I eventually made him laugh. He comes across as quite a serious man ... I'm an irreverent soul ... death at this stage has no power over me, and I think Dick might worry he needs to save my soul ...

I don't know how we got there but he said to me, as though it was a minor confession that there were 'even Liberals in the family' ... I said, 'Oh well, Dick, family are meant to bring you down' ... we had a laugh.

He is a good man and I owe him a lot for his care of Tom, and I hope he will conduct my service. Hopefully before that, I will get to know him better, and we can laugh some more.

Had coffee with Serg and co this morning ... Serg is a good soul, who I feel I am getting to know a little better each time we meet. I want people close to me, I want people to talk about real stuff in their lives, I think I seek intimacy ... if that's the right word ... why shouldn't I, for Christ's sake, if I'm going to be dead in such a short space of time ... anyway, I think Sue and I feel closer to him each time we meet.

Marty Hanson also there ... I think truly a very good soul ... gentle and strong, with a true sense of what is right and wrong. He is the sort of man you would want watching your back in battle.

Gary O'Rourke also ... I find myself surrounded by exceptional people. Rightly or wrongly, I think they care about me ... it gives me strength.

What is the old school bond about, Michael? ... We came from vastly different backgrounds, pursued vastly different careers, are a mix of quite different people, and yet a bond remains.

I know Serg rightly says it is partly because we grew up together, literally ... but I often wonder if the physical, sexual and psychological abuse we either suffered or witnessed also is a contributing factor ... even if it was just the loneliness and partial abandonment that comes from boarding ... but somehow, like the veterans of a military operation, we share a bond ... I think just about anyone from our time could come and sit with us and it would be good ... even those we didn't even know at school ... just bring along the annual for proof of membership, coffee would be ordered, and all would be well. It's not too bad, even if we are a crazy bunch of bastards.

As I understand the last scan, left kidney has shut down ... unless I'm a freak, that only leaves one ... joked with Sue I could consider donating the right, but I mightn't be so cheeky when the time comes. I don't know, Michael, I will die knowing less than I thought I knew 20 or 30 years ago.

Anyway, back to my kidney ... that's a joke. Oedema is being managed a little better at the moment ... In with the physiotherapist a couple of days ago ... Sue in the room, me stark naked on the couch, the physio (poor girl) doing battle with my giant scrotum ... Christ, I thought, this is what old age brings ... Looking like a frigging freak, no shame, no embarrassment, just letting it all hang out ... making me up a bag into which to place my totally useless genital bits, so I can carry them around, waiting improvement.

Anyway, still need to walk like a duck (waddle) but at least it is a little less painful.

I hope the wedding planning is still progressing according to plan ... most probably not your plans, but progressing anyway.

Friday, October 30

Might call it quits on this effort ... I find solely writing about myself incredibly selfish, and somewhat unrewarding.

198

I had an old mate in Toowoomba, he was 60 and I was about 30 when we met. We became pretty good friends. I had sold the final lot of flats in Toowoomba in 2001 … I called in to say goodbye and thank him for his friendship over the past 25 years.

He said, 'Jim, it was equally rewarding for me … It is impossible to have a good friendship if it is not mutually beneficial to both parties.'

So … I don't know … the story of my life.

I should be asking you about your life, the stress and strains of meeting daily deadlines, the drawbacks of having a public profile, being subject to criticism from random members of the public, and people who don't hold back on the abuse and venom they spit … but no … I ramble on about the size of my scrotum and other such matters …

I hope all is well for you and yours, and the Liberals are not taking over. I've been a faithful conservative all my life, and lo and behold up sprouted a couple of lefties. What do you do, Michael?

Be good old mate.

Love Jim

October 31, 1.06 pm

My dear mate

There's a lot in this letter of yours that has been turning over in my mind for 24 hours, pre-empting a couple of questions I've wanted to ask you, one from thinking back of the beauty of your farm and your obvious pride and pleasure in it, the other – perhaps related – prompted by various coal seam gas claims and counterclaims. But I'll get to that.

I wouldn't worry about my brother thinking he has to save your soul. He knows it's a good 'un and is already taken care of. He is a good man – bloody stupid sometimes, drives me mad with some of the messes he gets in, but even when he has made mistakes it's been with good (albeit sometimes misguided) intentions. I hope you feel at ease with him.

And, as you say, Sergio is indeed another good soul. The drive to and from your place was good for us, or at least for me, to understand him better – a conversation you can maybe have one-on-one that you don't in a group. I didn't realise the problems he was carrying with his mother at present. And, like all of us, he worries about his children. He volunteered that line 'parents are only as happy as their unhappiest child'. He doesn't have a problem there but that doesn't stop him worrying. A good soul.

I suppose that's what love is, or a big part of what it is: wanting to reach out and lift the load off the shoulders of those you love – your family, your dying friend, your worried friend. And that's the frustration and sadness that you can't.

I had a funny little insight into love last weekend with Chris back from Dubai for a bit and Tim up from Canberra. It's good to have the boys back for a while. Anyway, we're talking and I realise they've got some washing that needs doing and I take it and leave their mother talking to them and put it on to wash. (By way of explanation, I am the son of a man who mostly did the family washing – something that was unusual back in his day – and I am happy to do it myself. There's something about it that links with my dad that I can't rationally explain.) While I was hanging out the boys' things, it struck me that I was enjoying doing it because I was doing it for them, that it was something I could do for them. There was love in hanging out some shirts and underpants. And I wondered if my father – not the best verbal communicator with me – had felt something like that too.

Writing that, I realise it is of course just a variation on what many a family cook has said, that the preparation of a meal for those you care for is an act of love. Maybe it's just selective. I'm a happy cook as well, but not keen on tidying up, and it has to be a dire emergency for me to even think of ironing someone's shirt.

It is strange how we express our love, though, how intimacy is experienced. I think I know what you mean about sharing time with people who care and the strength that comes with it. It is shared, Jim – I certainly feel your strength and am uplifted by it. And people certainly care for you. It's probably the desire for boasting rights of being a mate of the bloke with the biggest balls in Christendom.

The Nudgee bond is interesting, especially in the strength of it that can be felt after many years of separation. I don't have as open a heart as you, Jim, so the blokes I didn't much care for then I still wouldn't much care for. Having a copy of the annual wouldn't be enough. There was a brotherhood forged there, a sharing of life and laughter and trials and growing up. I don't want to sound like a rugby tragic but I think it is an even stronger bond when you've pulled on that jersey together, when (at least in my case) you've overcome physical fear together, relying on each other. As mere boys, I doubt that we consciously thought much about who was a good soul and whose welfare you cared for, but we still did it. Once formed, it's a bond that can lie dormant for decades but remain strong. It's a very fine thing – perhaps the finest thing about Nudgee. And we only become aware of it much later in life. As for the abuse that we witnessed – it was of the times. Proctor excepted, it was pretty 'normal'. We got on with it. What would now be considered rough just was. And not just at school. When I think back on it, I was doing next-of-kin 'death knocks' on *The Courier-Mail* when I was still short of my 18th birthday. If you sent a young graduate journalist to do that now, you could be up for psychiatric counselling and stress compo.

Or maybe it did send us all crazy, and because we're all crazy, we don't know it. I'm very glad to have had the opportunity to go crazy in fine company.

And now you've turned kinky as well, having Sue in the room while another woman plays with your balls. Time was a bloke had to pay folding money for that but you wouldn't want your wife to know. This is the Nudgee training coming in again – it's hard to feel physical embarrassment after being used to showering with the likes of Pedro with a Proctor watching. That was schoolboy fame – Pedro of the Giant Wanger.

Lifting the tone of the conversation, what I wanted to ask came from the way you said 'I suppose I'm a conservationist' when we were up on your hill, among those aptly named pretty-faced wallabies, the hills beyond. You put a set of quotation marks around 'conservationist', a little wink about the concept of you being a greenie when you clearly are a proud preserver of the land – a big journey from the boyhood wildlife slaughter. If you want a challenge, here's one: tell me how you feel about that farm. I know it means peace to you – even a city slicker like me can feel that – but I also know that it's more than that. When I have tried to explore my own feelings about the landscape, the country rather than nation, I have felt a bit of a fraud – a dilettante who's dropped in and out of it without the commitment to live it. I've written in another unpublished place that I fell in love with the country at 30,000 feet, flying over it a lot, visiting plenty of it, wanting to get down into the thing.

And after those thoughts came stuff on Twitter and the ABC this week about CSG, including the claims made about the farmer who allegedly topped himself over CSG pressure. It rang a little hollow for me, that there would have to be more to it than that, but I don't know. The impression I've had is that for every farmer strongly opposed to gas, there's a couple who just want more money and a bunch more who are being kept alive by it. Yet you can't doubt the sincerity of some of the opposition. You've obviously been a lot closer to it than me. I can't imagine you welcoming a rig down along your creek or next to the grass trees, but within the context of a bigger property ... ?

Time for me to stop. I'm smelling bacon cooking as Chris has a late lunch before going off to a mate's wedding – the reason for his visit, which we used to have Dom's bucks' party last weekend.

Take care, my friend. I can't lift your load but it is a privilege to walk beside you.

Love
Michael

Death knocks

It's the country on this drive, not the places. The journey of the road itself through the broad land, over its hills, around its bends, down and up its dips and gullies and curves through paddocks and bush, through grassland and eucalypt forests and over creeks and rivers. It's the land that's alive and triggering memory. Tamworth, a pleasant enough town – 'both kinds of music, country and western' – is irrelevant unless you need a petrol stop. Kootingal on its northern side is good to say, a word to play with, otherwise doesn't matter. Moonbi village matters because it's nestled at the feet of the range.

> 'Mid the great grey forests that know no change.
> 'I never have left my home,' she said,
> 'I have never been over the Moonbi Range.
> 'Father and mother are long since dead,
> And I live with granny in yon wee place.'[8]

One of Banjo's more forgettable poems. Those who stay, those who go.

Leaving Nudgee, slowly leaving boyhood working on *The Courier-Mail*.

Next-of-kin death knocks, my first a month after starting on the paper. Whiskey Au Go Go firebombed, 15 people killed, the paper short-staffed, the new intake of cadets paired off and given three names and addresses.

Memory paints a fibro house in need of paint somewhere in what were the boondocks on the way to Ipswich. Oleanders growing against the house, two steps up to a screen door. His brother answered my knock, the dead young man had worked behind the bar at Whiskeys, the brother had done some shifts there as well. There had been trouble, he said, a shotgun was kept behind the bar. At some point their mother approached the door from off to the side.

'Who is it, dear?' A trembling voice.

'*The Courier-Mail*, Mum.'

'Oh.' A handkerchief held to her face, a glance at me, a sob, and she kept moving into the inner gloom.

'Do you have a photograph we can borrow?'

A journalist for a month and you knew to always ask for a photograph, to personalise, to illustrate tragedy.

Her son dead a matter of hours and a gangly youth at her door wanting a photograph of him. For the paper.

The next one was easier. The girl shared a house with two or three others, sitting around wondering how they were meant to feel. Come in. She was nice. Yeah. Nothing really to say. Didn't have a photograph.

And there was no-one home at the third.

Forty-eight years later there's another inquest into Whiskeys and a million-dollar reward for information about Sydney's 1979 Luna Park Ghost Train fire. The stain of the crooked cops of those times, known and/or suspected, leaching into the future. Past crimes burned into the public consciousness, worrying at the still touchable edges of our history.

We boomers can plot our lives, print a timeline of our existence, by the more infamous crimes, universally starting with the kidnap and murder of eight-year-old Graeme Thorne in 1960. His parents had won the Opera House lottery.

And then they tumble out, the Nedlands Monster, Wanda Beach, the Beaumont children, Whiskeys, Juanita Nielsen, Donald Mackay, the Sydney Hilton bombing, the Ghost Train, Anita Cobby, Samantha Knight, Hoddle Street and on along with mass shootings we've forgotten unless they were next door. Port Arthur wasn't the first, only the biggest. Well, not counting blackfellas, which we generally don't.

I did more police rounds shifts than most cadets, the desk at the front of the newsroom, monitoring the police radio. Maybe some affinity for the work, or at least familiarity, not worried by the grit, by death. Fatals. Bodies. Got on with it. Still people in the force who remembered my father, who owed him something. A big motorcycle cop once told me he joined the force because of my father, who had kicked him up the arse and straightened him out when he needed it. I enjoyed the late shift, 6 pm start, driving the dark city to drop off copies of the first edition to the Valley, Roma Street, Gabba and Water Police stations after midnight, maintaining relations with various sergeants. Cruising in the old police rounds Falcon.

There were other death knocks. I never pushed. It was easier if you arrived first, before TV crews barged in. *The Courier-Mail* had presence back then, it was The Paper. Sometimes people wanted to talk, needed to talk, even thanked you. Other times – one time, a girl murdered and as I opened the front gate, her sister shouting from the veranda to go away. TV had already been there.

Public opinion convicted Lindy Chamberlain because of the way she reacted to her daughter's death. She didn't behave like mothers are supposed to, as they do in the movies. Public opinion hadn't done many death knocks.

Our little *Business Sunday* crew – cameraman Jim Crystal, soundman Nick Nezval, me – arrived in New York the Sunday after September 11, 2001. It felt like we were death-knocking a city over the next five days.

Sunday. No interviews. We dropped bags and caught a cab to shoot what we could in the deserted finance district. Without announcement, the barriers were being removed from the streets approaching Ground Zero, leaving an Australian television crew to wander past police and road workers up to the final barriers around the smouldering ruins, a silent rain of fine ash falling on us with the smell of burning plastic. We stood alone opposite the remaining skeletal girders of the World Trade Center façade, wondering if we should have face masks, shooting a useless piece to camera of forgotten clichés. Death at scale.

Two days later, there were souvenir sellers on that spot and smiling visitors taking selfies.

November 1, 11.25 am

G'day Michael

All Blacks won World Cup ... to be expected, I suppose, in spite of your efforts to rally the troops ... I don't take it very seriously, although I would have gotten quite nervous if I had watched it all. Sue and I awoke early this morn, just by chance, had a cup of tea and watched the final 5 to 10 minutes.

It is interesting to reflect on our schooldays and rugby ... I enjoyed playing, I liked winning and didn't like to lose ... but even then on some level I wasn't very serious ... maybe against Grammar under 15? ... a few of the boys enjoying a bit of the biff ... you would have been there. Steady on, lads, I thought, it's only a game we are playing here ... I remember the feelings quite clearly, but not really the details ... not going there, I thought.

Funny, reflecting on the World Cup brought that memory back ... so much lays just below the surface ... against Southport I think, in the Firsts, the opposite breakaway hit me as we packed for the scrum ... had a good black eye out of that one. Those were the days, Michael.

Read your letter last night and thanks for your reply ... I like doing the washing up, either by myself or with Sue ... wash and fold a fair bit, used to cook a lot at one stage ... like you, I think they are all great acts of love.

My Father used to get everyone tea and toast in bed every morning for years ... starting with my Mother, and then all the children, in order of age ... while at the same time working the property ... Milking cows, cutting up the weekly sheep etc ... what an extraordinary act of love that was.

Dad became very sick when I was 16 and still at Nudgee ... he died when I was 25 ... I was too young and stupid to really connect or thank him for his selfless love and duty towards us all ... it distresses me writing about it now ... maybe, though, like you and I, he received his own rewards from his acts of love towards his little brood.

I'm glad you connected so much with Serg on the drive down here ... you and he have a long and strong friendship with each other ... he does carry a heavy burden, and he is a gentle soul. I can't talk for you, Michael, but many of us, just below the surface, are really just children at heart ... we have whatever façade we have, and we show that to the world, but it is not the true us ... I suppose it is a very necessary part of us, to survive in this rough and tumble world, but it is only that. Sergio's façade is pretty gentle and loving when you think about it ... I think mine is too, but my girls shoot me down whenever I make such assertions. I think Serg would welcome your support and love ... I hope and believe he gets some from Sue and I.

'Conservationist' is a word that is thrown around loosely ... I do love the land, the animals and trees which survive upon it, I like to preserve it as best I can ... but I am also a realist. I would imagine, without much thought, it does become pretty obvious that our current living standard or way of living is unsustainable ... maybe for a few we can sneak through, but for the many, no.

I laugh to myself as the conservationists board their 747s on way to their luxury hotels in Rio, where there awaits fine food and wine, prostitutes, and whatever else is necessary to combat the scourge of climate change and social and moral degradation. So, Michael, I put 'conservationist' in inverted commas when I talk about it ... I try to be kind to the various animals I run here, but at the same time I also send them to be slaughtered.

So who am I to pass judgement ... Nature, for all its beauty and wonder, is cruel and harsh, almost beyond belief. Most that we find fault with in mankind occurs in nature ... why do I separate mankind and nature ... are we but one and the same? ... Maybe it is part of the grand plan that we destroy the planet. Little old Jim with his grass trees and pretty-faced wallabies, while we have comets and asteroids flying by, all with the capacity to destroy it all in a moment.

Nudgee College? ... You seem to go more along Sergio's line ... we grew up together, we showered together, we lived together ... and hence a bond.

You made me question my theory, and maybe you are right ... maybe we just need to belong ... the Reds, the Blues, South Sydney, the Broncos etc ... It is interesting to contemplate, but whatever the case, we are Nudgee boys, we have a bond, and I am grateful for it.

As for people being welcome, depending on the annual, of course, I did say almost, almost anyone would be welcome. Depends on where we are coming from, Michael.

You may have been more inclusive of people in your Nudgee days ... I hope I would never have been exclusive (well, not too badly), but I was a loner of sorts, so many were excluded, or not in my sphere ... if that's the correct word ... many boys who were intellectual types, not good at sport, from the city etc ... They are the people I would welcome to the table ... in theory, of course.

When talking communication, less is definitely more ... as you found out with your one on one with Serg ... I know a couple of mornings the group has become larger, which is great, but the dynamics do change.

As for your love of country ... you are no fraud ... just because you don't have 'a home amongst the gum trees' ...

I think you have written before about that sense of belonging, of feeling a part of it ... you don't need to be in possession to feel that love for or affinity with something.

Part of my love of this patch of dirt was to do with unfinished business arising from my growing up, and the subsequent loss of the property I grew up on ... we have talked of that before ... that is changing though.

Two reasons ... One is I have resolved those issues arising out of my past, and the unfinished business is no longer unfinished ... Two is I'm dying, or at least preparing to die ... property and material things don't quite have the sway they had over me ... I think I'm letting go ... I hope I'm letting go ... and that is not just of the farm.

As for coal seam gas ... They have a moratorium on CSG in the Scenic Rim for the present ... Arrow Energy put a well down about 4 km from the house before the moratorium ... I don't know the results, but you would think there would be no shortage of gas around here.

Nielsen Developments owns one of the big hills very close to here ... They purchased it a couple of years ago and are big suppliers of gravel and concrete to Brisbane and Ipswich councils ... the Warroolaba Creek runs through the middle of the hills, quite a sanctuary for koalas and other wildlife ... but money talks louder than koalas.

We all need energy, gravel, road base etc, and all is well with that, so long as the operation is not next door. As for suicides in relation to these developments, I tend to think along your lines. Suicide is a mental health issue ... generally we don't suicide for causes (religion aside), nothing is worth killing yourself for. Acceptance ... a lot of things happen that we don't like ... I suppose there is a line somewhere between standing up for our rights, and accepting the law of the land ... even if we disagree with it.

As for the potential gravel pit here, I would be in the minority by thinking of it in a negative way ... most, even those close would see it as a good source of employment, and good for local business etc.

With respect to CSG in the broader perspective ... it just happened before anyone realised ... then British Gas came in and paid $30 billion (correct me if I'm wrong) for a number of the companies operating in Queensland, and it sort of became an unstoppable juggernaut.

When all the associated pipeline work was in progress (some still is) it was part of this amazing transformation of inland southeast and southwest Queensland.

Between CSG and coal, I think it kept the commercial real estate market of inner Brisbane alive. John Dwyer and Paul DeLuca have talked about that ... oh, the old Nudgee connections.

All that said and done, I think it might be a very questionable industry ... I think its amazing growth even surprised those people in it ... underground water must be one of the biggest questions ... What is your point of view, Michael?

Money ... and lots of it ... it wasn't really about the farmers' point of view ... They had about as much say with CSG as I would have with the gravel pit or a coalmine. It is the surrounding business and local communities who rake in the money.

Brian was saying the other day he does 8 days on and 6 off ... but 2 of those 8 days on are travel ... I don't know what Brian earns, but it would be good money. Tom was earning $1200 or $1300 per day, admittedly he had put in the hard yards, but he was still in the field.

Now I know a lot in Sydney would earn this before they get out of bed, but we are talking rank and file here ... You go out to Miles and Chinchilla and that is phenomenal money.

Anyway, Michael, you know more than me about these economic issues, it's your job ... but you did ask.

Well, old mate, this is same day return mail ... something got me up early, and feeling a little ordinary today, so good for me to write.

Notice your note re reality and football result ... maybe on some level a lot of Aussies are like me ... they don't like to lose, but they also don't really care all that much ...

Is that the difference between the teams?

What is life and death for one side is a game for the other.

Thanks for your love and support.

Love Jim

Moonbi Hill

The road rises very nicely indeed up First Moonbi Hill now, double lanes in both directions, well separated, inviting you to drive again after rolling through the towns, feel the power again, the tension between the car and the incline and sail effortlessly over a range that used to break bullockies' hearts. On the original track, they'd hitch multiple teams together to drag a single load up The Pinch, straining beasts under wooden yokes amid whips and curses, every inch an effort.

My father's father was a teamster with a dray and horses, not bullocks, to cart wool from the western Queensland stations to the railway line. He was killed by a milk cart, stepped into its path on a Barcaldine street – a suggestion alcohol might have been involved – leaving eight children, my father the second eldest, the responsible one, six boys, two girls.

There's a photograph of Dad and his siblings gathered in Barcaldine after the war, all bar Peggy who married an American, a war bride. They were a hard-looking bunch, eyes squinted against the western sun, mouths tight against the flies. And in time they were scattered. Alf, the eldest, was considered no loss – 'a liar' and no help, according to short and dismissive conversations. Johnnie, the youngest, was some sort of trouble and died young from a heart condition. We kept in

213

occasional contact with Morrie and Herb, the tallest of them, and more so with Phil, Dad's favourite brother, the brother he was closest to. Phil worked at KR Darling Downs. For a time there was an annual ritual of Phil getting a Christmas ham for us, the two families together for afternoon tea in the police station house, cousins to take down the river. I would have liked to have gone to Phil's funeral, too, but didn't. Couldn't get there for some reason. I would have liked to have shown respect for my father's brother.

Families scatter, were scattered, out of the bush unless wealthy enough to own land to hold them. None of Dad's family did. One of Uncle Phil's sons, a fitter and turner, lost an arm at the elbow and I innocently thought it was the most terrible thing that could happen. Much more recently one of Phil's grandsons made contact through Twitter, an IT infrastructure strategist in Melbourne. We move on. Working class is about getting out of it.

Another ritual at Christmas, to ask if it was a 'good' ham and confirm that it indeed was. My parents must have known times when a ham might not be good.

There's a lookout at the top of the range I've never visited and there's time to stop this time, time for a stretch and gaze out over Moonbi and the Cockburn Valley. The local council has built steps up a granite boulder and the valley floats away amid the ranges and spurs and hills into the blue haze and sky. The Cockburn Valley, where poultry is a major industry. Which came first then, the chicken or the egg? The name Cockburn or the vast sheds full of chooks?

No-one else has taken the turn-off, there's nobody to share the lookout with, nobody to be mindful of, to volunteer to take a photograph of to prove they were here. The sound of the vehicles making the run up the hill, of trucks in low gear grinding down, is muted, allowing you to listen for the silence of the bush noise beyond, the silence of trees moving in light breeze and bird call.

The valley is green away into the blue, the season has been kind. The Cockburn River would be running into the Peel, the Peel into the Namoi, the Namoi into the Barwon, the Barwon into the Darling, but there's been no flood to carry it on to the Murray and the Southern Ocean, unlikely to be any movement, barely any river out at Wilcannia, gone to climate change and to irrigation and livestock and towns further up. A billion square kilometres where the Western Rivers flow, when they flow. Generations since a paddle-steamer could make it up to Walgett.

Hard towns, hard times permanent in the hard towns out there now. But below Moonbi Hill is just the bush, not the outback; rich enough land, easier to love but still capable of cruelty, of years-long drought and fire and plague. The big drought before last, the politician's photo op was a farm somewhere in the Tamworth foothills, the media circus all over the dust and emptiness of livestock gone, Bob Carr the premier, posing with a woman fighting to hold her dignity in the face of going broke and losing her land, fighting to hold back tears as the cameras zoomed in for them, getting what they came for. Her devastation was a prop for the city politician to announce some welfare funding, to declare a Natural Disaster.

It wasn't. It was the weather. Always has been. A couple of good seasons, more not so good, some horrendous. A flood and start the cycle over again with the odd bushfire thrown in.

And now the climate is exaggerating the weather, accelerating the heat and the storms and the fires, promising harder years to come.

'Don't think of this is as the hottest summer of the past hundred years, think of it as one of the coolest of the next hundred.' An American academic trying to reset the prism of perception.

Yet the land sinks into the blood, or rather, the soul and blood sink into the land and bind with it.

Only for some, of course, the children of the land. Judy doesn't feel it, a girl of the coast, of beach and surf and green headlands. At the end of yoga, during shavasana, she goes to her happy place, Sunshine Beach. The endless drama of surf, the white sand sweeping for 16 unbroken kilometres from the Noosa national park down to Coolum. The ever-changing hues of water, the moods of water. Wild often enough, capable of a vicious sweep and rip, surf to dump and break you. Or flat, an endless millpond. Nor'-easters bring in bluebottles, scattering their air sacs along the beach to be popped with your heel, the long tentacles shrivelling, 'O death, where is thy sting?' Bluebottle, such a gentle Australian euphemism. Portuguese man o' war. If you're lucky, if the onshore wind has been strong, you might find blue dragons, the fantastical nudibranch that eats bluebottles and absorbs the poison to use for its own protection. In season, whales cavorting, dolphins in the waves, the silver flash of fish near your legs. And, sometimes, perfection – a pale green surf, water so clear you could see through it to New Zealand. No sweep, no rips, reliably lifting your body to ride, to caress and play. Shallow dive under the waves and feel the power of them run along your back and legs, tug at you, massage you. And out the back, beyond the break, swimming out as far as you dare, diving as deep as you can, a depth of quiet and isolation. Sunbeams filtering, glittering down through the water, weightlessness, sand patterned by tide and current stretching away into unfathomable blue-green distance, a peace beckoning you to stay until your lungs burst.

You could go that way, out beyond your ability to return, panic setting in, lost at sea.

Brian's shirt

On November 11, Judy and I turned left at Warrill View, dropping in on Jim and Sue, forewarned, at the farm. We were driving up to Sunshine in the Mazda CX-5 with stuff for the unit and a pair of chairs for Richard, the SUV at home on the gravel. The wallabies worried Judy – they could jump our way – Judy who would swim at Sunshine untroubled by thoughts of sharks, who would walk the length of the beach at dusk and city streets at night with apex predators all about but had no desire to get out of the vehicle and walk through the grass any taller than mown lawn. Jim, who stayed in the car while his girls played in the sand; Judy, scared of small furry animals if they weren't dogs. She said if it was a choice between being in a room with a lion or a wallaby or a bandicoot, she'd take the lion. I think she might have meant it.

The kitchen table, late afternoon coffee and tea, not for long as we needed to get on to Brisbane.

Jim said an old friend from Mitchell days, Howie, not seen for many years, had dropped in and he had been surprised how very glad he'd been to see him, how he brought back a rush of memories, how he hadn't wanted the visitor to go. He found himself more and more thinking about the early days, about childhood. Life was all about letting go, but your childhood you wanted to hold on to more than ever.

'And I'm not just saying that because I'm dying. You let go of your 20s, your 30s, your 40s, it's all past and gone, but I was so happy to have that link to childhood.'

A brief stop, not for long. We were expected in Brisbane for dinner. Shadows lengthening, the wallabies more active preparing for their evening parties, warned by Jim to take it very slow around the gate and back to the bitumen. He was right – there was a large mob in the first gully, taking off in all directions from the Mazda, Judy glad to see the back of them.

Time.

I have a shirt that was black, now grey, missing a button, too big for me, showing the mark of having spent long years on a wire coathanger. My brother Brian gave it to me when we visited him on Long Island, said it was too big for him. Every time I do a cull for St Vinnies, it stays.

Ellis Bugg, a friend, someone who could give banking a good name, a wealth of markets wisdom for a young finance journalist, died in his armchair on his farm outside Coffs Harbour. When I begin to type an email address starting with E, his name and address pops up. I can't delete. My phone retains Ellis' mobile number and those of others who have died, Jim's, Kev's, others'.

It's silly, perhaps superstitious.

But I can't let Brian's shirt or Ellis' address or a dozen phone numbers go.

November 18, 4.16 pm

Dear Old Cowboy

I'm looking forward to the Ascot Gentlepersons' Coffee Club tomorrow, though it will be hard to leave Sunshine Beach if the water is as brilliant as it was this morning. Not that that would interest you.

Something you said has been turning over in my mind since we dropped in, and it received a further boost today with the news of Jonah Lomu's death. (I read an interview he had done during the World Cup – he said his ambition was to live to see his sons turn 21, to become men. They are five and six years old. The first and biggest superstar of rugby and his greatest ambition came down to living to 55, only to die at 40.)

But that's not what I've been pondering upon. You told us how the visit of your old and older mate Howard had brought back a lot of memories, a rush of memories of what sound like your tearaway times, and that you had seized upon them and Howard and didn't want to let him go. And from that, how much time now is given to thinking about childhood and where we've come from and who formed us.

It's probably obvious and has been put in other ways, but it strikes me that that is what our lives are: memories. The reality of what we did yesterday or last year or 40 years ago is a memory. The things we possess are only physical confirmations that those memories are true, assuring us that we didn't imagine it.

There are a bunch of thoughts here that might just add to confusion. Real philosophers have played with the memory and perception business forever. There's a line from a poem I've looked for and can't find about the death of a bushranger, something about the tortured char of a match and 'past and present touch alone at the instant and are gone'.[9] The pleasures I might take now in a sip of wine or a kiss are immediately just memories of that pleasure, added to all the other

220

memories that have been my life. Maybe not 'just' memories – they are us.

So it makes all the sense in the world to be focused on memories now – it is being focused on life.

A confession: I'm given to daydreaming, hopelessly so – I can happily while away time (that I don't have) on flights of fancy, imagining this or that possible action or deed. Sometimes I have thought, what's the difference between re-running some real memory in the private movie theatre of the mind and imagining what you might like to imagine? And that probably sounds very silly indeed. Some of that daydreaming thing is creative, leads to thoughts that get filed away, but mostly it's indulgence. Some of it is thinking 'what if' I had turned left instead of right at different times. Some is mental wank – just what would I really do if I won Oz Lotto in a big way – and some is considering how other outcomes, terrible outcomes, might best be handled.

I'm not sure where that fits in (aside from leading you to think that Pascoe is losing it), but it has something to do with what we choose to think about and the memory thing.

One of my favourite movies is *Blade Runner*. Do you know it? Science fiction of the highest order, not about the gadgets but artificial intelligence and what it is to be human. A highlight is a short but brilliant speech by a replicant, Roy Batty, as his time is up: 'I've seen things you people wouldn't believe. Attack ships on fire off the shoulder of Orion. I watched C-beams glitter in the dark near the Tannhäuser Gate. All those moments will be lost in time, like tears … in … rain.'

If you've seen it, you know what I mean. If you haven't, see the aforementioned comment about Pascoe losing it. What I think I mean is that we are our memories and therefore it is a fine thing to share them, to record them for those you love, to take them out and play with them. And the older they are, somehow the more precious they seem.

Re Lomu, everyone has a memory of him. Everyone knows the footage of the 1995 World Cup. I was one of the lucky 109,000 at the Sydney Bledisloe Cup in 2000 when he scored the winning try right at the death of the greatest test. I met him once – he was speaking at a conference, and

221

I thought he wasn't comfortable with the speaking gig but had worked at his act. He (like many people) was better at being interviewed, more relaxed if they don't have to maintain their own structure in discourse. But he was such a nice, humble sort of superstar that he didn't have to put on a good show to be a good show, if you know what I mean. He was the real deal.

And so Jonah Lomu is now the summary of everyone else's memory of him. The reality of him has gone but he is just as real now to those who weren't actually close to him as when he was alive. What it is to be an international superstar.

And other people are defined by their interaction with him. Mike Catt, the English fullback, will spend the rest of his life as the bloke Lomu ran over for that World Cup try. I particularly remember noticing and marking the first person to tackle Lomu solo: little Elton Flatley playing for Queensland in 1996 when Lomu was still god status. Twice Flatley stopped him head on by dropping down and grabbing one of those massive shins. No surprise Flats had to give the game away from too many head knocks! Cripes, I thought at the time, there was a Nudgee boy to be proud of.

It's all memories. To be embraced, revelled in, celebrated. Our lives, I mean – not Lomu. But Lomu too today.

See you tomorrow – if you don't think I've gone so weird I should be given a wide berth!

Love
Michael

Shrines

The contemplation of what it is to be alive, to be sentient, must be our very oldest. I've seen a dog I had to shoot know it was about to die. It's not awareness of death that elevates us. Seneca – 'Roman stoic philosopher', there's a job description – declaimed the present is all we have. 'All the rest of existence is not living but merely time.' Wonder how he felt about running out of present and time when Nero ordered him to kill himself.

Blade Runner was released in 1982 – it's that old. The movie is set in a 2019 where everyone is smoking.

And like so many movies, it wasn't quite as fine as I remembered when I caught it again in a lockdown binge. Read somewhere that what we remember is our latest remembrance of any particular memory, not the original, and thus end up with the degradation that comes from copying a copy of a copy of a copy back through our time, a mechanism that loses detail and concentrates focus on honing and polishing aspects we want to recall, or can't avoid recalling. Unreliable memoirs indeed.

Time.

Pretty little Bendemeer coloured by deciduous trees – poplars almost as popular here as in Glen Innes – is slipping past on the left, the Oxley Highway turn-off to Walcha and

Wauchope and the coast on the right. If you turn into the village, there's the Macdonald River and an ancient wooden bridge and a grand old two-storey hotel with broad verandas you could spend your days on. The Macdonald rises on the western slopes of the Moonbi Range and flows north-west to join the Namoi, flows through a manicured park at Bendemeer before it goes into deeper country and the outback, in a good season. Bendemeer was a Persian river in the turgid and interminable *Lalla Rookh* by Thomas Moore – not the saint but an Irish poet whose greatest achievement was burning Byron's memoirs. The book-length oriental tale must have seized 19th century colonial imaginations – Lalla Rookh was the nickname given to Truganini, the woman generations of us were taught was 'the last full-blood Tasmanian'. An oriental fantasy visited on genocide.

Captain Thunderbolt held up the Northern Mail in Bendemeer, too. Well, it was the local mail and he was the resident bushranger for more than six years, so it had to happen more than once. Further up before Uralla – a fine open stretch of country, less populated – there's Thunderbolt's Rock, graffitied granite tors where he would sometimes keep watch and not far from Kentucky Creek where he was shot. And Thunderbolt's Cave off the highway at Black Mountain south of Guyra and Thunderbolt's grave in Uralla. The grave and death sites are heritage-listed. Two kilometres on from Kentucky Creek is unlisted Terrible Vale, the scene of one of the many massacres of First Nations people. I've never found or heard of a memorial to the murdered Anaiwan and Kamilaroi in these parts, all along the New England, but there is the Myall Creek memorial out on the western edge of the tablelands,

115 kilometres from Glen Innes. The only exceptional thing about Myall Creek is that seven of the 12 perpetrators were tried, convicted and hanged. The site is vandalised from time to time.

There used to be a Banalasta visitors' centre a little beyond Bendemeer – Banalasta, another word to play with. I've never stopped or asked a local to find out if it's Banal-asta or Ban-alasta. I want it to be Banal-asta, filed in my memory with Gladesville's 1960s housing commission complex, Blandville Court.

I'm not stopping. Acknowledge this country's many ghosts in passing, the bloodied land, but don't stop to seek them out, to talk to them, to find their final fears, to feel the horror of the children beheaded, the woman 'kept for a few days'. Keep going.

The driving is good, the day is kind and traffic light and I've been blessed with a stalking horse pulling out of Bendemeer, a Holden ute in a hurry. The Giulia has radar-guided cruise control you can set to stay a distance behind whatever's in front. Set the speed at 140 and the car's radar will keep it your desired distance behind the ute doing 110, 120, 130, allowing you to relax a little about cops, letting him be picked up by a police speed trap first, react to the sight of a highway patrol car first, letting him cop the ticket. You're playing tag with him when a truck or car or caravan intervenes, needing to overtake them soon after your stalking horse to stay in touch. And you wonder if he wonders about the red Alfa determined to stick behind him at whatever his speed.

We're in luck – there are no police cars, no radar traps until the ute turns off into a property a little short of Uralla and as you slow down behind him slowing for the turn, you catch sight of a shrine further ahead on a sweeping bend with a wide enough shoulder to pull off.

I've been watching the shrines all the way, always do on drives now – the wooden crosses and plastic flowers that mark the site of someone's death. Sometimes more ornate – a biker's site back near Scone with handlebars and more. We've given up cemeteries and replaced them with roadsides; it's not where you're buried but where you die that's remembered. Some roads have more, some less. Some councils have tried to stop it. We're largely immune to them, you barely see them unless they're fresh or particularly large, or if you find yourself more attuned to death.

There's a swelling of the land on the west not far out of Canberra on the way to Cooma that had four white crucifixes, two larger than the others, that don't bear contemplation. I first saw them in late afternoon light slanting through gum trees behind, golden spotlit in silhouette.

When Billy and Sam were killed on Mona Vale Road, boys from the year between my Christopher and Dominic, a Riverview rugby jersey was nailed to the tree the next day. It hung there until replaced by a wooden version, anonymous classmates' love in cutting out the template of a rugby jersey, painting the blue and white stripes, somehow scaling that tree. Catching the eye every time we drove that road, back when we drove it often.

I've pulled over. I want to visit this shrine. It's not a good place to stop on the bend, so I wait and do a quick U-turn, go back to the previous turn-off, turn again and stop. I've thought about these roadside shrines to death, have daydreamed about chronicling them on this road, tracking down each fatal accident in the local paper, putting names and photographs to faded ribbons and peeling paint. A testimony to our ability to kill ourselves at speed. I've also daydreamed about photographing cups of coffee for a literalist coffee table book.

I'm contemplating walking the hundred metres beside the highway. I get out. Cars, SUVs go by. There would be a glimpse of a tall white-haired man beside a red car. I stretch, bend, the little 'uh'. The verge looks rough and hard, the way it normally is in the bush. It's due for slashing. I get back in the car. What would I expect to see up close that I can't from here? What inner wisdom, what insight into a vehicle leaving the road on that mild bend, the gravel on the shoulder of the road, careering through the rough into the tree and death? It's an unlikely place, but many of them are.

Draw a line to the coast from here, go back down the Oxley Highway and up to Kempsey and there's the spot where Peter Fox's Ferrari went straight off a mild bend like this at 10 o'clock one night when he was driving from Sydney to Noosa. He was in his new Testarossa because his private jet was being serviced, or maybe the creditors were already moving in on it. The Ferrari became airborne and hit trees two metres off the ground. An expert witness told the coroner's court the Ferrari would have been doing 160 or 165, the 'critical speed' to lose traction on that bend. Fox had a blood alcohol score of 0.16 and it couldn't be established where he had done the drinking that day in a couple of missing hours after he left his Sydney home sober. He had a large insurance policy and the company, Occidental Insurance, was very interested. Fox's empire, Adelaide Holdings, the planes, the cars, the vineyards, the movie investments, the land deals, collapsed after his death, were collapsing before he died. And a business cycle later, Occidental Insurance was one of two insurance companies Dick Pratt sold to a conman who used the companies' reserves to pay Pratt, who was having his own problems at the time. I had doubts that became one of only three times I've cost an employer money over defamation – settled by a $50,000 donation to a charity of Pratt's choice. A commercial settlement, cheaper than defending it. There was no public apology. The deal stank. Still stinks. The wheels and cycles keep turning.

And on the same page of the *Australian Financial Review* that recorded Peter Fox's death there was an advertisement for a Ferrari dealer. Murphy's Law never sleeps either.

It happens easily enough. The first or second time we drove back to Brisbane after moving to Sydney, in the cream Mitsubishi Sigma, came to the crest of a hill beyond Tenterfield and there were two sets of headlights in front of us on the two-lane road. Younger reflexes flicked the Sigma left into whatever was there – missed a guidepost and into long grass, a glimpse of trees, fought the wheel, 180 degrees and stopped. Lucky. No close trees. Didn't roll. Room to get off.

The other driver came back – a woman, a mother with young children in her car, to see if she had killed people, then to apologise, to explain she wasn't thinking, that a teenage son was in some sort of trouble and she had to go get him in a hurry. She was more shaken than we were. What do you say? 'Doesn't matter why, you never overtake blind, never ever overtake blind.' And you go on your way, taking your chances and it doesn't matter.

I was the 12 or 13-year-old passenger in the front seat of Terry's Mini driving into Brisbane from Petrie. On the Bald Hill flats – daylight, clear vision – inexplicably someone pulls out of the oncoming traffic in front of us to overtake. Terry is off the road quicker than it registers on me and back on again. Says nothing, keeps driving, no drama. Somewhere in a boy's psyche, the behaviour of his hero big brother registers. The way to be. Carry on.

She came back that night. She would have seen the cream side of the Sigma veering off sharply at speed. That flash of speed and anticipated collision would sear. Her children in her car. Was it guilt? Did she have to know what happened, if she had done it? To help? She was putting her hand up. Must have been old school.

Maureen ran her little Mazda 2 into the back of a 1965 Holden station wagon – a car only has to be old to qualify as historic now – stopped at traffic lights at the turn-off for the Mona Vale Hospital. Convenient that. Ambulance didn't have far to come or go. Wrote off the Mazda but it had done its passive safety job well, the 88-year-old relatively undamaged. They had to slide her out of the back hatch. Bruised and a cracked sternum but that was it. And no memory of how it had happened. A story grew in her mind that someone had run into her. She gave up her licence and the police were happy enough with that.

And Maureen bemoaning the day she surrendered her licence became part of her litany of woes and regret with the story evolving along the way. By the time she was 93, another story had taken root: she was convinced she had nudged another car while parking at a shopping centre.

'I thought, oh, there could have been a child in that car, I could have injured someone, so I surrendered my licence. I told my doctor and he laughed. "Maureen, you bumped a car and you gave up your licence? You should have called me and I would have come and sorted it out." Oh, he thought it was hilarious.

'Maybe I was a fool to give it up. You're trapped if you can't drive.'

For a while, you try to set her straight, remind her of the real accident, of how lucky she was, of how she did the right thing. But the new, preferred version becomes set in her mind, grows more details in the retelling, and you let it go. We all have our preferred versions of history.

Her mind moved along its one-way path, forgot about the accident altogether while she sometimes mused about getting a little car again.

Memory begins to play games, or not play. There are too many passwords in the world, too many PINs. It's inevitable that they'll jumble. Maureen only had one she needed to remember, for the ATM, but she started forgetting it and then it was forgotten.

'We need to go to a bank so I can get some money out,' she used to say at some stage of most visits, searching for her debit card. It's OK, I'll give you some cash and transfer the money from your account – that's easier than having to go to the bank.

That's something to fear: standing at the ATM with a couple of people behind you waiting and the four numbers disappear. Or accidentally mis-key and you have two more chances to get it right or the machine takes the card. Mis-key and you doubt yourself – have I forgotten? Press the buttons carefully the second time, don't bother about covering your hand, you want to see your finger on the numbers clearly. Press 'enter' and for a long moment, hope.

Because you know the odds. You've seen the movies. You've read the articles. You've observed Maureen, but hers is only a little senile dementia, not the darkest fear. Mike Carlton nailed that:

My mother turns 90 today, but she probably won't know it. Alzheimer's disease and the onset of nameless fears have hollowed out what was a lively and humorous mind. My brother tells me that when I go to see her in the nursing home near Brisbane this weekend there is every chance she will not recognise me, her firstborn child. If she does, she will not remember the visit five minutes after I have left.

Her life has no quality to it. She has no knowledge of her five grandchildren and one great-grandson. Once she was a voracious reader and a keen gardener and knitter, but all that is beyond her now and she is too frightened and confused even to turn on the TV. We had to take her telephone away because she was running up huge bills making the same call to say the same anxious thing to the same person, every half hour. Her days and nights are spent lying on a bed in a small, beige room, staring at the walls and waiting to die.

I owe her a lot over a long life. My father died when I was five and she never remarried, which left her raising two boys on the small wage of a doctors' secretary. But, honestly, I shrink from seeing her again. I will find it hard, even surreal, to reconcile today's frail wraith with the vigorous young woman who changed my nappies, tended my grazed knees, bought my first long pants, corrected my table manners and my English, and pulled every string she knew to find me a job when I left school.

But I will bring her the red roses she has always liked, kiss her on a feathery cheek and tell her that I love her, and hope that there is a miraculous spark of the mum I once knew, even for a second.

There must be hundreds of thousands of Australian families in a similar frame. If only there could be a better way to go when your time is up.[10]

November 26, 8.08 pm

G'day again Michael

I was waiting for you to write ... I didn't want to be pestering you with emails ... so just a slight breakdown in communication.

Sort of jotted thoughts ... maybe boring, I don't know ... dying can't always be exciting you know ... sometimes it is just very boring.

Started smoking again about 2 weeks ago ... for the first time since 1996.

Always said I would if confronted with a terminal illness ... so since 2010 I have regularly contemplated a smoke ... a couple of issues stopped me ... mainly the addiction side of the habit, and the subsequent loss of control ... most other issues fairly irrelevant.

To sit in the squatters chair on the veranda in the dark with a cigarette is a beautiful thing. To control the urge to smoke all day long is a struggle ... not much new in such struggles. Point two, is it worth struggling with? Fuck it, so to speak.

At this point I would call the experiment a success ... I want the time out ... it is like running, I drift off into a private place in my head ... alone, with my thoughts ... I can disengage.

Downside ... it can give me a head spin and I feel a little anxious.

My need for people ... To feel their love and support, but more importantly, I think, for me to be able to give love and support. Currently I think there is more in the giving than there is in the getting ... I don't need to contemplate or explain at this moment because there just is ... I think much of it has to do with the fact that time and the option of giving or receiving love is limited. It has become my scarce commodity.

The false feeling of wellbeing is doing my head in ... only 17 days ago I was 10 kg heavier, unable to ride a horse or sit on a tractor ... swollen up and very uncomfortable ... my deterioration and eventual death seemed a reasonable proposition ...

Now I'm looking bright and beaming ... it seems ludicrous to say I am dying ... the old feelings of being a fraudulent drama queen, shouting death, death, death ... at any opportunity I can get.

So it buggers me.

I add a little PS here ... watching TV last night and a KM Smith funeral ad came on ... it made me feel quite uneasy, so there are still plenty of unresolved issues here.

No amount of resistance is going to change the outcome ... it will only spoil the journey ... and reflecting on the last 60 years ... enough time was wasted growing up ... it would seem almost criminal to waste time as a mature and experienced adult ... youth has a reasonable excuse ... age has none.

I feel a little cheated I have no contact with Tom ... why do I think I should have some connection with Thomas and not with my sister Sue and Dad? It is a very good question and most probably underlines the unreasonableness of my desire. I sense some sort of bond with Tom, but nothing has transpired since Tom died two years ago.

Love Jim

November 26, 11.38 pm

Dear Jim

Mate, please don't wait for me to write if there's something you feel like saying – your emails are a delight to receive and absolutely in no way pestering. Sometimes a saddening delight in making me realise what warmth I have missed the opportunity to share and with the awareness of indefinite time. But it's trite to say our time is always indefinite – yours just a bit less so than many.

As for purple patches, long may they bloom. And I think you can be forgiven a durry or two on the veranda at this stage of the game. It's a long time since I had a smoke – gave up for good when Nicholas, my first son, was young – but I can remember periods before that of having quit for a while and the first one or two back seeming powerful. Cheap head spin, or at least it was back then. I don't think I could afford to smoke now!

I was thinking of you and the land a lot driving back to Sydney. I didn't get far that night – the worst of the traffic out of Brisbane I hoped to avoid, I didn't. Stopped in Tenterfield where I was lucky to find a feed, albeit best forgotten. The payoff was the morning drive across – the northern New England must have had reasonable rain as it was looking rich and often covered with wildflowers. And I must be getting soft as I stopped a couple of times to take pix of them which I subsequently tweeted. Spectacular. My intimate knowledge of flora can fail me, but I know some paddocks were white with daisies and what looked like yellow daisies or small sunflowers formed rich honour guards down parts of the highway.

Which reminds me of visiting Ireland for the first time in 1979, when the place was still dirt poor and animal-drawn carts a hazard on the roads. We stayed for a while in a farmhouse B&B somewhere, County Mayo, I think, and daytripped from there. It was autumn and we seemed to be among the last of the tourists. I remember the daughter of the house being a delightful girl, clearly keen to make the most of life and opportunities and learn more from exotic guests – my guess is that the B&B was her idea. We went for a walk one afternoon along the lanes through postcard Irish farms – pretty but small and poor then. There were lots of daisies about and when we got back to the house, the girl asked us if we'd enjoyed ourselves. Yes, we said, it was beautiful, and so many daisies about. I clearly remember this young woman, a teenager, looking a little wistful and softly saying, ah, around here the daisies are a sign of poor land.

Weren't we fools – praising the pretty farms, we thought, but unknowingly saying the land was rubbish.

And I've never checked to see if that was an Irish myth or that daisies do indicate poor soil. So maybe the country around Guyra was actually crap, but it looked grand.

Bedtime for me. I'll come back to you about your memories, feelings and people wisdom. The complexity of relationships with our loved dead, how you feel about Tom now, is too much for me at this hour. There's something about a conversation we can choose to have with them that is one-sided, but a conversation nonetheless. I've told you that I can swear I heard my mother and father answer me once each. That was quite a while ago. But I still sort of talk to them on occasion, or perhaps talk to the idea of them.

For now, though, goodnight. May the purple light continue to shine on.

Love
Michael

Therapy

I never pictured Jim as a choirboy, but he writes back about sitting on his veranda with his daughter Catherine up from Sydney and recording a few songs on her phone. 'Good for the soul,' he says she says.

I can see them on that veranda and it warms me. Father and daughter focused on time together, enjoying each other's being, a favour granted the living dying that's denied those of us gone suddenly.

And he says recording a conversation with Sue was 'good DIY therapy'. I allege a business opportunity, Warrill View Ashram – Wallaby Singing Therapy.

Jim's not dying in this purple patch. He's living with what will eventually kill him, as are most of us, whether we know it or not. The microscopic seed or genetic fate buried within for years, for decades, from conception.

I would be presumptuous to try to tell Alison something like that while her prognosis is fresh. I think she's only half joking when she says she will be able to eat as much as she likes as it doesn't matter now. The shock of the diagnosis is reverberating – she's listing the music she wants played at her funeral, starting with Leonard Cohen's 'Dance Me to the End of Love'.

You're not dying yet, Ali. That will happen to you and me and everyone else, but you're not dying now or for ages. Anyway, how long is the perception of time when your eventual mortality is underlined, when you're focused on life each day? Time is elastic, stretching away forever into the distance for a child waiting for Christmas, snapping back past you as you age. Faster heartbeat, faster metabolism when you're a child, slower when you're old. Maybe the hopping mouse perceives its three years to be as long as the elephant's 60.

A time to be childlike.

Easy to say.

December 10, 8.34 am

Jim

Welcome to the 60-year-old club!

Hope you have a good day, feeling the love of friends and family.

Now where do you apply for that senior's card …

Love
Michael

December 10, 8.40 am

Currently Ascot Gentlepersons' Coffee Club … Thanks, old mate.

Love Jim

Sixties

'Sixty isn't old; 60 is the new 40,' they say. Everyone says. No, the sixties aren't old age. But you can see it from here.

There are changes, a friend quietly admitted. You start to think a little differently. A friend of the friend, a wealthy, well- and often-travelled man, said he had started to plan his holidays on the basis that he wouldn't be back there again.

The rosy view of new experiences reads well, presents well. The beaming faces on the billboards for 55+ enclaves. *The Best New Marigold Hotel* world of opportunities. It's the sensible, rational, optimistic view to take. Optimists win. But somewhere deep or shallow in our hearts, we know it's bullshit. It is what it is. Options are closing down. Not wiped out completely, but they become more limited by the year. You have to choose more carefully as you may not get to choose again.

And along comes COVID and takes away the choices. A regular refrain: 'When do you think we'll travel again?'

Age or COVID or both, it's the loss of possible lives, of alternative lives that you know will go unlived. The things that you might do start shrinking. To spend three years in New York – one to get to know it, one to enjoy it, one to have had enough and be ready to go home – recedes from possibility to improbability. Perhaps not impossible – yet, maybe – but not a reality.

Marianne Faithfull's 'The Ballad of Lucy Jordan', bemoaning at the age of 37 she'd never ride through Paris in a sports car, viewed from well out the other side, at 37 anything remains possible. And at 47 and 57 – 67? Not so much.

Flying north from Sydney on clear days, there are long scimitars of beach towards the Queensland border, their handle a village and you wonder what it would be like to live there, to move in and go local and explore the detail of the waterways, eat at the bowlo, get to know the fishermen, the characters, the secrets and lives, walk a dog from headland to headland, maybe write again. You wouldn't. You wouldn't really want to when you already have the place at Sunshine – a better beach, better coffee – but you could. You could have.

Then COVID shuts down more possibilities. Friends turning 70 not just wondering but saying they may never travel overseas again, frustrated enough with our state borders shutting and opening and shutting and opening and …

When do you think we'll be able to travel again? As if any of us have a clue.

In a few months, the wee virus changed the world. In two years, it changed us, changed what we might hope for.

So many waves of hope: that there will be a vaccine, that the vaccines work, that the virus doesn't mutate beyond the vaccines, that the vaccines can be rolled out quickly, that the vaccine we'll get will be the best one, that the vaccine is safe, that the boosters will boost. So many unknowns, watching politicians make it up as they went along, the scientists learning more and less every day. Incredible science brought to bear, genomic sequencing of the virus within hours as tracers chase carriers. Yet the mysteries of how it affects people so differently. Then the Delta variant came barrelling through and the Omicron and the time between infection and becoming infectious is quicker than testing and contact tracing.

'It is like a police car that can only do 150 kph chasing a car thief who has stolen a car that does 200,' was a friend's analogy. The thief won't be caught unless he crashes or runs out of fuel.

So make the best of it and party on, maybe. Something becomes a little urgent in our ventures. It's not enough to enjoy a band playing the songs, it's 'how good is this!' We seize the dictum of dancing like nobody is watching, but we are watching and watched, and often it's not pretty.

There are compensations – the freedom of not needing to compete, of letting go. The wisdom of acceptance. The sharper appreciation of beauty the way the warmth and brilliance of an autumn day can be all the finer for knowing it won't last. Apricity – feeling the winter sun's warmth.

But getting old remains a bastard. Getting closer to one kind of end or another and knowing people who die from natural causes is shit. Getting old is only better than being dead while it's better than being dead. At a point, a point of pain, a point of losing the memories that make us, a point of options reduced to nothingness … fuck it.

Among the visitors to the Ascot Gentlepersons' Coffee Club, John and Paulo have survived cancers that, statistically, should have killed them and continue to threaten Paul. Serge's wife and son have had thyroid cancer. Gary doesn't know it on

Jim's birthday but he's carrying inoperable tumours, the caring doctor too busy to have his own colonoscopy. Judy's had two melanomas cut out. While I'm having chemo, Serge has a prostate cancer operation. Peter the same the next year. I finish chemo and Sue starts it for breast cancer. And Kev Carmody, a drip in his arm, giving cheek, purple blotches over his body as he lays beneath a sheet in his Mermaid Beach bedroom, back from hospital that morning when I visited on December 1, died on January 4.

Mark Triscott, with a bit more weight to offer in the scrum, pipped me for the final spot in the First XV second row. He moved to the US as a graduate student and died there in December 2017. With Barry Kennedy gone, four of the 15 members of the 1972 Firsts would not make a 49-year reunion. I'm beginning to think I'm glad to have been in the Seconds.

No, the 60s aren't old, but you're sure not entering the prime of life either. The averages will have their way.

And if it's not ourselves, it's our parents and older siblings. My father was 73 and one day when he died, a heart attack on the eve of having his cancerous bladder removed. My mother was 77, declining to undergo chemotherapy after bowel cancer returned. My genes don't promise old age anyway. One less thing to worry about.

And it could be worse. My mother's greatest fear wasn't death – it was that she would live long enough to lose her mind.

At some point I realised I dropped things more often. I dropped the Alfa 159's keys down the gap between a lift door and the floor once, a few hundred dollars' worth of expensive keys into the well of oil at the bottom of the lift shaft. They were in my hand, nudged by the lift door, nothing really, and down they went in that little gap. Then other things, any little thing, more often and without nudging. Pegs at the line. Keys certainly. Always held tight getting in and out of lifts though. Once bitten.

And my hands had been good – could catch that lineout ball at the peak of my jump despite the shoves, the gouging and elbows and competition. They were safe under a high ball. The kick-offs that tended to come to where second rowers stood on the field, tumbling down out of blue Brisbane winter skies as the enemy pack charged towards you, as set on committing mayhem on you as you were on them. Ignore them, don't see them, ignore the thought of them, watch the ball, have faith in your brothers to envelop you as you catch it and them, the thump of bodies colliding but the ball safe. Half a century ago.

December 16, 6.32 pm

G'day Michael

Just a short note to wish you well for the soon to be wedding celebrations. Hope all is going fairly well and you can relax and enjoy what will be a wonderful day.

Eloping would be more my style, but I'm sure you will be very much the proud Father of the Groom ... Something you will do well.

Thanks for the 60th birthday call ... Good to hear your cheery hello.

Maybe six of us old regulars from GPCC. Hard to believe we are all turning 60 ... what happened to us young fellows on the flats at Nudgee?

Have a great Xmas, old mate ... look forward to catching up whenever that may be.

Love and best wishes for the Xmas season.

Love Jim

December 16, 7.54 pm

Dear Jim

We've almost had a case of crossed emails as I was sitting down to write to you, turned on the machine and found your kind wedding wishes – more things to have to think about at present, more sets of decisions to be made and details to be remembered.

Now I'm sounding like a cranky 60-year-old. No doubt it will be a great party and the silly details will be forgotten. 'It'll be all right on the night' and 'the show must go on' and all that.

What sparked my intention to write – aside from the need to spur you into replying – was that I met Julia Baird last night when I did *The Drum* with her on the ABC. After the show as we were exchanging pleasantries, I thanked her for the cancer piece she wrote and said I had sent it to an old mate who didn't have a favourable prognosis and he enjoyed it. Julia said she very nearly didn't write it, didn't particularly want to write it as it was very personal and she felt a bit of a wanker doing it, but then she felt she just had to, that she had to have it all said. I told her that I was glad she did and that my mate was. I suggested that sometimes writing a personal piece isn't about pleasing you, the writer, but you do it for the reader – put a little bit of yourself out there for better or worse. I'm not sure that she bought that.

And now I'm not sure how much of that is the case, how much of writing is for the reader and how much of it is to fuel the ego of the writer. Certainly when an audience responds favourably, it's a warm thing – and considerably better than when they throw rotten tomatoes! In honesty, when I write the usual journalistic commentary, I hope it takes off and gets a decent-sized audience and stirs some thinking and will be appreciated and all that. You hope people will think you think something worth thinking about – and there's certainly ego in there.

246

But when I have written personal pieces from time to time, there is a slightly different hope, more that other people will connect with it, that sharing the human condition will provide warmth all round. Or something like that. Still plenty of room for ego-stroking – and that's not necessarily a bad thing anyway.

Re my duties as the FoG, I might surprise you by saying I don't know what to say in my speech yet. I'm leaving the run a bit late. There are a couple of anecdotes about Dom I can work in, but I don't know where I want it to go. I had been at a similar sort of loss before Nick's wedding, but the message came to me for them about the adventure they were setting out on, working off Julia's migrant story, about being brave to face whatever happens next together. Somehow that doesn't fit with Dom and Carmen – and I can hardly repeat the speech anyway. For them, it's something more about being a blessed couple, both born into supportive families, both able to do what they wanted, both happy people, quite untroubled in their lives. And I don't know that those thoughts go anywhere.

Oh well – journalists work best to a deadline. I have until about 7.15 on Saturday night.

Time for dinner and then some bookkeeping before I can go to bed ahead of an early start (early for me) picking up Chris and his girlfriend from the airport, morning arrival from Dubai. Tim's up from Canberra tomorrow afternoon and we're all off to see Cold Chisel tomorrow night – a grand way to get into wedding and Christmas mode.

All the very best for the McCormack Christmas, Jim, in the peace of those you love and who love you. See you when I can next go north – at the moment that looks like the start of March.

And keep writing if the mood takes you. I'm thinking about collecting a list of Life's Lessons Learned – so far the only three I've come up with are:

1. There is no elegant way to pick up dog shit.
2. Never lean over a toilet bowl with a mobile phone, or anything of value, in your shirt pocket.

3. The same distance measured on two different pieces of wood, when cut, may not result in the same length.

Any contribution by you would raise the tone!

Love
Michael

December 17, 7.33 am

Michael

Your thoughts re writing and ego spurred my thoughts.

The obvious difference is you write for a living ... I'm writing to try to process a life lived, but still ego is involved in all.

Is our ego the trigger to encourage us into action? ... Why did I pick a journalist friend with whom to share my dying experience? ... I'm fairly sure I didn't do it with the hope of personal publicity.

I did it because:

1. You offered to do it with me, and
2. I see you as a kind and gentle and generous soul.

But also somewhere in there I also wish to spread a message, anonymously, about death and dying ... which on re-reading might just be a terribly egotistical thing to do.

'And now I'm not sure how much of that is the case, how much of writing is for the reader and how much of it is to fuel the ego of the writer.'

I'm not sure either, even in my case ... I'd hate to think I'm writing to teach, but I am writing to share, and maybe teaching is not such a giant leap from there.

'... put a little bit of yourself out there for better or worse.'

It's much easier for me to do this than you, Julia Baird or any other public figure ... but still it requires some sort of personal abandonment to put it out there.

A lot of this is just pure personal therapy ... and you are the catalyst ... the conduit ... If you get my drift.

Well then why can't I write about it anymore? ... Maybe my message is getting more and more jumbled the further I get into the dying game ... It's getting complicated.

I've lost my way, or more to the point, I've lost my positioning. All through the last 5 years I've known where I stood on the 'path', as far as the progression of the disease goes.

It was able to be plotted on medical graphs ... I knew what the various timelines were, I had some idea what the various PSA levels meant, I knew the terminology.

By June 2014, the cancer quickly in a matter of a couple of months engulfed a large portion of my body ... chemotherapy and/or death ... pretty straightforward. Well, the chemo worked, settled into a nice weekly routine until July 2015, when kidney function began to decline and treatment began to fail, still pretty straightforward outcomes and decisions. Stop curative treatment and begin palliative treatment.

Almost certainly would not make Xmas ... sometimes we are wrong, but this looks fairly straightforward ... is what the doctor said to my daughter Catherine.

Come Xmas, I still look a healthy person in the GPCC ... Underneath the clothes is a deformed mess ... externally it's deceptive. My scrotum so swollen at times I have trouble getting my penis out of the mess to have a pee ... then it disappears back into the swollen mess.

My masculinity in tatters ... my genitalia is a large part of my self-esteem or who I am.

Anyway, I digress ... come Xmas I'm very much still alive ... Just a few parts missing, or at least badly disabled by collateral damage.

Had blood test results today ... very impressive, said the doctor ... kidney function pretty good, most other levels very good ...

The graphable and predictable pattern of events has now turned random ... I don't like random very much ... It's like playing with an injured fish on a line.

I am and should be very grateful to be alive ... I am and should be very grateful to be able to be here to comfort and support my loving wife ... To watch my beautiful children and grandchildren prosper and grow.

I need to embrace and be grateful for the opportunity I have been given in this lifetime to experience loss and humiliation … not everyone gets it.

Keep well, old mate.

You are a good friend.

Love Jim

December 21, 7.39 pm

G'day Michael

Hope wedding went well and you behaved yourself.

Just read the Julia Baird article 'Web encounters reveal kindness of strangers'. It is almost word for word what I feel about sickness, death and dying. If you meet her on set again, tell her she nailed it. I know it is unfair to ask one writer to compliment another … but you're a big-hearted soul.

I also thought that this back and forth we have going on is a web encounter in its own way.

We relate differently (most of us) via the web than in person.

So until next time, old mate … hope you are relaxing and enjoying the post-wedding days.

Love Jim

December 21, 11.56 pm

Jim

At this late hour, after writing a script for Fairfax for tomorrow's video and generally trying to catch up after a fantastic long weekend, you have sent me off to read Ms Baird's latest piece. I will tell her of your approval.

I won't write more now – I want to put your mind at rest about what I managed to come up with as the peg for the theme of my speech, that positive human encounters, whether by web or chance meeting or grand design, are indeed fine things. As Julia writes, when death is a reality instead of something perceived as being far over the horizon, all sorts of mundane barriers come down, it erases divisions. The money shot for me was 'Perhaps it's the recognition that we are all vulnerable'. Mate, I think she's onto us, has been reading our letters.

We spend our lives avoiding the deep and personal until the threat of loss of life makes them the only things that matter. How could I, an Aussie bloke, tell you, an Aussie bloke, how much I admired you if we were just going through the usual social rituals? It's just a shame that it takes mortality to get us to shed veils.

But now, I have a couple of good bemusements to send before sleeping.

I'll write soon.

Love
Michael

P.S. An elderly man went to his doctor and said, 'Doc, I think I'm getting senile. Several times lately I have forgotten to zip up.'

'That's not senility,' replied the doctor. 'Senility is when you forget to zip down.'

Speeches

To speak at your child's wedding, to speak at your brother's funeral – a chance to express love publicly that Jim was denied, that big heart bursting with it in silence. For me, my sons' weddings and three eulogies.

For Chris and Bianca's wedding, the magical 'WedFest' at Muldersdrift outside Johannesburg, the inspiration again came late. I was asking my mother and father and it came: sliding doors. All the sliding doors moments that had to happen just right, all the accidents and happenstances, things going right and wrong across their lives to bring them together at this point of matrimony from so far apart – Chris from Sydney with his Australian–Irish Catholic heritage, Bianca from Joburg with her Saffa Jewish heritage, meeting in Dubai, so well matched. The blessing of all those moments that made it possible.

Eulogies – my brother Brian, my father-in-law, David, my dog Max. OK, Max's wasn't a funeral, not a spoken eulogy, but one nonetheless.

There should be a core to such speeches, a core for the living as it's too late for the dead. For Brian, it was for his optimism, an openness to opportunity that he wanted for his three daughters.

When Dad died 14 years ago, this was Brian's job, and of course he did it brilliantly. The heart of that fine eulogy was Brian's memory of the childhood and youth our parents gave him.

He said that when he thought back on those years of growing up in country towns, the farm in Goomeri, going off to Nudgee and the holidays therefrom, that it all seemed to be a golden summer.

As far as Terry and I can recollect his exact words, Brian said: 'We lived in the summertime of our dreams, a long golden summer of love.'

I said Brian made a small mistake with the tense – he had continued to live in the summertime of his dreams, expecting a generous, honourable and fair world, where adventure and whimsy were to be admired and pursued, where everything was possible. He knew it wasn't, but he chose to live in defiance of that knowledge, chose to maintain the sense of honour he had inherited, of good form, of taking responsibility for your actions, of a generosity of spirit, persevering with that inheritance for very nearly 58 years.

For David, it was for his widow, as it was a funeral for her as well, a funeral for their life together, the death of the major part of her life. David had always been the leader, the joiner, the social engager, Maureen always waiting to be invited. I tried to bring some sort of comfort, a roundness of no regrets in his death, a genuine celebration of a good, full life, from war service to marriage to business to family to grandchildren to retirement. And I failed, inevitably failed. Maureen dissolved into an inconsolable widowhood.

Last weekend, after a good but still too short innings of 84 years, David Paul Grey Edmondson died what doctors call 'a good death', to the extent that any death is 'good'.

It was peaceful, relatively quick, with no suffering, with appropriate medical care, in the comfort of his faith and the last rites, and, most importantly, surrounded by the love of his family. It was a death we all might wish for.

And in David's case, it's entirely appropriate, in keeping with the rest of his life really: a good man, having led a good life – with an appreciation of the good life as well – with a hand of greeting open to the world and a word or several for everyone he met. Well, it's no wonder His Maker would in turn want to welcome him in as friendly a manner as possible.

In time, Maureen came to believe David had died quite young. 'Not many of the men back from the war made old bones,' she'd say. She thought he'd had a long illness in hospital instead of the stroke he suffered at home. She had been so lonely since he died, she thought it must have been a long time ago.

David begrudged the minor deprivations of age he was beginning to experience. I think a slow death would have annoyed him, an incapacitated life infuriate him. 'It's not for me, let's get out of here,' I could hear him say, but I don't know what peace or fear he lived in for the few hours between his stroke and dying, how long that time would seem on the banks of the Lethe.

As the years without David have passed and Maureen's grip has weakened, she forgets she was married at all, regrets that she didn't get married and have a family.

'Well, who do you think I am, Mum?' asks Judy.

'Oh, you came to live with us when you were a little girl. I know you call me "Mum" but I'm not your mother. I would have been much too young to have you – my parents would have died of shame if I had a baby then!'

It hurts Judy. She knows it shouldn't, but it hurts.

Maureen is regressing into her childhood, confusing photographs of David with her brother, Kevin. Thinking her family is that of her childhood, talks more of her father and mother. When we take her out from St Paul's, there's a ritual reciting of it being just like boarding school when her parents would collect her. She sometimes calls the fine woman who runs St Paul's activities program 'the sports mistress'. I think that started as a joke but now is not.

Some days are better or at least clearer than others. She is increasingly given to wondering if she should try to get back to Brisbane, to see if any of 'them' are still there.

'Who do you mean?'

'You know ... my family, my brother.'

'Maureen, Kevin is dead. He died 40 years ago.'

'Oh, thank you for telling me that. I was wondering why he hadn't tried to find me ...'

The good days are getting fewer, the lack of memory more confusing and made worse by the inability or unwillingness to accept its failings.

'You can't be my daughter! I mean, you're very nice and a friend, but I'd remember giving birth. Don't treat me as a fool!'

It's senile dementia, not Alzheimer's. If her heart holds, delirium is waiting for her somewhere up ahead. Possible terror, possible imagined but real pain, possible violent swings, not that her frail little body seems capable of any violence.

Terry's similar-aged mother-in-law, the most prim and proper of women all her long life, erupting: 'You're all sluts! This is a sluts' house!' Possible curling up and withdrawal, not eating, not drinking, dehydrating into death. And then bouncing back until next time.

The first lines of my mother-in-law's eulogy already composed: Maureen died twice, maybe thrice. The first time when David died ...

For Max, well, Max was a fine old dog.

We are better for having had Max, for him increasing our ability to love another, for the pain of missing him, for making us more human.

December 25, 1.08 pm

Dear Jim

There's a ham to be sliced, a decision to be made about heating the turkey or serving it cold (it is cooked, I hasten to add – we're not hardcore paleo down here), Judy is having the usual last-minute panics about where some candles and particular glasses might be, there's smoked salmon to be arranged on blinis and hummus to be bowled, with people supposed to be coming at 2 pm for a long Christmas lunch of excess – but before all that, I want to wish you and your girls and boys a wonderful Christmas Day together.

We've been in various degrees of recovery and preparation since the wedding and ahead of having lunch today, so I haven't been able to sit down with my thoughts on the keyboard. A couple of things are running through my head.

1. How, on the morning of Dom's wedding, we boys played some beach cricket and went for a swim. I found myself bobbing around in the Palm Beach surf (outside the flags – I know you'd love that) with my sons, four grown men. And I wondered where they had come from so quickly. When they were little I'd take them out in the surf in my arms and sing a modified ditty that I think came from Play School about bobbing all around in the deep blue sea ... and decide together whether each approaching wave was a 'bobber' or a 'diver'. There was some strange mixture of peace and pride and sadness in the water, not talking, just seeing them, being with them.

2. The whole religion thing with weddings. I feel a bit like the Fiddler on the Roof – Nick and Julia were married in a Catholic church, full nuptial mass; Dom and Carmen had a Christian wedding in a beachside park; Bianca, Chris's girl, is Jewish, so they'll be up for a non-denominational or civil wedding; so I guess Tim won't get married at

all if the trend holds! Dom and Carmen (well, mainly Carmen, methinks) didn't want much God in the wedding ceremony, but Richard fitted enough in. Having spoken to Bianca last night – she explained why she wouldn't join us for Christmas Day mass – I think I saw it through her eyes today, the assumptions we make, that all religions make. The Christmas story remains a fine one though – a better core for a faith – until religion gets hold of it and complicates matters.

Anyway, Christmas remains a fine tradition and excuse to be together in love and hope and celebration. I better go get stuck into it.

Hoping you are travelling well, my old cowboy friend. Just stay away from the deep water and big waves.

Love
Michael

December 25, 3.24 pm

Hello Michael

And a very Happy Xmas to you and all your family.

Thank you for your Xmas wishes.

We have finished our celebrations ... started with tea, coffee, champagne and treats at 8.30 this morning at our place, with an extended family collection. All very nice ... I need family more at the moment than I used to.

Later around to my brother's place for a quiet lunch ... The girls and partners and Jo's in-laws had Xmas lunch at Jo's place ... I hope they are having fun.

I could feel the feelings you felt in the surf with your boys ... peace, pride and sadness ... there is a feeling of melancholy that comes with age ... it is hard to avoid.

One minute they are just children, and then these adults turn up ... we were Jo and Ben just a couple of years ago. Then there is the pride that comes with watching them flower and grow.

Enjoy your day, old mate ... Your hand of friendship this year has meant the world to me ... a great source of comfort and support.

Love and best wishes
Jim

Saudade

Saudade, Jim, sometimes it's saudade, the Portuguese word with no exact translation, something more than nostalgia, more than fondness for the past; a sense of longing for something grand that's been lost, for lost love, for lost grandeur, for lost innocence and all of history; a melancholic wistfulness that underpins fado, the tightly structured Lisbon shade of blues I fell in love with one night without understanding a word being sung. An intensity and quality of performance in the closeness of Clube de Fado that took me by surprise and overwhelmed me, tears in my eyes from music I had never heard before, only felt. Saudade.

And Jim's music? Archie Roach, a man who would understand saudade. 'Old People Singing'.

A morning in the Sunshine Beach surf, a man and his daughter swimming near me out where waves of not inconsequential size were breaking. The girl quite young but a little water nymph. Locals. The girl talking away about treading water and swimming and how big the waves were, the dad calling when to dive under or ride over them before they curled. A slight note of urgency in his voice – just to be sure the call was heeded – as a bigger set looms, calling the dive a little early, to dive deep so a small body might not be plucked up and rolled and dumped by the ocean's endless power rising, crashing.

The girl comfortable with it all, confident with her dad. She surfaces, picking up her chatter where she left off, says something about getting out of breath sometimes.

'Maybe that's because you're always talking,' says her father with a gentle smile. She ignores him and talks on.

I'd like to tell him to lock in this memory, these moments with his little girl diving under breakers in bright sunshine, the light shining through the advancing green walls; to photograph her smile in his mind, to never forget this perfect morning together whatever else happens in their lives, uncomplicated minutes forever happy in trust and love.

I don't. It would be presumptuous, might be creepy, some old bloke saying stuff like that. Entirely hypothetical anyway – I wouldn't be able to get those words out, just the thought threatening to tear me up. Dive down and further away from them, silently wish them well and know their magic will be lost in time, too. Tears under the ocean. Saudade.

January 16, 2.11 pm

Dear Jim

Now I'm the one who has gone quiet. I don't know where the first half of January has disappeared to, but I'd like it to come back so I can catch up. I seem to have lost the plot a bit, thinking I had some time to get stuff done and finding it rapidly growing. I might be catching a bit of what my mother-in-law has.

How are you travelling, old cowboy? I hope your medical balancing act is remaining happily on the high wire. Keep singing.

A friend of Judy's who was a friend of Nick Masinello told her this morning that Rosa had died. I emailed Sergio – one thing both more and less for him, that dear emotional soul, to deal with. I welcomed him to the orphanage. However ripe the time, there's the rush of memory and loss.

Rosa has made me think of my own mother's death – she was ready to die, chose not to have chemo when her cancer returned – and I think much of that feeling, emotion, might be the loss of your own childhood that is so caught up in your parents. What should be such an obvious celebration of a long life remains tinged nonetheless with loss.

I suppose that's part of what I admire about your recognition of wanting to leave good memories and feelings.

You must be bored with the offerings of much less involved writers about the process – the chickens in the bacon-and-eggs analogy. If you are, don't bother reading 'How to have a good death' in *1843 Magazine*.

I found it an honest attempt to deal with some of the complexities of death – some good ideas but eventually overcome with the individuality of every person's experience. Or maybe that's the point. The idea of death being a normal part of life is something you have written better.

In the meantime, to paraphrase that Snoopy cartoon, every day we're not dead, we're alive. So we'd better get on with making the most of them.

Love
Michael

Lost

In the rhythm of our correspondence, Jim would normally comment on a piece I'd sent. He didn't for that one, a fine Maggie Fergusson feature from *The Economist's 1843 Magazine*.[11]

In the 1970s and 1980s, cancer was the illness we feared most. Now it's dementia. Whereas cancer, on the whole, leaves people in command of their thoughts and memories, dementia wanders through the corridors of their minds, switching off lights. And the darkness left behind often crepitates with phantom terrors – scrambled versions of the anxieties that preyed on sufferers when they were young and fit. For my Dad, it's that he's lost his job, and run out of money, and is about to be cast out – not, like Lear, onto a blasted heath, but into the parking lot of the suburban care home where he now lives.

Her father had a little dementia that went into overdrive after the general anaesthetic following a fall that smashed his hip.

Lying in hospital over last Christmas, with the skeleton nursing staff moving about in tinsel haloes and reindeer antlers, he became increasingly confused and distressed. Through the thin wall dividing his ward from the next was an elderly lady much more deeply demented than he was. 'Help me! Help me!' she wailed. It sounded as if she was drowning or being tortured. I thought, listening to her, of the 19th-century German housewife Auguste Deter, and her plaintive cry to Dr Alois Alzheimer: 'Ich habe mich sozusagen verloren,' – 'I have lost myself.'

That night in the Mona Vale Hospital emergency department after her car crash, Maureen bruised and swollen and scared and confidence broken, nearly every bed had a little old lady in it. There was a youth who had been in some sort of accident and one elderly man with his heart being monitored, but the rest were elderly women. Falls.

And one repeatedly calling, 'Where am I?'

January 28, 10.18 pm

Dear Jim

Another week has run away from me somewhere – wish I knew where – but a couple of things have passed by me that I thought you'd find interesting, or perhaps annoying.

In the latter category, I saw *Spotlight* last night, the movie about the Boston Globe's investigation of priest paedophiles, showing how widespread it was and how the cover-up was institutionalised. In one way, there's not much in it that we shouldn't already know, but in another way, it remains shocking. It also sheets home how 'we' were all to blame for not blowing the whistle sooner – including the journalists who eventually did. It might make you angry to see it, but I think it's worthwhile. (Mind you, the most enjoyable movie I've seen in a while is *Paddington*, about the bear of that name. Might say something about my taste in movies. No, *Paddington* is good stuff.)

The other is part of a few exchanges I've had with an economist mate, a child migrant from Glasgow, someone who has always appreciated the opportunities Australia provided for him. We have long discussed the great migrant story of Australia and I mentioned attending Rosa's funeral and the death of the Holocaust survivor father of another friend. My Scot told me that he'd had a sad Christmas as his younger brother had died on New Year's Eve after a short illness. He wrote his brother's triumph was 'the simple one of how much people, especially his nephews and nieces, loved him, and in how much he'll be missed'.

He said he had remarked only that night to two of his children still living at home 'what a remarkably generous and hospitable country we occupy. I guess that's why children in detention and Stan Grant's statistics about Indigenous kids are, like the peace of God, beyond understanding.'

Amen to that.

And goodnight.

Michael

January 29, 7.39 am

Hi Michael

I was going to write to you yesterday so it was interesting to find a message from you in the inbox this morning. It was good catching up with you last week, albeit sad that it had to be at the funeral of Sergio's Ma.

You sound a little pissed off by the tone of your email ... if I read it correctly. We live in an extraordinarily mad world, populated by extraordinarily mad people ... sadly, you and me included. We draw lines on maps and kill each other over them.

We should never try to find reason in an unreasonable world.

As for the movies ... I like to keep it simple, so Paddington Bear would always be a winner with me.

To the subject of blowing the whistle on paedophilia at boarding school during our time there ... I was subject to an advance from Proctor ... So I suppose you could say I witnessed it, and I think at the time I would have come forward and reported it, if there was the avenue to do so. A pointless exercise. 'How dare we defame the name of this man who has given his life to God.'

Would I testify to support another Nudgee boy in a case against him now?

Sadly, the answer is no ... To have my mental and emotional health, my struggle with alcohol etc, laid bare before the court and the daily press ... I think I will give it a miss.

As for my health ... Everyone at the funeral said I looked very well ... So I will take their word for it. About 104 kg, the heaviest I have ever been, mostly excess fluid. Nothing much has changed except for my weight. I have been at the farm since last Friday (a week), three of those days on my own. It has been good for me in a way because I am literally stranded down here. I have the ute, but I can't drive. I can drive around the farm but go to sleep if I try to do too much.

The experience of loss is very real. I've lost my physical strength … If I try to run or move quickly I just fall over … I had trouble getting up on the tractor this morning … My skin is like tissue paper, and tears at the slightest rub … I am finding riding a horse difficult and uncomfortable … The future for me no longer exists … etc etc. So loss is my current life experience.

I no longer read the news or listen to the news. That is a freedom I appreciate.

I have no more to add at this stage so will call it quits at that. I hope you and family are all well. Keep writing if you can find the time, Michael, as I look forward to your emails.

All the best.

Love Jim

February 15, 11.56 am

Jim

I didn't ask Sergio's permission – I hope he doesn't mind – but I've included his mother in a piece I've done on the 24 millionth Australian.

I think her story, the migrant's story, is something to be proud of.

Michael

Alex and Rosa

The ABS population clock ticked over again on February 16, 2016 – 24 million of us. Having made the 23 millionth Australian a newborn and with Rosa's funeral fresh in my mind amid swirling anti-immigration commentary, I decreed the 24 millionth a migrant on the eve of their arrival:

In some foreign city, you, the 24 millionth Australian, are experiencing the mixture of fear and excitement that comes from leaving family and the familiar to make your life in another land.

That takes bravery or the direst necessity. To abandon 'home' with all its certainties and support, the streets and buildings and sources you know, the people and friends you grew up with, perhaps even the language you speak, is not for the fainthearted. The adventurous migrate, the people who have what we hope is that most Australian trait, the willingness to have a go. The timid stay behind, or sometimes are dragged along behind.

In the wee small hours of tomorrow morning – February 16, 2016, a date you will never forget, another birthday of sorts – you will be warned against trying to bring food from your old home into this new one. You will have your passport and visa examined and stamped by Border Force at curfew-free

Melbourne Airport. You'll clear customs and wander, tired from the flight, into the arrivals hall, all your most precious possessions down to what you can drag or push in those couple of suitcases. The summer night will be cooler than you'd heard to expect of this country. There's a possibility of showers. Welcome to Australia.

You could be from just about anywhere and could be just about anything – a refugee who has lost everything and everyone or a multi-millionaire who has effectively purchased the passport.

I have a treasured quote from fellow Queenslander Lloyd Rees who said he felt sorry for people born in Sydney because they never saw it with fresh eyes. That pretty much applies to the Australian-born about Australia.

Each year, a wave of migrants arrive, look around and say in various languages words to the effect of: 'How bloody good is this? Let's get stuck in!'

And, mostly, they do, working with a drive and enthusiasm that shades we skippys. Of course, it doesn't last – their grandchildren as slack as the rest. But by then more have landed to keep reinvigorating the economy and culture.

You tend to have to be a risk-taker to migrate and it's risk-taking that grows us.

At the extreme edge of risk was Alex Graus, pushing 90 when he died last month, an event largely unheralded beyond his family.

His is an almighty story, one of many. After being among the last Jews to be deported from Czechoslovakia in August 1944, it took calculated risks and luck – a camp doctor was from his village – for a boy to survive Auschwitz-Birkenau, Ravensbruck,

274

and Sachsenhausen and to leave Czechoslovakia in 1949 for Australia.

His family tell me he did not like to speak of the war years and rarely did. He found it hard to trust anyone and kept his emotions locked down, but he broke his silence to help a granddaughter with a sanitised version for a school assignment. In part:

'For many migrants adjusting to the new life was challenging. Alex recalls, "It was reasonably easy. No-one actually wants to leave their home country but my family perished in the war so a fresh start was good. Ben Chifley was the prime minister at the time and Australia was fair to me. I remember there was a strike for eight weeks, which left us with no electricity for a week."

'Alex's experience of Australians as a migrant was generally very positive. He recalls that "they were not hostile. They felt sorry for me, I think, and were very sympathetic. I mean, if you weren't arrogant there was no problem. They were actually very helpful and personally, I didn't experience any racial discrimination."'

Her eulogy began:

'Grandad is the bravest person I know. Although we will never be able to truly understand what he went through in his early life, I can imagine the strength and bravery it must have taken him to live through the horrors of the Holocaust, the loss of his family and come to a new country.'

Alex Graus and his brother, Walter, who had escaped Czechoslovakia before deportation, eventually started making neckties, establishing Boston Ties, employing 100 people at its height. Alex had two sons, themselves continuing to build this country, to make it better, as are his granddaughters.

His descendants tell me Alex was always optimistic, no matter what happened. I suppose after you've been to hell, any purgatory would look like heaven.

The 24 millionth Australian could be the makings of another Alex Graus, a survivor of war and horror who would be forever grateful to the country that gave him or her a fresh start.

Or maybe the 24 millionth will be a much younger Rosa Masinello, a nonagenarian who also died last month, the mother of my schoolmate Sergio.

Rosa was a young woman when she left all the closeness of Filicudi, one of the Aeolian islands off the coast of Sicily. Here she married Frank, also from Filicudi, forming a partnership to raise four children and build businesses, helping to literally build Brisbane.

'Mum, in her quiet, humble way, achieved great things for her family and friends,' Sergio wrote to me, also with characteristic humility.

Rosa, like Alex, was part of that great postwar wave that changed Australia forever, just as the present wave does. She remained more at home with Italian than English, certainly more at home with Italian food, but, with Frank, she very much wanted her children to be Australian.

The most powerful economic driver on earth is a mother's desire for her child to have a better chance in life than she did. There'll be Rosas arriving tomorrow, for sure.

Or maybe the 24 millionth will be like an economist friend, a child migrant who admits he might bore his children by reminding them how fortunate they are to be born here. He's a fine man, a servant of the country, who says he has had opportunities that would not have been afforded him elsewhere – yet his mother never stopped missing Glasgow. It could be harder for partners dragged away from family.

Or maybe the 24 millionth will be like his brother who died before Christmas.

'He wasn't one of our migrant triumphs,' my friend wrote. 'He was a single man whose life took a different path from his brothers. His triumph was the simple one of how much people, especially his nephews and nieces, loved him, and in how much he'll be missed.'

To be loved and missed is great success indeed. It is to be a successful human being – the rest, merely trappings of one type or another. Pericles: 'What you leave behind is not what is engraved in stone monuments, but what is woven into the lives of others.'

Whoever our 24 millionth person is and our 24th million people, they will make us richer through their diversity, by bringing their experience and desire, their fresh eyes. In time they will seep into the land through their bones and children and their children's children and the land will seep into them, as it has for millennia. Australia would not be as promising, as fine, without them.

Jim said he liked the article. Sergio had forwarded it to him. 'I think Sergio would be really chuffed – what a lovely way to remember his mother.'

Alex Graus was Alison's father-in-law. Philip, her husband, told me that the first time the survivor of hell met Alison, Alex told him, 'You have won the lottery,' and Alex wasn't one for saying much.

'She doesn't call me "Lucky Phil" for nothing.'

They continue to see themselves as lucky as they go on in the company of a terminal cancer, ticking off the YPLL.

Snow gums

Time.

Armidale is anchored by its university and schools, big enough to have a diversity denied most country towns, big enough to have Catholic and Anglican cathedrals diagonally opposite each other on Central Park, both of fearsomely dark and cold Armidale blue brick. Tamworth has the Golden Guitar and buskers and the equestrian centre, Armidale has bishops and professors and deans incongruous in the middle of the New England Tableland. Armidale is pretty in autumn and a cold hole in winter. We've stayed there, back when we were driving with children and it was too long to do the run with them in one day. Had two tyres replaced there on the people mover after waking to find them flat, riddled with echidna spikes from the dark bump experienced on the road the night before.

A coffee would be good, but not worth the detour into town for the McDonald's. There would be good coffee in Armidale if you knew where to buy it, but I don't and keep driving. The highway skirts the place at 80 kph and on the outskirts is a new housing estate that, like a couple of other towns along the way, features uniform boxes cheek-by-jowl on small blocks typical of expensive and limited Sydney land. Beyond the estate, empty paddocks stretch forever.

The paddocks are civilised around Armidale, ordered and well settled, until you hit the bush and the hills around Black Mountain. It's good driving again to Guyra. If Armidale is cold in winter, Guyra is bloody freezing, one of Australia's highest towns. Once on the way back from Queensland in July we were caught overnight by snow, just made it into town before the road was closed and glad to find a nondescript motel.

And from here to the border there's a flinty quality to the land that I love. This and the high country from Cooma to the snow, boulder-strewn, climate-hardened. A Judith Wright poem stuck from school:

South of my days' circle, part of my blood's country,
rises that tableland, high delicate outline
of bony slopes wincing under the winter,
low trees, blue-leaved and olive, outcropping granite—
clean, lean, hungry country.[12]

The snow gums in particular entrance me. I stop when I'm skiing to photograph them, the gnarled persistence of them. Iced branches, the vibrancy of them in the snow, or wearing white after a fresh fall. The old survivors, twisted limbs, half dead, half living, ice fingers along dead twigs; the stunning beauty of their striped trunks as the bark undresses for spring. I try but fail to capture the silver sparkle of their leaves in sunlight, the constant variety of their shapes and battles. There's one in particular at Blue Cow, on the top of the Copperhead run, she could have been painted by Munch. Defiantly, strongly alive before a dead forest, a woman spirit, bent over by the wind, limbs flying away with the prevailing gales. I have a large photograph of her on my study wall. A bluebird day, the sky an unnaturally dark blue but her leaves and finer branches encased in ice. She is beauty and persistence, life among death.

I tell myself I would like to spend a full year in a cabin in the Snowy Mountains, to see and feel the four seasons come and go. Comfortable and warm, of course – log fire, electricity, internet and running water. Able to go walking through the tussocked landscape, my dog chasing rabbits. Try to write and watch the snow come and go and come again and melt.

South of my days' circle
I know it dark against the stars, the high lean country
full of old stories that still go walking in my sleep.[13]

There is a humbling quiet in the bush. You can be woken by the cracking of corrugated iron as an old house warms and stretches or shivers and pulls closer. And there's certainly birdsong, if only the inevitable crow, but those solitary noises only accentuate the deep stillness, a profound stillness of soul. I understand timelessness in the bush. The absence of the city's constant hum stops clocks. The quiet of trees and long grasses suspends judgements and demands. In the solitude of a bush hut, as long as you wish the mood to last, you can simply be.

I could have done it. I didn't. Another option closing off.

Sometimes – heresy – I fear the loss of the land's power over us, doubt the pull and spirit of this country to absorb us, its roots reaching up into our veins. I wonder if mine is the last generation to have a general understanding of country, a generation where everyone seemed to still have at least one relative outside the capital cities, a generation where visiting someone in the bush was the norm, not paid tourism. Twenty-eight per cent of us now were born in another country, the highest percentage since the gold rush days. How does that change us if we lose our mythology, if the kids no longer learn the bush ballads, if the sense of distance and resilience we shared, or at least shared the idea of, is gone? I wonder if there will be another generation of grey nomads. Saudade, Jim, saudade.

I recorded a parody of 'The Man from Snowy River' when Turnbull announced Snowy 2.0 and played it at a conference I was MCing. I lost the audience. Most of them had never heard the poem.

Time.

Year of the knees

G uyra has an annual Potato and Lamb Festival, but no
McDonald's. It's another 60 kilometres to Glen Innes for
one and there's a touch of hunger now you think about the
afternoon getting on. Drive on, be there in no time, driving
through Australian country that has the mark of Celts upon
it. Guyra to Glen Innes, past Ben Lomond, through Glencoe.
Dundee and Glen Elgin if you turn off at Glennie. This higher,
harder, further country must have appealed to Scots. Guyra has
its summer lamb and potatoes, Glen Innes has the Australian
Standing Stones, a copy of Orkney's Ring of Brodgar, and an
autumn Celtic Festival. No wonder it has a McDonald's.

Signs declare this the Land of the Beardies, which must
puzzle the passing tourist. Two hirsute convict stockmen
working on the northernmost station of the time had guided
the squatters pushing beyond, knew where the best land was
to steal from the Ngarabal people. 'Dispersal.' The flood had
taken another few years to creep this high up, the late 1830s,
and then surged with the discovery of tin.

This literally bejewelled country can break hearts. Diamonds
were found at Copeton, extremely hard diamonds of important
industrial use during the war, the old mines lost now under the
Copeton dam. More sapphires mined around Inverell than all

of Sri Lanka. Albert Joris, trained by his Antwerp diamond-cutter father, took me to Inverell to show me his vision for Arrawatta Holdings, to do for sapphires what De Beers had done for diamonds – establish a cartel, bypass the Thai buyers by treating, cutting and polishing the stones here, control and add value to the market. The Thais were buying the dark blue Inverell stones by the sugar bag, cash, taking them back to Thailand to be cooked – the rich inky darkness fades to a clear light blue crystal if heated just enough – and sold as Ceylonese sapphires around the world.

The vision wasn't shared. Arrawatta was taken over by those of lesser ambition, the Inverell operation with its cutting machines sold off, the company used as a backdoor listing for a tourist opal shop. And a generation later, Albert's grandson was a classmate of one of my boys, in a rugby team I briefly coached.

I've stopped for a coffee and burger in Glen Innes but I'm on the sidelines of Riverview's 13Bs against Kings at Kings. Their regular coach was indisposed by a knee operation. I had done a Level 2 coaching course with the sportsmaster who asked me to help out. They were a good team that had been unlucky. Fine, smart boys who had lost a couple of games they should have won, just needed an injection of confidence and a little more structure. They learned so fast, picked up lineout moves in two sessions that had taken Wagner weeks to drill into us in the Nudgee 15As of 1970. I knew that Kings field, knew it sloped away to the north, knew a ball booted long would roll on and away, knew the five-eighth, Sam Rarasea, from the Lane Cove team I coached, from primary school with Dom and had him drill that ball towards the corners, had the forwards pick and drive and barge and hustle over. Joris copped a whack on the nose, came off bloodied and bleeding. I remembered consciously deciding to put him back on for the last five minutes, when the flow had stopped, asked him if he wanted to get back into it, in the belief it would be good for him to get back on the horse. He did.

I remember that game of under 13s rugby better than any of the games I played. I remember bits of games, incidents in the play. I never remembered the opposition as individuals, as faces – they were all just jerseys to be stopped, to be shredded if you could. I remember the Grammar under-16 hands coming over my face, across my eyes, my foot being stomped as I was about to jump. My shoulder connecting perfectly with a BBC diaphragm, winding him, him spilling the ball. Missing a tackle against BGS in the under 14s, weakly falling for a 1–2 penalty tap switch 10 metres from our line and losing the game because of it. Of being part of perfect pack teamwork in the under 15s as we destroyed them, taking a high ball from the kick-off and immediately enveloped by my teammates to drive it. We seemed to fly into those rucks, boots working, the smallest, lightest pack in the competition but stronger as one, but the utter frustration of being simply too small against State High, of losing lineouts, of being pushed off balls. I'm sitting in a McDonald's with my coffee finished and replaying childhood football games as the afternoon grows old, remembering 1972, the Year of the Knees. Sergio, the First XV playmaker, a natural athlete in every sport, did his ACL and more in the pre-season game against Waverley – their turn to visit us – and never played rugby again. Jim wrecked his cartilage against Ipswich Grammar. No keyhole surgery then, the same big slash of a scar across his knee that my father had thanks to his foot getting caught in a stirrup. His left knee. Driving with him sometimes, he'd rub it after changing gears. When he was posted to Redcliffe after Petrie and his shift sometimes coincided with my school day at De La Salle, he'd drive me home, slipping the old Holden into neutral and letting it coast to save petrol. 'It's not the safest thing to do, don't you do it when you start driving,' he said, and rubbed the left knee when it was playing up. Jim worked and worked on his leg after the operation, the model physiotherapy patient, and ran his age 100 metres at GPS. And me against Toowoomba Grammar in the Seconds, playing number 8, corner flagging from a scrum but running too deep a line, the big TGS winger stepping back inside, propping on my left leg, all my momentum and weight and all his too as we hit and the ACL snapped. I remember the grass under my face as I lay there, not quite game to move. And I wonder why I bother to remember any of that, wonder how it's my childhood preoccupying me.

And memories further back. The night I stopped giving my father a kiss goodnight. In the lounge room of the police station house, maybe started primary school, maybe not. Kissed Mum, went over to Dad in his armchair and declared I wanted to shake his hand instead because I was getting too old. I think there was half a laugh from Mum, and Dad looked at her with only half a smile. I don't trust my memory that perhaps his eyes glistened a fraction in that instant. Mine do now. Another regret.

I wonder if we ever grow up. Nudgee was overwhelmingly a boarding school then and many of us went our very separate ways. I ran away from Brisbane when I was 21, to Hong Kong, to the *South China Morning Post*, to travel. I sometimes claim I grew up in Hong Kong as I did over those three years. Or grew up as much as I ever would. And then to Sydney, lost touch with nearly everyone from school until I went back for a 20-year reunion at Tattersalls. I walked into the room and wondered who all these fat and balding men were, but after a few drinks I realised that none of them had really changed, that they were still the same 13-year-old boys I had met in 1969. And after a few more drinks, I thought that if they hadn't changed, I probably hadn't changed either and was still basically a 13-year-old boy. And after a few more drinks, it hit me, one of only a couple of epiphanies I've been granted: if they hadn't changed and I hadn't changed, maybe nobody ever changes and the world is being run by a bunch of 13-year-old boys. Which explains everything – the wars, the stupidities, the failures, the grandiose games and greed and blindness. I thought it was brilliant – I'd tell men and they'd laugh in acknowledgement. But I'd tell women and they'd merely nod. 'Yes, we know.'

And it's later than I thought and the roos would be out soon. Get another coffee and into the car with a scrapbook of schoolboy ghosts and memories and head for Tenterfield.

February 28, 2.28 pm

Dear Jim

In the lounge in Los Angeles with a few hours' wait for the connection home. I was about to title this email 'weed' but then I thought Big Brother might be watching and I don't want to experience a cavity search as a welcome to Sydney. (We did spend a week of this trip in Colorado where weed is legal for residents, which opens up another question that will hold for another time.)

Anyhow, I wouldn't encourage anyone to smoke by buying duty-free, but for you, I'm prepared to make an exception. I hope you read this sooner rather than later and tell me what your preferred brand of durry (or is it durrie? not a word you see anymore) might be. I'll be in Brisbane for a breakfast job on March 10 – fancy some duty-free of what?

Your pusher
Michael

February 28, 2.40 pm

Winfield blue.

February 28, 11.05 pm

Dear Michael

Sorry for the abrupt two-word reply. We were in the midst of things when your email arrived but keen to get a reply to you.

Jim is in a bit of trouble with his back and basically can't walk. It happened suddenly and Karuna nurses are thinking it is a fracture but we will know more tomorrow.

Hopefully Jim will be back in action and writing to you soon himself.

Love
Jim and Sue

Bolivia

A sunset as big as the bush, as you'd hope for on this drive. Golden rays through the trees beside the road, strobing over the Alfa driving through the shadows. The tableland was uniformly lush the last time I was here, but it's dried off over the summer, dead grass all the more golden in this light.

There's Deepwater and Bolivia before Tenterfield. Deepwater optimistically named after the Deepwater River. The Ngarabal were more realistic, called it Talgambuun, 'dry country with many dead trees'. Economic with their words, the Ngarabal, said plenty quite quickly.

Bolivia isn't anymore. Bolivia Hill a landmark, a road to curl up and around, but if you turn off the highway in search of Bolivia, all that's left of the village is a community hall and a disused railway siding. What was the Great Northern Railway stops at Armidale, all the track and bridges and stations and sidings ghosts thereafter.

The bush is littered with such wreckage. Villages that had made sense as a settlement according to the time and distance farm families took to get to them by foot and horse. The motor car killed many; better roads and better cars, and more efficient farms with fewer workers killed more. Corporate farmers often don't even want resident managers now – insurance issues, on-costs – and use contractors instead. It makes for mournful colour stories – a piece to camera once amid sheep having the run of an old farmhouse, a home that would have seen generations of birth and death, felt hope and dreams and grief, the home yard's remaining fruit trees struggling. But that belies the larger regional centres doing well, the places with supermarkets instead of general stores.

I like driving through country towns where they never take down the football posts, towns with tiny schools. I like country towns with wide streets and shady verandas, with old hotels and solid bank buildings, albeit often no longer banks, and carefully maintained ANZAC memorials with the names of the district's sacrificed sons kept clear and legible. I like the old Greek cafes and Chinese restaurants, despite the coffee and food respectively being dreadful.

Country towns, with your willows and squares,
And farmers bouncing on barrel mares[14]

But I'm not innocent of such towns' class divisions and prejudices – townies versus those on the land, the superiority of the local squatter on the big property compared with the dirt scrabblers. Within the town there's the doctor, the council engineer, the bank manager and, in the old days, the teachers. Then the shopkeepers, then the working class, the mechanics and labourers, the railway fettlers, seasonal workers, carriers. Then the blacks, if there were any. Everyone's business known and discussed.

Police were somewhere in the lower middle class or upper working class of a small pond. Driving from Longreach to

Mount Isa once, a petrol station in a village nowhere, sussing out if radar was about, the bloke told me I was lucky it was the local copper's day off, pulled anyone over for anything. 'We had to tie a chop around his neck to get the dog to play with him.'

Not always, of course. There were good towns and bad. In my family's folklore, little Kumbia was an Arcadia, the country idyll where farmers rich and poor helped each other, the townies and the farmers could be friends and there was none of the usual sectarian divides of the time – the Catholics and Anglicans and Lutherans and Methodists went to each other's fetes, supported each other's cake stalls, attended each other's weddings. A Brigadoon where lasting friendships formed. Or that was their experience. No doubt there were people who hated the place.

One day soon he'll tell her it's time to start packing,
and the kids will yell 'Truly?' and get wildly excited for no
*   reason,*
and the brown kelpie pup will start dashing about, tripping
*   everyone up,*
and she'll go out to the vegetable-patch and pick all the green
*   tomatoes from the vines,*
and notice how the oldest girl is close to tears because she was
*   happy here,*
and how the youngest girl is beaming because she wasn't.
And the first thing she'll put on the trailer will be the bottling
*   set she never unpacked from Grovedale,*
and when the loaded ute bumps down the drive past the
*   blackberry-canes with their last shrivelled fruit,*

she won't even ask why they're leaving this time, or where they're
   heading for
– she'll only remember how, when they came here,
she held out her hands bright with berries,
the first of the season, and said:
'Make a wish, Tom, make a wish.'[15]

I stumbled on Bruce Dawe's 'Drifters' in the Nudgee library's only copy of a modern anthology that taught me poetry when the syllabus did not. The poem has haunted me for half a century. I had met her children, scrubby kids who would turn up at the Petrie State School for a while and be gone again before anyone made friends.

I drove my elder brother and sister back to Kumbia for a celebration of the little Catholic church's centenary. Richard two months short of 80, Annette a couple of years behind, back in their early primary school country, posing outside the police station house that was theirs, remembering the cows across the road, the backyard cricket and chooks. The chooks in cages strapped to the running boards, taken with them on camping holidays to the coast in the immediate postwar period. They didn't remember how many chooks came back.

Not too much had physically changed in Kumbia beyond the school being much bigger, the common overgrown and cowless, a few new houses, but there were very few people they remembered or who remembered them. Police families were itinerant – a half dozen years or so and gone to another station without the roots of extended family and intermarriage and ownership. Perhaps a lasting friendship or two – the Ryans –

another town, start over again. New kids in school, new copper, learning the currents.

But it's not the towns now, anyway, it's the country. The towns still punctuation for the road, a passing focus.

Bolivia. I have no idea who or what inspired the naming of a hill and village Bolivia, but I'm warmed by the whimsy of it. There are places on earth more dissimilar than Bolivia and this northern tableland but not much more. Paraguay next door had its crazy Australian utopian settlers thinking they were escaping the 1890s depression – such was utopia in 1893 that one of the founding rules was 'keeping white' – but Bolivia? Amid all the dour occupying Scots, I like to think someone carried a flame for the ideal of Simón Bolívar, for revolution and republic and independence. I'm probably fooling myself.

It's darkening by the non-existence of Bolivia and it's wise to drive a little more cautiously up Bolivia Hill. Zero road sense, your roos and wallabies and wombats and echidnas, the roos as likely to jump into the headlights as away from them. You watch for the reflection of eyes beside the road now more than the reflective paint of police cars.

A road upgrade has tamed Bolivia Hill, smoothed the descent, making it safer and probably saving some lives. I miss the old road.

Tenterfield's ahead, three hours or so from there to Brisbane. I could do it, could do it easily, have done it, but having dawdled with my scrapbook thus far, I don't need to. There's time. No necessity to arrive in Brisbane late and disturb people, later still to think of pushing on to the sanctuary of Sunshine Beach.

Tenterfield will do tonight; Tenterfield's fine enough. The scene of Henry Parkes' federation speech in 1889, a time when a speech in a country town in the middle of nowhere much could inflame the idea of federation across colonies dependent on telegraph wires and mail trains. Not that anybody cares or bothers to know anymore. Tenterfield now is forever Peter Woolnough's – a fine moniker for lean country growing superfine merinos, but not for cabaret. Peter Allen was a better stage name. And you overlook the odd corny line to retain a fondness for 'Tenterfield Saddler', hum it a bit, sing the snatches you know, be reminded that time travels every time you pass by. There are not many hit songs about someone's alcoholic World War 2 veteran father committing suicide.

It's good driving at night in the bush, another type of comfort with the dark closing in around you and the car and your headlights' tunnel through the night, the centre line leading you away from wherever you've come. Wildlife's a risk, but so's everything. There's not much roadkill about – unlike the Monaro Highway – so you're alert, but the odds are reasonable, the speed creeping up again.

I've turned off the lights driving under a full moon and clear sky on empty country roads. The effect is eerie, the dark tunnel gone into a blue-grey light, trees' shadows deeper, moving like a ghost yourself through the landscape.

The road's not empty tonight and there's no moon yet, just regular enough semitrailers lit up like circuses, the high windscreens black eyes in skulls. To be a long-distance truckie – the road a constant marriage through the nights and days instead of an affair, nursing a B-double through a dozen gears, inches to spare straddling the lane, the Brisbane–

Melbourne run on the Newell Highway and the Melbourne–
Brisbane run straight back – a different kind of solitude high
up there above the road. All that mass, unstoppable at speed,
hurtling across the continent. It's another dream, another life
imagined.

Our first classmate to die was taken out by a truck, driving
a tractor across the highway from the family tobacco farm in
Far North Queensland – FNQ. If I was the mayor of Cairns,
I'd rebrand the town, the region, FNQ before the title is
forgotten, like tobacco farming in Australia, wiped out in
FNQ by federal decree in 2004. I'd buy a t-shirt with just
those big letters in black on maroon. I reckon every second
backpacker would too, but I'd be the only person to think of a
schoolboy every time I put it on.

Laugh

'First World problems.' One of Judy's colleagues finds the concept amusing. 'You live in the First World, all your problems are First World problems.' No-one is starving, there is no war, there is running water, power, peace. He had been a young migrant from the Balkans.

An inexpensive random Tenterfield motel will do – a low red-brick building off the main drag, anonymous aside from its name. The essentials, warm, wi-fi.

Managing country motels, another life. Met a couple who did it as part of their retirement, locum motel managers, a few weeks at a time here and there up and down the eastern seaboard. Paid-for country travel instead of being grey nomads paying. I wouldn't last long as a host.

A feed of more than generous proportions at the bowlo. Reminded of another visit, the adjoining oval covered in grazing corellas. Evenly spaced, socially distanced birds upon the late afternoon dark green, the vast crackle chatting away as they fed. A small boy would like to use his unlimited energy to run across that oval, erupt a white cloud of feathers and chirps and marvel as they filled the sky in the pink-gold of a setting sun.

I stood for a while by the fence, admired their community.

Get up early, get petrol, be gone is the plan. Look down at the phone in my hand as I head towards the office to drop the keys and see it's the motel TV remote. Laugh. Laugh at yourself – the only thing to do. Return it to the room. At one point in Maureen's saga, when she was in a serviced aged-care room without a landline, I went in search of and bought her the most basic, simple, large mobile phone still available. Smartphone? I wanted the dumbest phone. And she still had trouble working it and complained to us that she didn't have a phone.

'But you have the mobile phone I bought you.'

'No, I don't.'

'You've rung me on it.'

'Oh, that's not a phone, that's something I rigged up out of the remote control.'

Maureen lost the ability to work any phone by the second COVID lockdown, a relief no doubt for the strangers randomly called by a deaf woman making little sense. Locked out, unable to visit, the staff rostered video calls – shouting at a screen when the only thing that could make any sense was physical presence, whether or not we were really her family.

But move over Alexander Graham Bell, my aging mother-in-law is an electronic genius with a TV remote. And I've reversed the process, turning my phone into a remote. Balance.

Laugh at ourselves. Laugh at our bodies deteriorating. A favourite meme, three old blokes out for a walk:

'It's windy, isn't it?'

'No, Thursday.'

'Me too, let's have a beer.'

Laugh at our minds. A lunch with men of a certain age, a confession by someone about the problem of going upstairs for something and forgetting what it was when they got there. Laughs all round, laughs of recognition.

Story of two elderly couples, the women in the kitchen making a cuppa, the blokes in the lounge, talking.

'We went to a restaurant over your way last night, quite good, you'd like it.'

'Oh, what's it called?'

'It's … it's … ah … what's that flower? You know, the one with the thorns?'

'Rose?'

'Yes, that's it.' And he turns to the kitchen and shouts, 'Rose, what's the name of that restaurant we went to last night?'

We laugh, the only thing to do – and do crosswords and sudoku and the quiz to keep grey matter ticking over. Declare being unable to remember someone's name deserves its own condition. Namelossness? Namacognosis? Denametia? Somewhere at the back of the laugh is the recognition that it's of age, not self. Nicks and tears in memory like the scars and tears of aging bodies. The little stiffness getting out of bed in the morning. My knee with the ACL reconstruction doomed to deteriorate, a shoulder not quite happy from a skiing mistake, a hip addicted to bursitis, a touch of arthritis in the hands, inherited Dupuytren's giving early notice of a slow contraction of the hand into a claw. And I'm in good shape, we laugh. Those only a little older awash with joint replacements and stents. Commence conversations with an organ recital.

The faltering performance. The arms that could swing from monkey bars for hours – you wouldn't want to have to depend on them holding you now. Those safe hands of mine – the dropped 159 keys down the lift well. (The red 159 sports wagon, a diesel, so much low grunt. Vince, the man who looked after all my Alfas, asked how we were enjoying it. His wife had the same model. We were loving it, I told him, but the diesel, it didn't sound like an Alfa. 'That's the way they mostly sound in Italy,' he said. The old preconceptions we carry with us.) Pegs at the line. The glass of two mobile phones crazed. No, not the start of Parkinson's, just joints and reflexes.

A family wedding tradition that started with my brother Terry's: the morning of, the menfolk would play sport. Squash for Terry's and my wedding; clay pigeons for Tracy-Ann's – Gavin was a grade tennis player, we feared he'd be far too good; basketball for Nick's; beach cricket for Dom's; touch footy for Chris'. The ball still good in my hands but a half gap and a hamstring torn. 'The mind making promises the body can't deliver.'

We had a badminton court marked up in the Petrie yard. Dad would play, competitive. Mum concerned about him trying too hard. I didn't know he had heart trouble until after he had died, my strong father.

And now – there's paranoia left behind by cancer if you let it. Am I a bit out of breath because the hill is steep or something else? I'm tired, did I get enough sleep? Is this normal tired? Is that a lump?

There's no simple test for lymphoma yet, no easy telltale marker in the bloods to look for. A matter of keeping an eye on your general health in case it comes back. A recipe for paranoia if you let it. Don't. I'm OK.

Add COVID. Is that a bit of a sore throat? Cough? Other people in a crowd coughing? We had practice with self-isolation and increased hygiene during chemo. Judy my guardian, stricter than I would be. No going into restaurants, tickets for a concert given away. Being COVID aware a little more of the same.

The chemo has left me with a drier mouth. Tastebuds have returned to normal, or what I remember as normal, but there's a shortage of saliva that wakes me in the night and means many mornings start with a throat that's a little raw. More raw than normal? Should I get a test?

Or perhaps the often raspy throat is something else. It was a top and tail session with Sandra. While her colonoscope was discovering the ulcer, the ironically named endoscope down the gullet found Barrett's oesophagus instead of Pascoe's. About 0.5 per cent chance of turning into a cancer, maybe or maybe not about the same chance that hosting the rona would kill me.

But I'm OK. Really. It's going to be fine.

When there was kerfuffling about who would get what vaccine in what order, I idly filled in an ABC website form that was supposed to indicate where you would be in the queue.

One of the 'yes' or 'no' boxes was 'diseases of the blood', including lymphoma 'diagnosed within the past five years'. That bumped a fella up from Group Three to Group Two. The people marshalling vaccine queues weren't assuming cure or the immune system coming back in a hurry.

An interesting concept that living five years is a cure. That's not quite right – it's being cancer-free for five years that's a cure. Time.

Alison learning fast in the first couple of weeks about her brain cancer, expectations rising from one year to between three and five. And, the doctors told her, they have one patient who has been in remission for five years. One. If given a choice between lymphoma and glioblastoma, grab the lymphoma.

A pleasant surprise from Luke at the last check-up, the 18-month turned 21-month check-up. The medical statisticians and better chemo have been at work revising data: 24 months cancer-free after the end of treatment, not five years, puts me back on my cohort's life expectancy. I've not been impressed by my cohort's longevity lately, but that sounds good.

The echocardiogram finds a valve leaking a bit, but not much, something to see a cardiologist about at some stage. Bloods are all good, you're going well.

And several days later, an email.

Dear Michael

There were two odd cells on your last blood test. These are not lymphoma cells.

It is best to check this with a repeat blood count (as attached). I am not sure when you are back in Sydney but if you could have it done then it would be appreciated.

Thanks
Luke

Glenalba

Terry wrote a letter of advice as I was about to sit the Senior exams. Terry, the generous big brother I idolised, the First XV captain, to me what Tom was to Jim, wrote in terms we best understood then – a rugby analogy, perhaps a rugby cliché over the years. Never mind that I didn't get the letter until the eve of my final exam, the intent was good and has stayed with me. I've refined it, deleting references to the possible inadequacies of coaches and referees, the pain or exaltation of the last hit, the noise from the sideline.

You play the game in front of you. What has happened doesn't matter, what might happen later doesn't matter, the eventual score doesn't matter, it's what's happening now that matters. You do what needs to be done now. You do it.

The life lesson of an old-school tight forward: you get up from the bottom of the ruck and run to the next one.

Up early, top up petrol, be gone – that's the plot.

Somehow it's not early, and laughing at the silliness of the motel remote slows me. There is no hurry. Find a likely looking cafe and have the full breakfast and passable coffee – the eggs over easy, thick bacon, more bacon than I would cook for myself, fried tomato, mushrooms, hash brown, thick-cut toast. Sun through the window. Another coffee. Read the papers on my phone. No hurry at all.

On the road again. A brilliant morning. Resist the temptation to find out what Boonoo Boonoo is like along the Mount Lindesay Road – that'd be an address to have, Boonoo Boonoo – or scale our biggest granite monolith, Bald Rock, a couple of football fields high and several long. Granite close to the surface in the lean high country, cliffs, boulders littering paddocks, thrusting slabs.

The border, Wallangarra, Queensland, soon enough. There used to be a tick gate here, you'd be stopped to check you weren't smuggling fruit flies. Gone now, just signs to warn about carrying fruit as you approach the Granite Belt, Queensland's home of stone fruit and apples and grapes and wineries, some not bad now, some good. Up through the thorpes – Stanthorpe and Applethorpe.

There's a faint sense of disappointment, a frustration, after the border. You've been driving to Queensland but when you get there, it's still three hours to Brisbane, closer to five to Sunshine Beach. This final stretch an annoyance. 'How much longer? Are we there yet?' And the road quality perceptibly deteriorates – Queensland a bigger state, more decentralised with fewer people, with less money for maintenance and dual highways. More fatalities per capita. More road safety signs admonishing drivers.

REST OR R.I.P.
DRIVER FATIGUE CRASH ZONE NEXT 95KM
BETTER TO BE LATE THAN DEAD ON TIME

78 FATIGUE ACCIDENTS LAST 5 YEARS
AND COUNTING

'Block' McMeniman was from a property around Stanthorpe. We were in the same team for four years, a powerful winger, a fine hurdler. Haven't seen or heard of him since the day I finished school.

I had an unusual mix of subjects and finished the Senior public exam a day before anyone else. 'That'd be right, Pascoe – your luck!' Dad and Brian, home on a rare brief visit, came to pick me up, Brian giving a smiling nod of acknowledgement to the lines on my honour blazer, schoolboy triumphs, schoolboy ego, on the last day I would wear it. I was the only one leaving while everyone else was cramming for their next exam, saying goodbye after four years to mates and those of the teachers I liked or at least respected. Gap years didn't exist in 1972. There were no big graduation events, no formals with stretch limos and pre and after parties. Just four years that came and went quickly and stayed forever, a well you didn't know you carried within until you found yourself peering into it, drawing from it.

The Texas Road heads west from Stanthorpe, an hour along it to Texas on the Dumaresq River, a name you'd never know how to pronounce if you didn't know how to pronounce it. Peter Deery bedevilled my jumping in the final selection trial for the Firsts, we both ended up in the Seconds, Peter a prop, me at number 8. We were in *Endgame* together in Year 11, won the Brisbane Arts Theatre Jean Trundle Memorial Prize. His family had the Story Bridge Hotel in Brisbane. Did medicine and died young and alone in his Texas surgery one night. Another ghost down another road.

I guess I would know someone in most districts of Queensland, maybe every district. Or know of someone in every district, someone who was at school around my time or with one of my brothers or nephews, connected with 1.85 million square kilometres of the state and up into PNG.

I couldn't wait to get out of Brisbane, away from all that connectivity, off to the adventure of the world, to get away from the claustrophobia of everyone knowing everyone. Go out with a girl and be subjected to an inquisition on one degree of separation. There was no question about moving to Sydney when we came back to Australia, of getting away from the closeness and certainty of the solicitors we went to school with giving work to the barristers we went to school with and using the accountants we went to school with and the doctors and real estate agents and architects, or the lawyers and accountants and doctors we had played rugby against, of whose sister was married to what cousin.

And now you find these men taking care of each other, knowing who needs some help, who has had troubles, friendships and community I had left behind for the isolation of perhaps living more broadly but certainly more shallowly.

First year at *The Courier-Mail*, trying so hard to be older, wiser, harder. Drinking black coffee, smoking non-filter cigarettes, growing a beard, trying to grow a beard. Kev O'Donohue was the deputy chief of staff and cadet counsellor, experienced, charitable and wise. I said something that was meant to be smart. Michael, he said, don't be cynical. Be sceptical, you have a duty to be sceptical, but don't be cynical. If you're cynical, you can't recognise good when you do see it.

Time.

Through the thorpes to Warwick. John O'Brien from the class of '72 was from Warwick. Not the poet – a family of accountants, I think.

I was booked in the Alfa 164 in Warwick on its first long drive – didn't mean to be speeding, doing nothing, just accelerated a bit faster than I realised, than legal, after a food stop. You lose perspective about speed through the towns after the highway, the 164's V6 effortlessly deceptive. Judy couldn't believe it, accused the copper of just wanting to stop the Alfa, probably hadn't booked one before. It was all right. Remember it every time I turn that Warwick corner and careful to never speed there.

After Warwick the New England Highway heads to Toowoomba, but you take the sweeper onto the Cunningham Highway for Brisbane. A prime intersection for fatalities that one. Country boys coming down from Toowoomba inexplicably not heeding the stop sign. And you find machinery at work, finally building an overpass, a monument to the killed.

Cunninghams Gap ahead, select D for the Giulia and enjoy the twisting hill climb around crawling trucks going up, feel the g-forces under acceleration and in the bends. Thick forest, always listen for the sound of bellbirds ringing near the top on the eastern side, past the rest area with its tracks enticing you to walk deeper into the rainforest and be lost. And more slowly down, trucks in low gear, limited overtaking opportunities, as often as not part of the road blocked by a rockfall. Slow enough to lower your windows to listen for the bellbirds and Henry Kendall. Judy could rattle it off in the pretty schoolgirl cadence she had learned it.

By channels of coolness the echoes are calling,
And down the dim gorges I hear the creek falling;
It lives in the mountain where moss and the sedges
Touch with their beauty the banks and the ledges.
Through breaks of the cedar and sycamore bowers
Struggles the light that is love to the flowers;
And, softer than slumber, and sweeter than singing,
The notes of the bell-birds are running and ringing.[16]

Pull off at the crest and listen for them. There's time, plenty of time. Stretch and take the track into the forest, one of the walks, and find the road disappears in no time in this cool and ancient rainforest of no time, drawing the walker in. All the haste of the road lost in trees and ferns and earth, in its age and our irrelevance.

Down from the Gap, you're in Jim's country, his new country. Warrill View registers with me now. Can't miss seeing the turn-off promising 'historic site Cunningham Lookout in 3'. Can't forget his grin in the dual cab – a bit of a 'conservationist'. It's different country, his last country.

I've googled Glenalba, a real estate agent's 'sold' listing. The Maranoa district, 20 kilometres from Mitchell, 110 kilometres to Roma, 9721.4 hectares or 24,022 acres. Bitumen road access now, rural power, mobile phone reception.

It changed hands again, old cowboy. There are photographs of a good season, lush grass, cattle, red soil, dam full, a lone boab tree you'd know, Jim. The best shot is of a creek, mud brown, a bower of river gums. Jim's paradise. There would be yabbies in it for catching with a piece of string and a scrap of meat. Dad would tell me about the monster yabbies in the channels out

307

west when I would bring back a few from the gully in the police station paddock. You'd have swum in that creek, the youngster Jim, back from boarding school to the calming freedom of the bush, back from the nuns who bullied you in Mitchell and then Nudgee, 600 kilometres away. Without incident, 14 hours or so on the old Westlander train – did you look out the window at the Rosewood stop and ever guess you'd end up not far away? Out through Toowoomba and Dalby and Miles and Roma to Mitchell and then a boy could run free, roam free by himself, run and ride with his big brother.

March 16, 11.50 pm

Jim

You know it scares me when you go silent. Hanging in there?

Michael

March 17, 12.25 pm

G'day Michael

My silence scares myself.
    I've tried to write but the well is sort of dry.
    I really appreciate your communication and your visits.
    Hopefully I will and can write again.
    Don't give up on me.

Love Jim

March 18, 6.34 pm

No danger of giving up on you – too scared you might come back and haunt me!

What's your bedtime on Sunday evening if I was passing by in search of a little wi-fi?

March 18, 6.41 pm

Dear Michael

Good to hear from you again. I won't give up on you and I won't haunt you.

We are often still up at 10–10.30 pm, so if we had a reason to be up, we would make sure we were.

Hope all is well with you and family.

We muddle on some days easier than others.

Let me know your plans and we will try and fit in with them.

Love Jim

Jim

Jim is in a hospital bed set up in the back room, up against the window that is most of the back wall. The land is terraced at the rear, so the bottom of the window, the height of the bed, is nearly level with the backyard where his two dogs run about or lie and wait and watch him – mainly lie and watch. Where little Victor plays and Sue hoses the plants around the perimeter. Lying in that bed, he's close to the grass and the dogs and sky and trees at the back of their suburban home.

April 25, 8.08 am

Sue, Jo and Catherine

Thank you for the great honour of speaking about Jim yesterday. As I was wondering about how to put the prayer in context, I thought Jim would want me to do it for you three, to present words for you about your wonderful man. In our letters, it came out that Jim envied my ability to talk, while I was jealous of his rugby ability and courage – we always want the strengths we don't have. He said he would have loved to have spoken at family weddings, at Tom's funeral, but he just could not. So I hoped I was doing this for him.

But I also tried to speak on behalf of his friends and particularly his Nudgee mates – that brotherhood that was formed the better part of half a century ago and that became deeper in recent years. In the case of Sergio and Jim, they met in 1968. What a very fine pair of men indeed, with so much respect and love for each other. And I confess I spoke for myself. Jim was so quick to question ego – he always saw right through me – so I have to tell you I was proud to be able to (metaphorically) stand there with him one more time, to share your love of him.

For your record, the following is what I tried to remember to say yesterday. I forgot a few lines. And I couldn't quite work in something else I wanted to mention – his respect and care for his animals and land, something that went to his soul. But it is what it is:

Jim's Prayer of St Francis

I haven't met anyone stronger or tougher than Jim McCormack – Mitchell tough. His physical strength and athletic prowess I was jealous of at school, on the rugby field, but his real strength, his strength of character and will, has been inspirational for all since he was diagnosed with cancer.

I've long said if you were ever in a trench, you'd want Jim beside you. Where many would freeze or flee, Jim would step up, step forward to do what needed to be done, whether it was stopping a burglary at his neighbour's house or stopping traffic to help a toddler in danger, he just did it.

So none stronger or tougher – but also none softer or gentler.

Jim was a kind, forgiving man. Over recent months, we've shared a correspondence that has perhaps gone deeper than what we blokes normally manage, maybe because it was in writing rather than spoken. What was clear in that writing is that Jim brought his considerable intelligence to bear on people with overwhelming empathy. The cruelties that people suffered hurt him, he felt their pain.

He made excuses for people. He'd had his own battles; he knew how hard things could be.

I think everyone knows he hadn't had a drink since he was 30 – something that takes great strength and courage to achieve. What many people wouldn't know is that as a young man he suffered extreme anxiety, something he faced and conquered every day. There was no professional help in the bush then – still isn't much. He tried self-medicating with alcohol, which didn't turn out to be a good idea. So it was his own force of will, his great core strength, that defeated it.

He'd also be pained to hear me saying these things about him as he was particularly self-effacing, very wary of ego.

In the death notices, we all end up as 'loving husband of', 'loving father of', but Jim really was. What mattered to him above all was loving his girls, his family, his friends, and their love of him. He didn't fear death, but he regretted that he wouldn't be able to help and watch over his family. He was annoyed sometimes that his fine athlete's body let him down. Just a week or so before he died, he was disappointed that he couldn't help round up the last of his cattle, he was worried that Jo had to do it on a horse by herself. He was worried about her. But Jim taught Jo and Catherine to ride, so he really didn't need to worry about them and horses.

Spiritually, Jim, like many of us, became unstructured over the years, but he did have a favourite prayer, a prayer that he wanted read out today, a prayer that explains much of Jim. It was a prayer he tried to live by, the Prayer of St Francis.

Lord, make me an instrument of your peace.
Where there is hatred, let me sow love;
where there is injury, pardon;
where there is doubt, faith;
where there is despair, hope;
where there is darkness, light;
where there is sadness, joy.

O divine Master, grant that I may not so much seek
to be consoled as to console,
to be understood as to understand,
to be loved as to love.
For it is in giving that we receive,
it is in pardoning that we are pardoned,
and it is in dying that we are born to eternal life.

Amen.

He tried to live by that prayer – and he did.

Love
Michael

April 26, 12.08 am

Dear Michael

Thank you so much for sending your words to us. They are such a comfort to us and we are so pleased to have them. I sent them on to Jim's mother and brother and sister and they equally treasure them and thank you for being so thoughtful.

Life is very hard for the three of us. Maybe the adrenalin is wearing off and we are left feeling very sad. My longing to have Jim back, to hold his hand, is so overpowering – I want the comfort of his physical presence. He always comforted us in our times of need and it just feels so wrong that he is not here with us.

Jo, Ben and Victor went to the farm today with my niece and her husband and three boys. Jo was filled with sadness riding without Jim. The day has been full of things that only Jim would know what to do about – a brown snake in the house yard that went under the house, and one of our horses, Buddy, collapsed in the paddock but then recovered. Jim always said I would have to sell the farm, that it would be too much for me, and today I thought he was right. But we will soldier on – I don't want to make any big decisions for 12 months or so and I couldn't part with the farm emotionally yet – the whole place is Jim.

Jo, Catherine and I have a strong desire to keep close to you and Serge and a few of Jim's other friends, a way of keeping a connection with Jim and because you are such wonderful people.

I hope you are having a good break, Michael, and thank you again for your email.

Take care.

Love Sue xx

Spirit rising

He knew he was going and did so quietly, calmly, helped by pain relief, strong to the end.

My words weren't Jim's eulogy – Jo and Catherine did that, said they were left with the inheritance for their lives' guidance of being able to ask: WWJD? What would Jim do? Sue had asked me to read the prayer and said they'd welcome any words I wanted to put around that, anything I wanted to say. The business and ritual of words, attempts to capture lives in a few sentences, to balm, to hurt.

Jim and Sue planned his service with my brother. In a funeral parlour, not a church. Jim's music, 'Old People Singing'.

Time.

The vignettes that flash by make a drive. A field daubed pink and grey by galahs now on the right. A few months ago it would have been bright yellow with canola, or covered in giant sunflowers. Near the Amberley turn-off, a man, a farmer under a battered hat, a figure in the bare, tilled landscape, walking down the dirt drive towards his house, a modest Queenslander. Déjà vu, only it's FNQ: a drive the back way from Cairns to Port Douglas, passing a school bus coming towards me and then a boy in a wide floppy school hat walking down the gravel driveway to his home, another modest Queenslander, but set back, half in rainforest. A depth of green around it, afternoon sun, the kid in shorts and sandals and I'm back in Petrie, barefoot, coming home from school, down Old Dayboro Road past the Queensland public service cream hall that was the police station and court of petty sessions, where Dad might be behind his desk wearing heavy-looking black-rimmed glasses. Across to the police station house, the dog waiting, my first duty to check in after school. The only unforgiveable crime was not to come pretty much straight home from school – Graeme Thorne's murder scarred a generation of parents. The gun, lighting the fire in the paddock, all Mum's cosmetics tipped in the bath, smoking, the paint under the house were all misdemeanours, but when the new monkey bars and gym set was installed and the big kids monopolised it, I waited till after school and they left and I climbed and swung and slid down the pole. 'Wait till your father gets home.' Dad whipped me with the cord of his electric razor, left a U-shaped red welt on the back of my leg, the only time I was belted.

Check in with Mum, grab biscuits, spoonsful of Milo and be gone till dark, down the river with Neville King, swimming in the gravel pits, riding bikes, hunting things, making things, breaking things.

I'm skipping Brisbane, passing through it on the freeways and tunnels, passing up the ridges and valleys of the town and the galvanised roofs and jumbled subtropical gardens, skipping people for Sunshine Beach, skipping the rituals of catching up, the canon of talking about the weather. There was a time when the weather talk annoyed me, made me impatient to be gone, when visiting Brisbane meant several sets of people, several sets of conversations and each one including the litany of the weather – the heat/the rain or lack thereof. It was a phase, it passed. I came to settle back into it, to appreciate it as social ceremony, a means of talking. In the bush it was as predictable as a handshake, almost an acknowledgement of country. 'Had rain?' 'Country's looking good.' 'It was looking dry through the New England.'

An Irish friend told me it was worse whenever he went home. 'How's the weather? You've got to ask. And it's always appalling!'

I wonder if we brought the cadences of our country weather talk into town or it was ever thus, when rain meant there was water in the tank and everyone could have fresh bathwater.

The road, the Bruce Highway, no longer passes through Petrie but you cross the North Pine River further down its course. My Tom Sawyer river. Neville King and I made a raft from the bamboo clump in the paddock one summer holidays. We were only nine or ten. Chopping down bamboo with tomahawks, some oil cans Dad had acquired for flotation, lashing it together with wire and somehow, God knows how, getting it down the river slung over our bikes. Our lashings were rubbish, the thing all over the place, our skinny legs slipping through bamboo, as much in the river as out. We'd need to rethink how we'd bind it. Tied it up to a pecan tree above the rapids and the next day the rain started, a flood took it away. I think we were relieved.

Crab pots and exploration, smoking cigarettes under the railway bridge, loving the noise, screaming against the noise as trains rolled over, putting a halfpenny on the line and then not being able to find it.

There's a fresh shrine on the northern side of the bridge, the other side. Flowers still alive, plenty of them. A quick death.

Another early, early memory: Driving back from Redcliffe at night in Uncle Emmett's car, a two-tone green FE Holden he bought new and kept for years, the seats covered in heavy plastic, a sticker on the quarter window for the hitchhikers he never passed by: *The pleasure's mine, the benefit's yours, but when you alight, don't slam the bloody doors!* We slowed down, cars, the police car, a tow truck, spotlight on the other side of the road, a little bridge over a creek – probably Fresh Water Creek – and a car's boot sticking up from the water. It was winter, cold, mist about the creek and Dad wearing his baggy swimming togs on the edge, seeing us, seeing me, waving us off, calling something to Emmett.

Talked about that with Jim at the Ascot/Clayfield Gentlepersons' Coffee Club once – the pros and cons of a quick death compared with his drawn-out sentence, the long notice of intention to quit. He said he appreciated the opportunity to prepare his girls, to try to make sense of things, some order. He was grateful for that, he said. Mostly, though, it was whatever hand you were dealt, it wasn't your choice. Every death the individual's, no-one else's to judge.

I think there's something in Terry's idea that we mostly die well. Nothing like death to sharply focus your priorities, on what's most important in life. That and a depth of culture and instinct in us for handling death better than we expect, if we still have our marbles, if there's not too much pain. There's sometimes denial, but nothing embarrassing. Whatever other changes we've made, we've inherited tens of thousands of years of breeding, of inculcation to praise a good death, to glorify the warrior's death, the martyr's. Our survival and success as a species at times, as tribes, has depended on a willingness to die bravely. Evolution at work, never mind inventing religions of every shade to tame death, to fashion it into a doorway to something more. I'm over religion, over the dress-ups and hypocrisy, the outrageous sexism of all of them. I used to wonder how women could support The Church, something so explicitly sexist – and it followed to ask myself how I could support something so explicitly sexist. Ditto homophobic. I'll talk to my God, my saints, but I'm past the old men's power clubs. Yet the culture underpinning religion remains in us.

Life might be but a poor player, but even the poorest player wouldn't want to botch their last performance. We're more likely to rise to the seriousness of the occasion than collapse and go whimpering. It's the living more likely to handle dying badly, the living feeling the pain. Tracy-Ann said the hardest part of Gavin's death was always seeing the grief in her children from missing their dad, for growing up without a father.

We're constantly dealing, only a card from it. Standing on the edge of the gutter in a city street and a bus's wing mirror flies by level with my head. A stumble, a shove – and gone. A mind obliterated. A card's thickness, a fraction of a millimetre, the size of a cancerous cell, the thickness of a blood vessel wall in your brain, a weakness, an aneurysm. Make a cherry out of a busted balloon: spread the latex over your mouth, suck it in, close your lips, twist the balloon to capture the air, a cherry. Rub it with your teeth to make it annoyingly squeak, bite a little too hard with sharp young teeth and pop the aneurysm – you're dead. Or sometimes worse.

A virus, a fraction of a fraction of a millimetre, blindly hunting the vaguely 'pre-existing conditions' and the old, mutating to hunt the young as well. A mysterious virus that barely kisses some and imperils others indefinitely. A wee thing that can overcome entire health systems if it is allowed to, if priorities are wrong.

I'm driving now with Death snoozing in the passenger seat, riding in all the cars coming towards me, riding pillion on the motorbikes, mopping up around the fresh shrine. Wave. Or give him the finger. Doesn't matter.

Sudden death's a depth charge for the living. A partner's world torn apart in the instant, a family's certainty shattered. The emotional equivalent of bTBI, blast-induced traumatic brain injury, the 'signature injury' of Iraq and Afghanistan. And all those poor shell-shocked bastards from earlier wars told it was psychological and now they find it is physical, deep neurological damage in the grey goop. Cut loose from your spouse's anchor, cut loose if there aren't other ropes, other threads, left with your own mortality and its challenges. Not scared of death, only of pain. Everyone's death their own. Not to be judged. Not to be known.

Sue came down to Sydney to visit Catherine a few months after Jim's service and we all had dinner, and again at Christmas. She was back at work, glad for that. In July there was a conference in Sydney. I picked her up in the Giulia, drove to dinner for Sydney's best pizza at La Disfida in Haberfield. 'It's a beautiful car. You like your toys, Michael,' she said without malice, a woman used to speaking directly, wanting the comfort of talking at depth, of explaining how much she missed Jim, missed his presence, the ability to touch his hand. Work was good, it was good to be working, the girls were good, Victor, but the emptiness was endless.

In late spring, an email. Sue and Jo had bought 30 cattle. I called. She slept on the farm by herself the first night, wanting to keep them in the home paddock, wanted to be sure they settled down, but they had accidentally left the gate open anyway. Laughed. It didn't matter, it was fine, but Jim wouldn't have forgotten that. It felt good, buying the cattle, having them on the farm.

There are tethers for her, good tethers.

In the Ramtop village where they dance the real Morris dance, for example, they believe that no-one is finally dead until the ripples they cause in the world die away – until the clock he wound up winds down, until the wine she made has finished its ferment, until the crop they planted is harvested. The span of someone's life, they say, is only the core of their actual existence.[17]

A sentence from one of author/philosopher/satirist Terry Pratchett's Discworld novels, *Reaper Man*, rings long and true – the farm and Jim and life.

My younger sister reminds us on the siblings' WhatsApp chat it is the 85th anniversary of our parents' wedding, the official beginning of our family. 'Aren't we (and our children) all so lucky,' she writes.

Yes, fortunate indeed to have such heritage – to be their legacy. And sometimes when the wind is blowing, there is whisper to deserve it, a responsibility, a pressure to pass it on.

Quickest to stay on the Bruce Highway until the Eumundi turn-off, but the day is grand and warm and cloudless so turn instead at Yandina, through the green of the Maroochy River valley, through cane fields, to the coast at Coolum, the David Low Way up to Sunshine, the snatches of long, empty beach around Castaways and Sunrise to Sunshine. The ocean the deepest navy further out, shades of sky blue closer to the aquamarine surf and wash rolling, rolling in.

Somehow it's mid-afternoon. From the balcony there's the vista south to Peregian and north from the flags to the national park headland, the waves bursting on the rocks, spray to the skies. The nor'-easter is in, probably bringing a few bluebottles among the surfers. I'm tired. The swim can wait. It will be good to do our usual sunset walk on the beach later, the ritual up to the headland, pick up shells, a stick to sketch the eternal stretched S of waves and a woman's curves – the red slash from the Carmen LP cover. Touch the rocks at the end together and we'd walk back. A beer and fish and chips at the surf club. I'll be awake early anyway when the paracetamol wears off, the hip annoying and a dry mouth and persistent morning cough I need to get checked. Sunrise over the Pacific glorious with morning cloud, pinks and purples and golds reflecting darkly on the wet sand. It's the time to scatter the ashes, if you're scattering ashes, before the onshore wind starts and blows the powder back over you. You want this offshore breeze, the land breeze, that helps stand the waves up, that catches the spray and combs it back from the curling crests, that can pick up the pages of your scrapbook and scatter them away to eternity.

The Morning Star paled slowly, the Cross hung low to the sea,
And down the shadowy reaches the tide came swirling free,
The lustrous purple blackness of the soft Australian night,
Waned in the grey awakening that heralded the light[18]

The surf dark beneath it, the water unfathomable, unknowable and endless and empty.

The call

L uke calls. It's two weeks since the second blood test.
'Hello, Michael. How are you?'
'Well, you tell me – how's that blood test?'

It was clear. No 'odd' cells. All good. Two more months to make the two years that drop me back with my cohort on the bell curve.

Take the odds as Alison and Philip now take theirs, as millions do, as we all do. We're born to this.

You're never too young to die. And Alison, a young 60, starts radio this week with a brief text: Saw oncologist so two to five years. He said to think more like two than five for my bucket list but there is a bell curve and I could well fall on the latter side. Basically he said it's shit, which I liked him for saying.

She's strong, I'll wager will stay strong, living dying.

There's time.

'Do you remember the lily lake?
We were all there, all five of us in love,
Not one yet killed, widowed or broken-hearted.'[19]

WE GATHER TO REMEMBER, CELEBRATE AND GIVE THANKS FOR THE LIFE OF

Tom McCormack

16.07.52 - 05.11.13

In Loving Memory of

James Robert McCormack

10.12.1955 – 19.04.2016

POSTSCRIPTS

The river

Sue

Hello. Hope the Brisbane heat hasn't been getting to you – I was talking to my sister Annette – they were changing the power poles outside her place on Thursday, she couldn't even have a fan on. Or have you been down the farm applying ice packs to the cattle?

Meanwhile, there's a decision to be made about the attached manuscript. The odds are it won't be published, that it will purely be for domestic consumption. But in case it is published, Jim wrote that he wanted to be anonymous. I don't think he should be. He can't vote now in the fullness of seeing what I've tried to write, but you can, so it's your decision.

It's pretty much finished. Some tidying to do, but pretty much there. The computer ate my original email history, luckily I had copied and pasted our correspondence, but the group jokes and bemusements are lost. I've only changed a couple of things in the emails, a couple of minor corrections, a couple of names changed or omitted for the privacy of the innocent.

Anyway, I am sorry if this causes you pain to read. It caused me pain to write at times. But it is what it is, as Jim might say.

Let me know about that decision.

Love
Michael

Dear Michael

Thank you so much for this. It is a wonderful record for us to have.

You offered Jim such friendship during his last months. I will be forever grateful. You gave him occupation in the hours when he could not sleep or work and you made him laugh and gave him an opportunity to process what was happening and his life.

Your writing about your growing up has brought so many memories to light for me – of Redcliffe school buses and Nudgee dances and your father doing the washing, my father with his two jobs, electrician by day, night shift at the Petrie paper mill, then doing the washing for his seven children and he was never appreciated – we only saw what he lacked as a father.

The girls and I agree that you should use Jim's name.

Talk soon, Michael, and thank you

Love
Sue

The paper mill has long since closed, a university's branch campus is being established on the site. When we first moved to Petrie, people would drive from Brisbane to swim and picnic by the river down the hill from our house. Old Mr Sweeney, possessor of a World War 1 German soldier's helmet and other souvenirs of his time, had a small kiosk that rented canoes and sold ice-creams and sometimes gave one to a mischievous small boy who had run away from home down to the river to visit him and Mrs Sweeney, to see the helmet. Theirs was the only house down the hill from us, built on high stumps, cut off by the occasional flood. I taught myself to dog paddle in that river by watching Pal, Terry's dog, the dog that dived into long grass just in front of me in the paddock to seize the brown snake I would have stepped on.

Cars ventured further as the roads improved, discovered the North Coast before it became the Sunshine Coast. The mill did the river's water quality no favours either – a stink sometimes, tidal below the rapids – but we still went crabbing. People stopped coming, the kiosk closed. We would swim in the deep gravel pits instead, swinging out over the water on a rope from a tree, working up the nerve to fold into a dive instead of bombing.

The river still bumps over the tame little rapids above which a rickety bamboo raft once was briefly tethered, but it's mown parkland now, Sweeney Reserve. The country town of my boyhood is not even an outer suburb as change rolls on, as the land absorbs and waits, we passing ghosts irrelevant.

Nixon and Chilli

We thought we would not have another dog, that Max could not be simply replaced. And there would be the commitment of a dog tying us to the nest as it otherwise was emptying. And the mess of training a puppy again and the backyard no longer a toilet.

In time we bought another dog, or, more accurately, were acquired by him. I was away for work more, Judy felt the emptiness of the house coming home, missed the canine companionship, there was the knowledge that walking the dog was a good thing for all, I had grown up in a family that always included a dog, a dog as much a part of a house as a yard.

But we didn't take the advice of Silverdene Emblem O'Neill's Last Will and Testament:

One last request I earnestly make. I have heard my Mistress say,

> *'When Blemie dies we must never have another dog. I love him so much I could never love another one.' Now I would ask her, for love of me, to have another. It would be a poor tribute to my memory never to have a dog again. What I would like to feel is that, having once had me in the family, now she cannot live without a dog! I have never had a narrow jealous spirit. I have always held that most dogs are good (and one cat, the black one I have permitted to share the living-room rug during the evenings, whose affection I have tolerated in a kindly spirit, and in rare sentimental moods, even reciprocated*

a trifle). Some dogs, of course, are better than others.
Dalmatians, naturally, as everyone knows, are best.

So I suggest a Dalmatian as my successor. He can hardly be
as well bred, or as well mannered or as distinguished and
handsome as I was in my prime. My Master and Mistress must
not ask the impossible. But he will do his best, I am sure, and
even his inevitable defects will help by comparison to keep my
memory green. To him I bequeath my collar and leash and
my overcoat and raincoat, made to order in 1929 at Hermes
in Paris. He can never wear them with the distinction I did,
walking around the Place Vendome, or later along Park
Avenue, all eyes fixed on me in admiration; but again I am sure
he will do his utmost not to appear a mere gauche provincial
dog. Here on the ranch, he may prove himself quite worthy of
comparison, in some respects. He will, I presume, come closer to
jackrabbits than I have been able to in recent years.

And, for all his faults, I hereby wish him the happiness I
know will be his in my old home.

One last word of farewell, Dear Master and Mistress.
Whenever you visit my grave, say to yourselves with regret but
also with happiness in your hearts at the remembrance of my
long happy life with you: 'Here lies one who loved us and whom
we loved.' No matter how deep my sleep I shall hear you, and
not all the power of death can keep my spirit from wagging a
grateful tail.[20]

And that is the way death should be. But, no, we did not follow
Blemie's advice. Somehow another dalmatian would be trying
to replace Max and he couldn't. There were practicalities:

dalmatians aren't small dogs, and Max was taller and stronger than most of his breed. A smaller dog would be easier to control on walks as we got older, easier to care for – less going in would mean less coming out – and at some stage there would be the prospect of downsizing.

So I went to look at cavoodle puppies, the poodle/cavalier cross being all the rage at the time, promising not to shed and a particularly happy temperament.

Turns out you're a harder man than me if you can go to merely 'look at' puppies, especially if among a group of Ewok-impersonating cavoodles there is one who came out very spaniel, a tricolour with a longer snout and legs than a King Charles. So you go home with a dog that will both shed and need clipping.

He was nameless for two weeks. Judy liked Jaspar. Tim, our youngest son, came home from a year in North America and declared him to be Nixon, that Jaspar was a cat's name. And if you caught the pup looking serious, he did indeed look a little like Tricky Dicky.

But the journey that forms us rolls on. We didn't acquire another dalmatian – our son Dominic did. Our grandchildren are growing up with Chilli, a most noble and forbearing dog. A happy, loved dog, a generous soul, an excellent companion for a walk or to have lie on your rug, a great help in the kitchen in case anything dropped and needed cleaning up.

And, in time, maybe a bit earlier than Judy wanted to, a real estate agent talked us into selling our family home of 23 years. Nixon adapted easily to having a paved courtyard rather than a lawn, doesn't seem to miss the yard as Max would have, as a younger dalmatian would. We take pleasure in meeting a fine local spotty dog on our walks or waiting for coffee. We also acknowledge to ourselves that he, like the splendid Chilli, is a good deal more to handle than Nixon.

It would not be true to say the old house was our Glenalba, our country. It wasn't our lives. But much of our story had happened in that home, there were lives invested in it, warm ghosts in those walls and doorways, looking from and in the windows.

I left a note for the new owners, a couple with two children.

Congratulations – you now own a home that, even allowing for our bias, is very special indeed. We never tired of that view, of having the city and bridge and Woodford Bay laid out before us in all its changing moods and patterns, whether watching a southerly roll in or a sunset gild the towers. And on the other side, the oval is joy. In any other suburb, to front onto the park would be a wonderful thing in itself.

Enjoy the space and its potential. It has been a wonderful place for dinners both quiet and raucous, for New Year's fireworks, for 18th and 21st parties, for wakes and christenings, for pre-wedding gatherings and farewells.

I hope your children will enjoy it as much as ours have and appreciate the area in general, join the local sports teams and form lifelong friendships over mud and balls and nets and water. It has been a great house for children to bring friends home to, both as little kids and young adults.

The studies have been places of creativity for us, places to think and maybe grow. Events were recorded, thoughts shared, stories imagined. I hope the muses of your fields take up residence there as well.

Photograph

Downsizing is going around. My younger sister, Tracy-Ann, needed to unload what she could of all the stuff that had filled her big house of five children. Among it, what was left of our mother's collection of school annuals. Some were missing, victims of a past flood and silverfish, but the 1971 Nudgee annual survived. It included the official version of the Sydney football tour and a photograph of the 16As. Serge, Jim, Kev, me and the others in a small black-and-white photograph. It surprised me – we look like such young boys, mere boys.

We were just boys, boys forming bonds we didn't know existed until we dared reach for them and found them strong.

Acknowledgements

Most obviously, Jim and Sue McCormack – I hope I've done you proud, old cowboy.

The Twitterverse for its serendipitous connection to Mary Cunnane who wisely advised on the manuscript and then kindly agreed to star in a revival of *Call My Agent*. (Who knew a cat could play the role of Jean Gabin?)

Publisher Alex Craig for not only 'getting it', but feeling it, for having faith that a book that didn't fit a single category nonetheless worked. And, hence, the Ultimo Press team.

Nixon, constant companion and sounding board through every sentence, albeit mostly asleep not too far from my feet.

Endnotes

Thanks to the Copyright Agency's Rosanna Arciuli for helping to track down some of the rights, particular thanks to those copyright guardians who were a pleasure to deal with, no thanks to the music publishers who were not.

Some elements of *The Summertime of Our Dreams* were first published in *The New Daily*, *Sydney Morning Herald*, *The Age* and other newspapers formerly known as Fairfax.

Epigraph
'I Know a Man', *Selected Poems of Robert Creeley, 1945–2005* by Robert Creeley, © 2008 by The Regents of the University of California. Published by the University of California Press.

Foreword: The times
1. 'Holy Thursday', *Songs of Experience* by William Blake, 1789.

The drive
2. *The Wind in the Willows* by Kenneth Grahame, 1908.

Timing
3. 'Because I Could Not Stop for Death' by Emily Dickinson, 1890.

The land beneath
4. 'Ozymandias' by Percy Bysshe Shelley, 1818.

The brothers

5. Lines from 'Australia' and 'A Blason' by A.D. Hope © Melbourne University Press, *Selected Poetry and Prose*, Halsted Press, 2000.

Faith

6. 'Was it cancer?' by Julia Baird, published by *Sydney Morning Herald*, 2015.

Sequent toil

7. 'Sonnet 60' by William Shakespeare, 1609.

Death knocks

8. 'Over the Range' by Banjo Paterson, 1923.

Brian's shirt

9. 'Thunderbolt' by John Blight, permission of his family. Papers in Fryer Library, University of Queensland.

Shrines

10. 'Oh for a glimpse of the mum I knew' by Mike Carlton, published *Sydney Morning Herald*, 2012.

Lost

11. 'How to Have a Good Death' by Maggie Fergusson, *1834 Magazine* © The Economist Newspaper Limited, London, December 21, 2015.

Snow gums
12. 'South of My Days' by Judith Wright, *Collected Poems* © HarperCollins Publishers Pty Limited, 1945.
13. Ibid.

Bolivia
14. 'Country Towns' by Kenneth Slessor, *Selected Poems* © HarperCollins Publishers Pty Limited.
15. 'Drifters' by Bruce Dawe, *No Fixed Address*, 1968, used by permission of Liz Dawe.

Glenalba
16. 'Bell-Birds' by Henry Kendall, 1920.

Spirit rising
17. *Reaper Man* by Sir Terry Pratchett, © Dunmanifestin Limited, 1991.
18. 'The Australian Sunrise' by James Lister Cuthbertson, 1907.

The call
19. 'Last Day of Leave' by Robert Graves, *The Complete Poems of Robert Graves* © Carcanet Press.

Nixon and Chilli
20. 'The Last Will and Testament of a Most Distinguished Dog', Eugene O'Neill Papers, Yale Collection of American Literature, Beinecke Rare Book and Manuscript Library, Yale University, 1940.

Michael Pascoe is one of Australia's most respected and experienced finance and economics commentators with nearly five decades in newspaper, broadcast and online journalism covering the full gamut of economic, business and finance issues. He's most recognised through his many years spent reporting on business and finance on Channel 9 and 7, in addition to his past role as Contributing Editor for the *Sydney Morning Herald* and *Age*. He's now Contributing Editor for *The New Daily* and a regular conference speaker and guest commentator on television and radio.